A People and a Proletariat

A People and a Proletariat

Essays in the History of Wales 1780–1980

edited by *David Smith*

Pluto Press in association with Llafur, The Society for the Study of Welsh Labour History

First published 1980 by Pluto Press Limited
Unit 10 Spencer Court
7 Chalcot Road, London NW1 8LH

ISBN 0 86104 321 9 paperback
     0 86104 322 7 hardback

Designed by Colin Bailey
Cover illustration: The Strike in South Wales:
    Amusements of the Colliers—"Stepping", from
    Illustrated London News 1873
Photoset by Promenade Graphics Limited, Cheltenham
Printed and bound in Great Britain at
    The Camelot Press Limited, Southampton

Pluto Press acknowledges the financial assistance of
    Cyngor Celfyddydau Cymru, The Welsh Arts Council,
    in the publication of this volume

Contents

Contributors

Gwyn A Williams	Professor of History at University College, Cardiff.
Ieuan Gwynedd Jones	Professor of Welsh History at University College, Aberystwyth.
Brian Davies	Schools Services Officer at the National Museum of Wales, Cardiff.
L J Williams	Senior Lecturer in Economics at University College, Aberystwyth.
David Jenkins	Senior Lecturer in Welsh History, Department of Extra-Mural Studies at University College, Aberystwyth.
Emlyn Sherrington	Lecturer in History at University College, Bangor.
Peter Stead	Lecturer in History at University College, Swansea.
Hywel Francis	Lecturer in History, Department of Extra-Mural Studies and Librarian, South Wales Miners' Library at University College, Swansea.
Kim Howells	S.S.R.C. Senior Research Officer, South Wales Miners' Library at University College, Swansea.
Merfyn Jones	Lecturer in History, Institute of Extension Studies at the University of Liverpool.
David Smith	Lecturer in the History of Wales at University College, Cardiff.

Introduction

The true picture of the past flits by. The past can be seized only as
an image which flashes up at the instant when it can be recognised
and is never seen again . . . Only that historian will have the gift of
fanning the spark of hope in the past who is firmly convinced that
even the dead will not be safe from the enemy if he wins. And this
enemy has not ceased to be victorious.

(Walter Benjamin, *Illuminations*)

What history we were taught in the elementary school was a
poisonous brand of romantic and medieval Welsh
chauvinism . . . The reading was dreadful—nothing but how such
and such a medieval Welsh prince defeated the Saxons, and took
from them great quantities of cattle and gold. I threw up on that. It
wasn't only that it didn't connect. It was absolutely contradicted by
how we now were. The irony was that when I entered the grammar
school we started to do the history of the British Empire . . . the
whole imperial expansion . . . The curious result was that I later
had to reconstruct for myself the main lines of the history, not just
of England, but even of my own region. I did not feel any loss at
that time. But I felt it enormously later, when I had to settle down
and read the main body of British history—including, of course,
the history of Wales.

(Raymond Williams, *Politics and Letters*)

For the history of Wales, both in its articulated past and its
mumbling present, this is the best of times and the worst of times.
Never before has there been such interest in the links between past
and present nor such written history, journals and societies to
meet this urgent need. At the same time, in our anxiety, as
professional historians and lay consumers, to arrive at the front
lines in our streamlined taxis we can be in danger of neglecting the
equally essential lines of supply and communication. The latter
require an open assertion by historians that they have a duty to

speak out, even at the risk of vulgarisation, beyond the audience of trained initiates and, in parallel, that historians have the right to assert the validity of their measured craft even if it brushes against the grain of contemporary expectations. The following essays are not an alternative history of Wales since all history stands on the shoulders of earlier practitioners, nor do they all agree with each other over methods of approach or required questions or even the fundamental shape of the terrain. Paradoxically, this is their strength for each of these historical motor-bike riders is scrambling forwards or backwards, often away from the beaten track, in order that *all* avenues to the front are kept in mind. These historians are acutely conscious of the importance of their role, and utterly convinced that only a people with a tingling memory can ever catch the omnibus to a meaningful future. Memories can be painful. Our intention has been to probe dark corners by isolating troublesome themes or events over the past two hundred years. This is not a complete history, either in the chronological sense or in its detailing of problem areas, but it is intended as a manifesto (self-justifying, we hope) on the importance of historical understanding of the Welsh experience, and as a challenge to various assumed notions.

That assumptions should flourish inside and outside Wales is an intriguing historiographical matter. Inside, as a number of the contributors show, the domination of most areas of Welsh sensibility from mid-nineteenth century by a particular constellation of social and cultural forces led to the formation of a class whose inner coherence derived from denial of its class function. The stressed values were those of community, of religion, of material progress, of respectability and, binding these together, of language and nationality. When the latter two began, respectively, to break or failed to appear fully then the more amorphous, but nonetheless powerful, concept of Welshness was substituted. From the 1880s to the 1920s there was a determined production of Gwaliakitsch of an iron-souled feyness that was out to lobotomise all the Welsh on behalf of some of them. A random selection of books, all in need of some acute investigation, makes the point in brief—Charles Wilkins *Tales and Sketches of Wales* (1879), T. Marchant Williams *The Land of My Fathers* (1889), Alfred Thomas *In the Land of the Harp and Feathers* (1896), O.M. Edwards *Wales (The Story of the Nations)* (1901), John Evans *A Popular History of the Ancient Britons or the Welsh People* (1903), H. Elwyn Thomas *Where*

Eden's Tongue is Spoken Still (1904), T.R. Roberts *Self-made Welshmen*
(1907), J. Vyrnwy Morgan *Welsh Political and Educational Leaders in
the Victorian Era* (1908)—and so it went on before losing the rich
vein of self-congratulation after 1914. It continued down to the
present in the thinner seams of *belles-lettres*. Its power in its own
time could only be met by bold counter-assertion. Hence the
counter-histories that worker auto-didacts like Noah Ablett, Mark
Starr and Ness Edwards strove for. Gwyn A. Williams, in the
opening essay, reminds us how mistaken it is to believe these men
were, in their attempts to locate their own identity, dismissive of
Welsh history. On the contrary, it was their ability to stay rooted
in a specific world and still be able to look outwards from it that
gave the writing and action of such men a bell-like resonance.
Most academic accounts of Wales, as it altered from the late
eighteenth century, still foundered on the blurring together of
material advance with that particular nineteenth century society
which was, *ipso facto,* justified; they still founded themselves in the
records and materials of that dominant class whose most conscious act was its own presentation. No wonder the best history
either stalled in the misty, castellated past or merged, with a silent
scream, into the icy waters of English historiography. The *Western
Mail*, a Tory newspaper in Liberal Wales, was able to be more
brutal, and accurate, about the mid-stream nature of the Welsh
rush into the 'Modern World'. It reviewed, on 1 January 1901, the
'Century in Wales' with all the pompous afflatus of that Wales
Rampant:-

> . . . every period and age dwindles into insignificance when
> compared with the nineteenth, the era of growth and development
> in all directions. In this century Wales at a bound emerged from the
> obscurity in which it lay in 1800 so that in this year of grace 1901 it
> is one of the brightest and most truly civilised spots in the Queen's
> dominions. . . . it is a tale of growth in material and industrial
> prosperity, in social well being, in educational progress, in
> religious life, in literary pursuits and in musical attainments . . . a
> veritable romance . . .
>   With the development of the coal and iron trade began a gradual
> exodus from the rural districts, until the latter have been
> depopulated and Glamorgan, Monmouthshire and East
> Carmarthenshire gorged with toilers and moilers as thick as bees in
> a hive . . .
>   Two of the chief ports of South Wales a century ago were

Carmarthen and Cardigan. It was thence people emigrated to America, and it was there home-produced and foreign corn was imported. What if the veterans of a century ago were permitted to see the swarming hosts of Glamorgan and Monmouthshire engaged in their respective occupations, with the black mineral pouring into the lap of Cardiff, Newport, Swansea and Llanelli, where the argosies of the nations await its arrival to convey it to the remotest parts of the earth? What if they saw the transformation of the Rhondda valley from a sleepy hollow into the most active and thriving community in Great Britain or the world . . . The social changes . . . are equally noteworthy. Popular weddings and biddings have disappeared, fairs are largely things of the past, the monthly market, the middleman, and the train having killed them . . .

Goblins, spirits, corpse candles and other unearthly visions have died a natural death and the country has been freed of the incubus of superstition. The 'wise man' who was consulted on all crucial points by our grandfathers, and even later, is as extinct as the dodo. There is no 'Cwrt y cadno' in Wales at present. Witches, wizards and sorcerers are incompatible with institutions of intermediate and higher education.

. . . With the exception of a little pilfering and poaching in the rural districts, the Welsh are a very moral and self-respecting people. The majority, however, are too Puritanical. They look upon sport as degrading, and football especially is to them an abomination.

It is useless to try and divine the future, still one cannot help surmising what is in store for Wales. The Welsh language, now spoken by about half the population, will be confined to the rural districts—some six counties probably. The English language and literature will become general. The Welsh intermediate and university colleges will have transformed the whole life of Wales before the close of the century. Still Wales will preserve its national entity and will be more than a mere geographical designation. Decay of language and modes of life and local customs notwithstanding, national characteristics will outlive the centuries.

The editorialist's prophecies, albeit not far removed from this present existence (and the twentieth century is not over yet), are not, perhaps, so interesting as his belief in 'national characteristics' from which most that is distinctive has been subtracted. What can he have meant by this abbreviated catalogue? Clearly it is the idea of blood and race to which he is paying fashionable homage even though this would prove a far weaker reed than the language itself.

However, the general social process at which he points makes the more sense since it is, in effect, a culture, historically and socially defined, that is the set of relationships which intrigues him. It intrigued his Wales, too, though this drive to a rational reordering of an older world, once dependent on its customs and practices for distrustful defence, did not evolve quite so readily, or painlessly, as this herald of progressive Wales would have us believe. The individuated valour of a 'mad' Dr. Price was, in some senses anyway, a protest against both the actuality and the mythology of nineteenth century Wales. That valour had a collective echo not only in the direct protests of the Welsh working class but also in a sly, almost pagan, refusal to lose 'the incubus of superstition'. Wales, in common with other European societies undergoing this socioeconomic process, produced its folk-lorists, its taxonomic collectors of tales, traditions and immemorial customs. Rural Wales, itself in a nagging toothache of a crisis, had its annoying features extracted and discarded by those outside tabulators who would place in aspic people who were in reality not only intimately connected to the forcing power-house of Welsh industry but also had a gimlet-eyed view of themselves, and of their observers. Folk studies, separated from the analysis of history, anthropology and sociology are frozen by their own time-bound origins. The 1893 Land Commission spent some time on the unwelcome decline of native Welsh costume and the more acceptable retreat of explicit sexual mores. There is no evidence that a peasantry has ever seen itself as anything other than exploited or done anything other than welcome the agencies of emancipation brought by material growth. They did not defend the old, 'organic' society. Their freedom was construed, of course, within their own world. Migration from or radical changes in the countryside was a species of defeat. Nonetheless, in the new urban world, the collective fairs, feast days and mutual, supportive structures of rural life had equivalents in the more open, constantly collective world of trade unions, sport and politics.

Language, whether Welsh or English, if taken as a code as well as a referential guide can serve historians of Wales well if they are intent on examining assumptions that lie deeper than politicians' guesses. The precise manner and implications of a further spread of anglicisation from the 1870s is, perhaps, the most yawning gap in current Welsh studies (though Professor I.G. Jones, here, and Glanmor Williams, in his collection *Religion,*

Language and Nationality in Wales, have struggled manfully with the Sisyphean boulder that blocks our light). In July 1909 at the monthly meeting of the Rhondda District of the South Wales Miners Federation the Chairman asked 'Is there anyone here who wants the resolution in Welsh?'—to which the delegate from Lodge 22 replied, 'Everyone here understands English'. Even so the Rhondda retained a heavy concentration of Welsh speakers for decades to come. From 1901 the District printed its rules in English and Welsh; from 1901 to 1907 they summarised every report in Welsh; from 1908 to 1911 they simply gave a synopsis of the whole minutes in Welsh; from 1911 on only the agenda was given in Welsh and, though this continued until 1931, in October 1928, a year of acute distress, a resolution was put 'That the Welsh translation of agenda be deleted for the present'. This linguistic slide was a social chute for a whole generation. What did it signify below this surface level?

It is apparent, now, that the Welsh experience, 1880-1914, was not, except in chronological terms, a mere equivalent of English history. The scope and type of militancy, both in religious and in labour history, cannot be understood without reference to the singularity (not, of course, the utter uniqueness) of that contemporary Wales. Nor does the specific localised close-up of mid-nineteenth century Wales seem any more amenable to an interpretation which would subsume Welsh history, there, within an English focus. At the same time this slow accretion of material about the shapes and sound of Welsh social history has not led historians into the seductive grip of models, such as M. G. Hechter's use of 'internal colonialism'. Why this enfeebled allegory, devoid of theory and crippled by innumerable errors of fact, leave alone interpretation, should have appealed to some intellectuals in the Wales of the 1970s is a question best left to future historians of myth. Present historians, and all who appreciate the craft integrity of this particular human discipline, have better comparisons to find in the enormously inventive and enlightening work of Eugen Weber on France 1870-1914, *Peasants into Frenchmen* (1977). Weber summed up:-

> After about 1650 ... the culture of the elite and that of the rural
> masses went their separate ways (The urban masses were quicker to
> assimilate rationalistic ideas, as befitted their place in the
> capitalistic scheme of things). When, after about 1800, the gap

began to narrow, it was thanks in large part to the rural world's increasing intercourse with the urban world. But material circumstances were crucial: increasingly, effective control of the environment opened the door to urban views suggested by like experience ... The rural convert ... could throw away his ragbag of traditional contrivances, dodges in an unequal battle just to stay alive, with the heady conviction that, far from being a helpless witness of natural processes, he was himself an agent of change.

The heady knowledge of such potential control came to the people of Wales wrapped up in their proletarianisation. This is the nodal point. The process has left us clear traces, especially at the junctions of social struggle, ideology and political shift. Arguably, though the evidence is thin, it was accompanied by the denigration of the popular culture of one class and the co-option of another—the bitterness felt by the latter when the warmth of imperial cousinage grew chilly led, among other execrescences of the petty-bourgeois mentality, to the absurd accusation, with its quite nineteenth century twitch, that the Welsh (but not the accusers) had an 'inferiority complex'. Loosely translated this means that those who chose or received other modes of life and understanding than those they were supposed to require (if only they had listened) were 'servile'.

Such an outmoded socio-biological interpretation of the history of Welsh people has had a surprising resilience, perhaps because it is so convenient a political cliché, in Welsh public life. We should be far more concerned at the continuing absence of any sustained history of women in Wales. A society whose dependence on female labour, at the work-place as well as in the home, has been lengthy and complex needs an analysis of the social culture erected, often with calculation, around this more real biological divide. Women were never 'outside' the actual history of Wales; they have been almost forgotten in our written history. No single essay in this book could have been anything other than tokenism. Arguably, they will require a separate history before they can figure in our male-dominated historiography with integrity, and therefore integrally.

Unarguably, we are still without a reconstructed political economy of Wales. So long as this continues, our history, however sophisticated its methodology and however many ignorances we remove, will be hamstrung. Nothing could serve for clearer example of the unity of theory and practice than the historian's ability, in this field, to clear the undergrowth. It is because historians have not been impelled by theoretical imperatives (other than those that stay, wisely, implicit) that in Wales such a central matter remains virtually untouched. At this stage, with historical groups, inside and outside Academe, sprouting luxuriantly all around, a co-operative venture may be needed. L.J. Williams' work on the Welsh economy, and here on the coalowners, tells us how little we know, how much we have neglected in our too quick polarisation of material. Agents of change could be victims, too, though in complicated ways, from involvement in riot to accidents at work. *Their* language can be heard, as well as read; can be seen in its attitudes as well as interpreted in its intonations. Ruling groups have been ever busy striving to order these aspects, for they are never incidentals to the 'real' world of politics and economy, all through the history of the last two hundred years. It is time to understand the sophistication of unstated, controlling factors (even in our written history) so that the interpenetration of what is indigenous and what is borrowed can be seen not as an unfortunate overlaying but as a quite necessary social process whereby a people became a proletariat without ever ceasing to be 'a people'. As the industrial economy of Wales in the early 1980s faces what may well prove to be the most serious, because final, threat to its existence, those who live in Wales will need to make a choice. If they do not know their own splintered history then they will prove incapable of holding together a world in which the pressures of past political economies have, momentarily, fused their lived experience into the weapon of self-knowledge.

Wales has been a plurality of cultures. These essays reflect this multiplicity as they reassess crucial periods or themes or dissect closely a particular view or event in order to suggest that we cannot be confident about the social history of modern Wales since, at each and every point that seems to matter (including the extent and nature of Welsh religiosity), the simplistic view should be, and now is, open to challenge. A few bold conquistadores of the historical profession over the last quarter century, from David Williams to Kenneth O. Morgan, have carved out and lucidly structured imposing narratives of the recent history of Wales. That was the first step out of the dark. The editor and contributors to this book would like to think, even if the new light shed is occasionally more blinding than illuminating, that this collection will encourage the taking of the next step. Anyway, with that phrase and that intention, we are already moving within one of our Welsh traditions, perhaps the best.

David Smith
Pontypridd. New Year's Day 1980

Locating a Welsh Working Class:
the Frontier Years
Gwyn A Williams

The chapel stands on the slope, square and uncompromising in the manner of Welsh Dissent, but with gracefully rounded windows and an unexpectedly Palladian aspect. Above it, on the tops, a big sky suddenly opens up on a breathtaking sweep of hill country running north to Mynydd Bach. There in the 1820s, men and women of Cardiganshire fought their 'Rhyfel y Sais Bach' (War of the Little Englishman) with their Turf Act and their huntsman's horn, their 'ceffyl pren' (wooden horse) secret society and their six hundred men in women's clothes, so many premature Children of Rebecca, under Dai Jones the blacksmith, to drive out an enclosing English gentleman, his soldiers and his hired goons, even as their cousins were similarly engaged, in similar style, as Children of the 'Tarw Scotch, gelyn pob dychryndod' (Scotch Bull, enemy of all fear) among the Scotch Cattle of Monmouthshire's militant and ingenious colliers. North, too, lies Tregaron, a black gnarled knuckle of a drovers' town in a crook of the moors; Henry Richard's town, the Apostle of Peace, first Welsh Nonconformist radical MP to be elected on working-class votes and working-class issues, when the men of Merthyr got their vote in 1868.

Look east; across the river down there is Llanybyther, famous for its horse fairs. In the nineteenth century it specialised in pit ponies for the Valleys over across the Black Mountain. And to the south and west curves the Teifi, threading its way from bleak uplands to the summer lushness of a coracle-haunted mouth, peopled with gentry mansions and the craggy chapels of radicalism—and peopled in the nineteenth century with woollen mills churning out flannel shirts for the Valleys' miners. The whole region in the nineteenth century was locked into the industrial world of the south-east, in its migrant workers, its chapel fraternities and its kindred networks, as the gravestones in its churchyards testify.

Not far from this hill Daniel Rowland used to hurl

thousands into those public ecstasies which earned Welsh Methodists the nickname of Holy Rollers and Jumpers. On this rock, however, he made no impression whatsoever. For this is *The Black Spot* of Calvinist demonology, the original Unitarian hub in Wales; this is Rhydowen, a mother church of Welsh Unitarianism, founded in 1726 in a heretic secession from the Carmarthen Academy. It was the Unitarians of Wales who were the motor force in the creation of the first Welsh democracy, the first Welsh populist nation, the first Welsh Jacobinism, the first Welsh working-class movement. It is a tradition which, in our own day, re-engaged its radicalism and experienced its most significant mutation.

For this chapel is Gwilym Marles's. It was built in 1834, the year in which two Unitarians over in Merthyr produced Wales's first working-class newspaper, *The Worker/Y Gweithiwr*, in the service of Robert Owen's syndicalist movement. Gwilym Marles took time off from becoming Dylan Thomas's great-uncle to fight a great battle against landlords. He was thrown out of his chapel and radical Wales built him a new one. This old one has become a museum. You'll see something familiar yet incongruous in one of the windows: a bust of Lenin.

A bust of Lenin alongside the pulpit is unusual, even for a chapel of Welsh radical Dissent. It was presented by a Unitarian from Aberystwyth who, rumour has it, is buried in the Kremlin Wall. For this was the final *persona* (to date) of Welsh Unitarianism's extraordinarily adaptable yet intransigent organic intelligentsia, personified in the Welsh-language poet, an Independent of 'unitarian' temper and Communist veteran T.E. Nicholas, 'Niclas Glais'; a dentist, he used to preach the Five Year Plan to his victims as he pulled their teeth: Suffering, like Freedom, is Indivisible.

The history of the Welsh working class in the frontier years seems familiar; the familiarity is false. Long neglected by a Welsh historiography created by the new 'nation' of a 'Nonconformist people' to which it was alien, it was marginal to the customarily ethnocentric historiography of the English, even the Labour English. The first recapture was by an act of will in the generation of militancy around the turn of the nineteenth and twentieth centuries, the enterprise of such as Ness Edwards. The work of academics in our own time has built a formidable structure, impressive in its scholarship and its sympathy, with David

Williams and Edward Thompson as twin if opposite architectural
supporters; recently there has been a shift into a deeper historical
autonomy. We have our *Llafur*, our societies, our workshops, our
miners' library. But we inch our way across continents of
ignorance. And the people whom we try to serve as people's
remembrancers, are a people without memory. Even 'traditions'
have been manufactured late and imperfectly; not until the 1970s
did Merthyr raise a plaque to its 1831 martyr Dic Penderyn (but
not to the leader Lewsyn yr Heliwr) or Gwent celebrate the March
on Newport of 1839.

We do not have many answers yet; indeed the first struggle is
to find the right questions. The first need is to rid ourselves of the
illusion that these frontier years from the 1780s to the 1850s are an
historical region whose contours and parameters at least have
been mapped. Maps we do not have; maps are what we need to
draw.

Perspectives

Some truths remain truths even if they are familiar. If the nascent
Welsh working class in the early nineteenth century had a
vanguard, it was without doubt the colliers of Monmouthshire
who staffed it, in the most consistent and most effective tradition
of *proletarian* militancy in early industrial Wales. And it was
Merthyr the iron town which produced the first working-class
martyr, the first working-class press, the first serious political
movement, the first red flag.

Other truths remain turths even if they are unfamiliar or
perhaps ideologically awkward. The first revolt against capitalism
in Wales broke out in Merioneth and Montgomeryshire, in rural
west and north; the first Welsh trade union known to have
affiliated to a national British movement was formed in Newtown;
the first Working Men's Association in Wales emerged in Carmarthen. In the 1790s, it is possible to detect a species of 'radical
triangle' in Wales, with its points in Montgomeryshire's Llan-
brynmair-Llanidloes-Newtown (with southern Merioneth as a
spiritual annexe until Britain blew its radical brains out across the
Atlantic), the southern Valleys and that complex in south Cardi-
ganshire/north Carmarthenshire/north Pembrokeshire which was
the human matrix of so many working-class movements. That tri-

18

angle appears and reappears in the years which follow, to find some kind of appropriate symbolic climax in Hugh Williams the Chartist leader *and* grey eminence of Rebecca, with his patriotic songs and his tricolour, linking in his person the textile workers of mid-Wales, the urban and rural sansculotterie of Carmarthen and its hinterland and the ironworkers and miners of the Valleys.

The first obstacles to confront are the related notions of isolation, backwardness and 'primitive rebels'.

Running across mid-Wales in the late eighteenth century, from Machynlleth to the English border, was the flannel country, a scattered industry of farm-based weavers and spinners focused on the mini-factories of the fulling mills and dependent on the 'Shrewsbury Drapers'. When industrial capitalism drove into the region on the backs of 'Welsh drapers' from Liverpool and Lancashire, the whole district was thrust into a crisis of 'modernisation'; the emergence of shoestring native entrepreneurs, the first factories in Llanidloes and Newtown, a massive growth in pauperisation as small commodity producers were turned into proletarians. The response was a distinctive and millenarian migration to the USA, highly Jacobin in temper, and the emergence of a rooted radicalism which was ultimately to debouch into Chartism. It would be ludicrous to talk of isolation, backwardness and primitive rebels in the Llanidloes-Newtown Montgomeryshire which was the stamping ground of Henry Hetherington, the *Poor Man's Guardian* himself, of Charles Jones and Thomas Powell and their kin. But it would be no less ludicrous to apply such terms to that rural Llanbrynmair to the west which became virtually a factory-parish in its own right, even if its inhabitants did speak Welsh. There, over the winter of 1795-96, great crowds assembled in defiance of the civil power, men made Jacobin speeches. Llanbrynmair, home of one of the most distinctive of Madoc migrations, was the home of the man who fathered the first native-born governor of the state of Ohio in the USA. Customary descriptions of the weavers of Montgomeryshire talk of 'part-time' work by farmers. In fact, the cloth trade was the vital margin between survival and desperate poverty; the first migrations in 1793 were stopped at Liverpool under the law against the migration of *artisans*; the leader, Ezekiel Hughes, had been apprenticed to a clock maker; their first concern in their Welsh liberty settlement of Beula in the USA was to create a rural industry, with which they had been familiar at home. This was a population of worker-peasants with its own breed of tough, literate and effective organic intellectuals. Desperate they may have been; isolated, backward and primitive rebels they were not.

Even more striking is the *web* cloth country of Merioneth, a belt of unremitting mountain poverty running along the Berwyn mountains to Corwen and north and west to the armpit of Llŷn. Over the winter whole families from this intensely poor and intensely Welsh people would meet to knit *en masse*, cheered on by the harpists, poets and singers who turned the district into a heartland of Welsh popular culture as it was later to be of popular preachers and craggy polemicists over Biblical texts. Peasants with primitive technique in a harsh environment, no doubt. But their production, which could sell 20,000 pairs of stockings at £18,000 a year in Bala and Llanrwst, was directed entirely at Charleston in the USA, the West Indies and the Gulf of Mexico, through the busy little port of Barmouth. There was a panic over American Independence in Dolgellau in 1775, and it was when Barmouth was closed in the French Wars, as the Welsh drapers moved in, that Merioneth suffered its crisis, with Jacobin toasts in the pubs of Bala, mass riots against the militia, calls for a 'government of the poor' and its own Madoc migration to the Land of the Free.

Much the same was true of the south-west, of the similar stocking trade concentration around Tregaron and Llandovery, of the hard-pressed artisans and smallholders of Cardiganshire encroaching without cease on the two-thirds of its stubborn soil owned by the Crown, of the deeply *American* temper of its southern district with its neighbours in upland Carmarthenshire and Pembrokeshire. This was the region most intimately in contact with America, the source of some of the earliest migrations. Here, the Baptist trans-Atlantic international, focused on Pennsylvania and Rhode Island College, with its own small fleet of four or five favoured vessels, its endless flow of Jacobin letters between Wales's unofficial consul in the USA, Samuel Jones of Philadelphia, and his brethren back home, found a firm and fecund anchorage. The American dimension is central, of course; it turned relatively affluent and literate Glamorgan, for example, with its coteries of craftsmen, artisans, small merchants and workshop owners, patriots Welsh and universal and Jacobins, into one of the nurseries of the democratic ideology in an age of Atlantic Revolution. But, once more, to apply such terms as backwardness and primitivism to such a region would be ludicrous; Joseph Priestley could bring pious divines in deepest Cardiganshire to the point of fist fights; the Unitarian hub was here, 'buried' in Welsh Wales. It was the Baptist Association of the south-west which committed itself to produce French translations of the Puritan and millenarian Canne Bible and to produce them *en masse* to serve Morgan John Rhys's crusade for Protestant liberty among the sans-culottes of Paris.

Even in the more familiar world of the ironworkers and miners of Glamorgan and Gwent, the primitive-rebel approach has been grotesquely overworked. Certainly God never meant men and women to live at those valley heads, but from the 1790s, the whole area was ribbed with canals and tramways; along one of the latter the first steam locomotive in the world ran in 1804. Before 1790 the 'primitive' frontier village of Merthyr could boast a bookseller taking weekly consignments from London; I repeat, *weekly*. Lewsyn yr Heliwr himself, charismatic hero of the Merthyr Rising of 1831, was the son of a butcher in the marginal mountain parish of Penderyn; he was literate in English, so literate in fact that on the convict ship *John* he was employed in teaching his English fellow prisoners to read and write their own language. The discourse of English radicalism, in its most advanced form, was commonplace in Merthyr and Monmouthshire by the 1790s; *Infidelity* was a periodic mushroom growth. It was not ignorance or isolation or primitiveness or the Welsh language which made the response of these men to sophisticated practice and ideology so apparently sporadic and discontinuous; it was their predicament, which was in fact that of American workers during their years of frenetic and revolutionising industrialisation.

That much of Welsh hill farming was primitive and at subsistence level, that communications were poor (at least before 1790 in the south-east), that many Welshmen were 'traditional' (as many were continuously mobile), that the Welsh language was an insulating factor (which I do not believe for a moment, having lived with it and in it through an English-speaking adolescence) have become truisms. A truism may be true, but it is necessary not to submit to useful simplification, even in a good cause; it is necessary not to see modes of production advance in a pre-ordained column-of-route. One minor but symptomatic fact: Volney's *Ruins of Empires* (1791) which became, as an exercise in revolutionary fantasy or science-fiction, a standard text of working-class intellectuals for three generations was available in

Welsh in 1793, just after the first English version and earlier than the first popularly effective version in English.

Two factors need to register in the mind: firstly, the autonomy of the 'superstructural', to quote the vernacular —primitive' structures are quite frequently exposed to quite unprimitive ideologies and secondly the coexistence of modes of production.

The only way for a serious historian of the working class, for a marxist historian, a people's remembrancer, to approach the early history of a Welsh 'working class', is firstly for him/her to shed all notions of backwardness-isolation-primitive rebels (however august their apostolic descent), to shed all notions of a linear progression in orthodoxy (and comprehensibility) and secondly, to accept, in its full reality (and analytical horror) the idea that modes of production coexist, that people can simultaneously live in different time-scales. Time is not indivisible. At one moment in the early nineteenth century, a man in Merthyr could be living within the world of a highly skilled worker in an integrated firm, probably the largest and most advanced of its kind on earth, while another man, tramping after sheep in some cloud-capped and barren valley, could be living in a world whose *mores* were fixed by the medieval, kindred and 'tribal' laws of Hywel Dda. More disconcerting is the thought that these men might well have been brothers.

Modes of Production

The industrialisation of Wales was imperial from birth and it hit a country which, almost uniquely in Britain, still had 'peasants'.

The Wales of the *Ancien Regime*, no less than the Wales of the Alternative Society, was a product of the creation of Great Britain with its Atlantic dimension. The historic British nation formed in the eighteenth century around the armature of Anglo-Scottish union, merchant capitalism and liberal oligarchy. Wales, subjected to the jurisprudence of capitalism from the days of the Tudors, was formed in the process. There was a massive shrinkage in the political nation, power in parliamentary terms shrivelling up into a handful of magnate families, often Scottish in origin and devoid of any Welsh content, just as the Church in Wales became the fief of broad-bottomed and Whig bishops *en route* to higher things (one of them was accused by his clergy of being an atheist); Wales's own judicial system, the Great Sessions, could be abolished in 1830 without an eyebrow raised. The multitudinous lesser gentry of Wales, product of its kindred social structure and critical to any distinct identity, was decimated, lost its foothold in public life, dwindled into a merely local and poverty-stricken prestige; men of long pedigree and short purse, they cultivated an alternative system of values, lending some power to Dissent, the new Methodism and the Welsh cultural revival. Challenging them were the multiplying professional and artisan groups which gained power from the rapid sweep of British Atlantic and mercantile empire. A peasant society living on the edge of subsistence characterised most of upland and pastoral Wales, but it was a society which also lived by the drove-herds of cattle seasonally tramping into England, bringing back currency and breeding banks, accompanied by the great droves of equally skinny people tramping no less purposefully into England to be fattened. And into and through this 'peasant' society throbbed the thrusts of merchant capitalism. Before 1800, the copper and brass industries of Britain were located, 90 per cent of them, around Swansea with its dependent mines in Anglesey under that Thomas Williams who clawed out a world monopoly. Tin-plate differentiated itself in the same period, located in Monmouthshire and around Swansea, almost totally directed to export, once more a British monopoly. By 1800, no less, the new iron industry with its coal dependency was accounting for 40 per cent of British pig iron production and was also geared almost wholly to export. Even Merioneth fed the Gulf of Mexico; the production of Montgomeryshire, through Blackwell Hall in London, went out to Europe and the Americas. The great thrust of British capitalist breakthrough during the Revolutionary and Napoleonic Wars was pivoted on Atlantic slave power. The British export sector in copper, brass, iron, tin-plate, plebeian cloth, was in Wales; the new Welsh economy was built on the backs of the blacks.

In consequence a plurality of modes of production coexisted within a country measuring scarcely 200 miles from end to end, to generate a bewildering complexity of popular response. Each mode of production produced its own working population; each working population had to live with others and with a rural population of peasants and worker-peasants in complicated interaction. It was the thrust of the iron industry, above all, after the adoption of the vital puddling process, the 'Welsh method' from the 1790s, which most closely approximated to Marx's model of an endlessly innovative, revolutionising, expanding process of self-generated contradiction.

The overall consequences are familiar but no less staggering. Over little more than two generations, the population of Wales nearly tripled; from 1841, most of it was sucked into the frenetically industrialising and increasingly English-speaking south-east. The Welsh, by the thousand, broke away from Establishment. Dissent, with the novel Methodism, may have accounted for perhaps 15 per cent of the population by 1800; by 1851, Dissent's predominance was so overwhelming that Anglicanism became a kind of historical joke. Together with Methodism, driven into Nonconformity by official repression in 1811, Dissent outnumbered the Establishment by seven or even ten to one in some places and averaged a five-to-one hegemony. The sects of Dissent threatened to become as much of a 'national church' as Catholicism had become to the Irish. From mid-century onwards, only the Nonconformist Welsh (maybe about half the Welsh on the ground) are historically visible. The rest, before the 1890s, are un-persons.

It is in this context that one has to locate the emergence of a Welsh 'working class'. During the 1830s, its presence is *visible* and *audible*; from the conjuncture of 1829-34, the Monmouthshire colliers' strike of 1830 with its remarkably sophisticated system of control, the Merthyr Rising of 1831, the penetration of the Lancashire colliers' union and the National Association for the Protection of Labour, the enrolment of the locked-out workers of Merthyr in the National Union of the Working Classes in November 1831; from that climacteric moment, through the revived but now quasi-political Scotch Cattle of the early 1830s, the upsurge of the Owenite movement with the first Welsh working-class journal in 1834, the massive and decisive intervention of the Merthyr working class in the election of 1835, the crystallisation in Chartism which united Carmarthen, Llanidloes and the Valleys, the abortive national uprising whose trigger was the march on Newport, the generation-long experience of Chartism which became virtually a sub-culture within British society, Welsh working-class consciousness, sometimes in revolutionary form, is an unavoidable *presence* in the history of Wales.

The 'disappearance' of that consciousness in the years after 1842, at least in the autonomous form which characterised it from 1829 onwards, no less than its formation in the preceding years, remain, in our virtually total ignorance of the things that matter, major priorities for the people's remembrancers of Wales.

Clearly the work situation was one determinant. The striking feature of the new working populations was, on the one hand, the high proportion of skilled men among them and on the other, their fluidity and class incoherence. Copper had the lowest proportion of skilled workers, maybe 15 per cent; tin-plate, however, with a skilled proportion of around 25 per cent was as stable as copper. The communities they created around the social and intellectual capital of Swansea had some of the worker-peasant characteristics of the northern slate quarries; there was no serious conflict in the copper industry throughout the period. To the east, however, the iron industry, 30-40 per cent of whose workers were skilled men, experienced continuous technical innovation and a roller-coaster growth; the collieries dependent on the ironworks shared some of their characteristics, while those of the sale-coal trade of Monmouthshire, run by under-capitalised Welsh entrepreneurs in cut-throat competition, witnessed some of the fiercest and most sophisticated struggles of the frontier years, led often by the skilled men who formed 20-25 per cent of the workforce.

Most works were a mosaic of sub-contractors, ranging from the master-craftsmen of tin-plate, through co-operative contracts with 'gentlemen puddlers' to the cutter commanding his team, with the *butty* or *doggy*, in effect a minor sub-capitalist of working-class origin, a distinctive figure—and an ambiguous one, now a staunch defender of the rights of property, now a spokesman for 'responsible' if militant protest. All over the coalfield, workers were mobile, flitting from job to job, following the shifts of an unpredictable iron-coal complex. The inflow from west Wales, at first seasonal, was continuous; the Irish started to flood in during the 1830s, when the huddled clusters of houses, chapels and pubs clinging to the valley sides went through their major ecological disaster; as many as 10,000 people could move through Merthyr in a year; men would tramp twenty miles to watch a foot-race; there were many Klondyke settlements alongside the model housing of the ironmasters and the indescribable tangles of cottages thrown up by middle-class speculators. The accident rate was high and, from the 1830s, became murderous; the infantile death rate was catastrophic; three-quarters of those who died were under five and average life expectancy at birth in the 1830s was about twenty.

The 'natural' death rate, however, was lower than that of country towns and the housing was superior to that of the west. Friendly societies were as numerous as the pubs which housed them and the chapels which confronted them. Wages were high if fluctuating, though sectional unemployment was rife and, in the Monmouthshire sale-coal areas, general unemployment was epidemic. Some of the more skilled trades had regular training systems and most had some kind of rough and ready approximation to apprenticeship, but with the continuous inflow and permanent insecurity, with the townships collapsing under the challenges, with no-go areas like Merthyr's *China* coexisting with a black economy of penny capitalists and drifters, permanent organisation proved extraordinarily difficult.

In the process, distinctive communities with distinctive patterns of action and response mushroomed. Most striking were the sale-coal villages of the lower valleys of Monmouthshire. Bleak, barren places, lacking even the amenities of a Merthyr, they were largely one-class settlements. Considered only half-human by their employers and the middle class, often quasi-permanently trapped in debt by the truck system, racked by the merciless competition of shoestring firms and by periodic bouts of miserable unemployment, this people, distinguished from each other often only by the presence or absence of window-sashes in their houses, proved the most militant and also the most capable of sustained and sophisticated struggle. More mixed in origin than most coalfield townships, they developed out of a very Welsh and semi-rural popular culture, highly organised and effective resistance movements and unions. From these villages came the hard core of the physical force Chartists; it was at Blackwood that the Newport insurrection was planned. By the 1830s these embattled men and women had created a vivid, living working-class culture, at once intransigent and cultivated, and had made themselves into a proletarian vanguard.

The ironworks settlements to the north, clustering around their capital of Merthyr, were more varied and richer in texture, with resident masters and a fashionable 'society', with a more complex (and wealthy) middle class. Skilled men like the puddlers were organising themselves early and *ad hoc* combinations of ironstone miners and colliers were frequent, with marginal, semi-artisanal groups like the hauliers playing a distinctive role. Artisan crafts were themselves strong and, above all, there was a persistent tradition of multi-class Jacobin democracy, very visible in Merthyr, but present throughout northern Monmouthshire. It was from the late 1830s and the 1840s that the *mores* of the colliers began to rise within this iron-dominated complex, as the valleys of Aberdare and the lower Rhonddas were opened up and Monmouthshire men moved west.

In that same period, driven on by its technical development, iron and its related trades were also shifting west to disturb the more settled pattern of the anthracite coalfield and to impose a more uniform style on the whole region from Pontypool to Llanelly. Beyond the latter lay a south-west Wales in quasi-permanent crisis and in continuous adjustment into a catchment zone for the south-east. Hit harder by the population explosion than most regions, Cardiganshire was the most disturbed county in Wales, a county of land hunger, inching self-improvement, smallholder resistance movements and seasonal migration, the Galicia of Wales. The Dissent of the region, heavily colonised by the newer Methodism, was moving out of the defensive and negative withdrawal of the west into militancy as the whole region slithered into an occult malaise and a permanent disaffection from an Anglican magistracy. It was this which tipped the already and traditionally turbulent town of Carmarthen with its press, its myriad small trades in crisis, its tribes of bloody-minded artisans, its brisk Bristol Channel commerce, over the edge into a kind of secession from public order. The endless faction feuds of Blues and Reds in Carmarthen took on a sharper tone, as its hinterland was riven by that tension between Dissent and the Church in which a populist 'nation' was shaping itself behind a language and religious line which was also a class line. There was a rooted populist radicalism in Carmarthen, fed by its neighbour villages, which could make it a 'sans-culotte' sort of place. In a sense, it served as a staging post between the south-west and the industrial complex; Chartism in Wales was appropriately born there.

Hugh Williams certainly found it a fairly easy jump from the textile towns of mid-Wales, with their small but alert and highly self-conscious factory population among a countryside scarcely less industrial in character. It was a tougher jump up into the north, where the relationships between the subculture of the quarry men of the north-west and the ironworks, collieries and mixed industry of north-eastern Denbighshire and Flintshire resembled those between Swansea and Merthyr at first. It was out of the Denbighshire of the 1790s, from 'remote' Cerrig-y-Drudion that Jac Glan y Gors, the Welsh Tom Paine, came; the north-eastern coalfield was the first seriously to respond to the millenarian unionism of 1830. The industrialisation of the north, however, ran into stasis, the population drain was continuous and Methodist-dominated Dissent a defensive reaction before the 1840s. With some brief exceptions, working-class radicalism in the north, before the great struggles of the late nineteenth century, was a matter of scattered groups and even individuals, though the quarrymen were already shaping that distinctive commonwealth of theirs which in later years would turn a lockout into a three-year civil war and a major crisis of community and tradition.

Each group, in its own particular environment, within its own pattern of authority and resistance, had to find its own way to cope with class incoherence and fluidity, to seek modes of thought and action within whatever traditions they brought with them from the sparse and bitter villages or artisan towns, whatever practices and skills they had learned from earlier struggles in industry, whatever they could marshal from their native cultures and the cultures to which they were continuously and often dramatically exposed.

What is clear, from a necessarily cursory and ill-informed survey of their actions from the 1790s to the 1840s is a pattern of episodic but frequent (sometimes annual) organisation to resist wage reductions and defend a traditional standard, occasional eruptions from what was, evidently, the familiar world of the 'moral economy' and a steady and ever richer elaboration of more permanent fellowship, whether in pub, craft, club, chapel or eisteddfod. There is quite evidently some qualitative change in the 1820s and at the critical conjuncture of 1830 a veritable 'explosion' of self-consciousness. Three factors seem general and influential: debt as the forcing-house and negative definition of a working class; a shift from consumer to producer awareness and, concurrent with the latter, a shift from protest to control as the objective. Indeed, control, of their workplace, their trade, their industry, their communities, moves centre-stage in working-class and popular action in the crisis of 1830. This drive for control, which was also a drive for dignity, found a more secure and a more permanent anchorage in a political outlook than earlier consumer protest had done. Indeed working-class consciousness in recognisable form emerges in the Valleys of South Wales with

abrupt and explosive force around 1830 precisely because a popular thrust for control, in the teeth of a debt crisis among a population which had elaborated a dense network of partly-occult
institutions, essentially cultural in character, coincided with an
equally sudden incursion of a political culture at the crisis of the
Reform Bill.

Politics had been present, in some form or other,
throughout; politics was in fact central. A radical and populist
political culture, providing a possible frame of reference, already
existed: it was there, to their hand.

For the birth of democracy had preceded their own.

Cultures and Ideologies

The ideology of democracy is pre-industrial (a truth whose
implications we do not seem to have thought through). The
Chartist programme was first published in 1780, in the reform
campaign of the American crisis. The Anglo-American character
of British Jacobinism, of which Thomas Paine is an appropriate
symbol, was even more marked in Wales, one of the sectors of
Britain in the most direct contact with America. In the last years of
the eighteenth century, the first Welsh democracy and the first
modern Welsh 'nation' were born of the conjuncture.

One of its strongholds was Glamorgan, with its big Vale
villages full of a bilingual artisanry and a patriot lower-middle
class, its Cowbridge Book Society, its Dissenting network linking it
to the tough-minded chapels of the hill country, with its own
Academy and its access to Bristol colleges. Such men as Lewis
Hopkin, craftsman extraordinary, his house full of books, Welsh,
English, Latin, French, grammars of the Welsh bards and the
latest number of the *Spectator*; John Bradford of Betws near
Bridgend, traditional nursery of Glamorgan's Welsh poets, a Deist
fuller and dyer, William Edward who built the bridge at
Pontypridd, Edward Ifan of Aberdare, apprentice in wood and
verse to Hopkin and on tramp like most of them before he settled
as Unitarian minister, created a lively, open but frustrated society
living in the interstices of gentry politics like some kind of diffused
Philadelphia. They nurtured the political culture of Morgan John
Rhys of Llanfabon, a Baptist Jacobin who travelled to France to
preach Protestant liberty, brought out the first political periodical
in the Welsh language in 1793 and founded a Welsh liberty settlement in America, and of Iolo Morganwg, Edward Williams, the

tramping stonemason of the Vale, a fantastic and maimed genius who invented the Gorsedd of Bards as Jacobin, Unitarian and Masonic inheritors of a Druid tradition turned into something akin to Rousseau's Natural Religion, and gave the newly-awakening Welsh a half-approximation to a national and radical ideology. Out of this world came two of the major British radicals of European and American reputation: Richard Price, the political Dissenter whose sermons on the French Revolution provoked Edmund Burke into his *Reflections* and who was invited by Congress to serve as financial adviser to the new USA and David Williams the Deist who may have supplied Robespierre with his Cult of the Supreme Being.

These people worked closely with the London-Welsh in their new and radical society of the Gwyneddigion, staffed largely from modernising Denbighshire, by such as Owen Jones, William Owen, David Samwell and the rest who tried to revive the eisteddfod as a kind of national academy and to re-engage an interrupted tradition. In alliance with Iolo Morganwg, these men, with some radicals of the Old Dissent, shuffled together into a loosely united organic intelligentsia in the 1790s with a journal and a campaign to create (in their own words, to 'revive') a Welsh nation conceived in liberty.

They made heavy weather of it, in the teeth of population explosion, wartime pressure-cooker industrialisation, government repression, loyalist witch-hunts, and Methodist advance. They used the revived Madoc myth to break through this wall and make contact with the disaffected working populations of west and north, whose migrations to the USA were charged with a millenarian passion, but their combative little 'nation' foundered on the rocks not only of the old regime but of the alternative society battling its way into existence.

For the real organic intelligentsia of the populist Welsh were the preacher-journalists of Dissent. It is from the 1790s that Methodism, closely followed by Dissent, surges forward in west and north, to disrupt Old Dissent itself. There was a profound difference in quality. In 1823, when Thomas Clarkson went on an anti-slavery mission to Wales, he found Dissenters of west and north, there mainly Methodists, almost an underground of withdrawn, inward-looking and defensive dissidence; the gentry would not sit with them on committees, subjected them to endless petty persecution and exclusion. John Elias himself, the Methodist leader who towered over many Welsh minds like a pope, did not dare meet Clarkson at home; they had to slink off to Chester. In the more varied society of east and south, Dissenters, among whom Baptists and Independents were more prominent, moved with far greater ease and sharper radicalism.

This distinction between 'quietists' and 'politicians' which, under the drive of evangelicalism, with its sensuous hymns and mass participation, actually ran *through* the Old Dissent itself, persisted. The first major press of Welsh Dissent, from *Seren Gomer* onwards, moved in an Independent-Baptist milieu to generate the radical *Diwygiwr* of Llanelly in the 1830s and to supply Chartism with many of its spokesmen, but a great body of Nonconformist opinion, particularly the Methodist, was a dead weight of apolitical quietism, often indistinguishable from a bilious Toryism.

As the chapels moved to embrace more and more of the working population of the industrial areas, the consequences were complex. The sweeping advance of Methodism and a 'methodised' Dissent into north and west could perhaps be interpreted in terms of the currently fashionable 'psychic compensation'; I cannot say. It was clearly a response to the disruption of traditional society. For a couple of generations, it locked its people away in a defensive bunker, a passive self-definition against hegemonic society. But there was a trend, a minority but powerful trend running in the opposite direction, driving men out with God's Sword to build a new Jerusalem. The Unitarian cause, minority but trenchant and highly influential, grew stronger right through into the 1830s; trends called 'unitarian' within Independency and Baptistry bucked the dominant evangelical drive. The Baptists were split wide open around 1800 as Independent chapels fell to Unitarians. There is a clear regional divergence; it is in Glamorgan-Monmouth and in mid-Wales that the minority Dissenting radicalism found some kind of permanent home, fed by the productive powerhouses on the Teifi and in Carmarthen. They produced a freethinking, Deist, Infidel wing of outriders and ran into congruence with the patriot Jacobinism of bohemians and unbiblical radicals.

After the great storms of the revolutionary decade, the migrations, the repression, the rampant evangelicalism, a new political tradition was rooted in Wales, in clusters of Unitarians, radical Baptists and Independents, Deists, Welsh revivalists scattered over the face of the south-west, mid-Wales and, most visible of all, in Merthyr and Monmouthshire. Merthyr village became a stronghold of Jacobinism, its freeholders 'sturdy old Republicans', with their Cyfarthfa Philosophical Society, their radical and, in 1831, freethinking and Deist eisteddfodau, their *Patriot* pubs and political societies of Welsh-patriot *Cymreigyddion*; Zephaniah Williams over in Nant-y-Glo and Blaina, with his Humanist Society and political clubs, sprang from the same root and all across the Valleys, there was a scatter of such men, some flamboyant like William Price, many, earnest moles of democracy who were often the backbone of working-class movements and ended their lives as Liberal municipal reformers.

The relationship between these people and the nascent working-class movements was complex, as the single, unified tradition of democracy splintered in the early nineteenth century under the pulverising hammer of class formation which ground society apart like some clumsy cast-iron mechanism. *Petty-bourgeois* many without doubt were, in social status and outlook, but it is not in fact possible to draw a clear line; there were working-class and artisan Unitarians and freethinkers. Much the same is true of the chapels, at least of the Old Dissent. Not until the mass Temperance movement of the late 1830s do the chapels in the Valleys play that unambiguously social-control role which English working-class historians unhesitatingly allot to them. It is quite possible that class structures and the ideologies which went with them created a quite different pattern in Wales; certainly the Welsh elementary schoolteacher of later generations did *not* play the role customarily assigned to him in England; very often he displaced the minister and challenged the miners' agent as a popular leader. Something of that *populist* order seems to have held good, at least in the Valleys, in the textile townships of mid-Wales and in parts of Cardiganshire, Carmarthenshire and Pembrokeshire. Many chapels were exclusive, battling for grace and respectability out of the sinful world of the 'roughs', but many were not and most chapels in the Valleys were strongly working-class from their foundation. It was the heavy commitment of Baptist and Independent spokesmen to the Welsh Chartist movement which was one of its distinguishing features. Certainly the cultural world of the chapels with their big and busy Sunday schools, their training in music and poetry, offered not only a home to the displaced but an arena for their talent. A rival to the pub world, the chapel world in the early generations in fact interacted with it. Not until the massive restabilisation of the middle years of the century and the impact of Temperance, does the more familiar dichotomy register clearly.

What is striking is that the radicalism of what one can call, loosely, the 'unitarian' connexion found an entry into working-class life through its popular culture. Ultimately derived from old Catholic Wales and settled by the eighteenth century into a form of 'folkloric' and customary adaptation to a hard life, this was rich and complex, with its 'cwrw bach' (little beer; self-help mutual loan and community celebrations rather like the American 'shower') its 'ceffyl pren' (cock-horse) extra-legal village discipline, its passion for games, for betting, for sometimes almost incredibly arduous foot-races, its admiration for physical prowess and pugilism, its folk-heroes like the red-haired giant Shoni Sguborfawr, champion of Wales (so he claimed), *Emperor* of China, army spy among the Scotch Cattle, mercenary hero of Rebecca and Australian convict dead of drink; or like Lewsyn yr Heliwr, the huntsman leader of the Merthyr Rising, a local Emiliano Zapata. Equally passionate, however, was the commitment of many of them to the standard-bearers of a culture ultimately derived from the old and dead bardic order, the harpists, the singers of the complex verse 'penillion', the ballad singers. Shoni Sguborfawr's boon companion in his Rebecca phase, after all, was Dai'r Cantwr, Dai the Singer, a hedge-poet. Dic Dywyll, Dic Dark, a blind ballad singer from north Wales, was the Voice of the People in the Merthyr of 1831; selling his song sheets on a Saturday night, he could make more money in a week than a furnace manager. It was in 1831 that Dic Dywyll won an eisteddfod prize—and the eisteddfod was that of the Merthyr Free Enquirers, the Zetetics who had been organised by Richard Carlile around his journal the *Republican*.

This amorphous and vivid world of the popular culture could find some organised outlet not only in eisteddfodau but in the choirs and verse festivals of the chapels, with their combative working-class conductors and teachers. Characteristically two of the recognised centres of this new kind of popular excellence in Wales were Merthyr and Llanidloes. It was the Unitarians who launched the secular eisteddfodau which blossomed from the 1820s in Merthyr and Monmouthshire to find a focus in Abergavenny, home of that dreaded figure in modern Welsh folklore, the eisteddfod adjudicator (it still produces them; Raymond Williams was born nearby.) And it is characteristic that it was out of this world that the first Chartist leaders in Wales came: Morgan Williams, a master-weaver of rooted local stock (there were harpists in his family), Unitarian like the brothers John, sons of a Unitarian minister. At the height of the rebellion of 1831, Matthew John walked alone up to the fortress of Penydarren House to present the rebels' terms and to make clear his hourly expectation of national insurrection. Most striking of all was John Thomas (Ieuan Ddu), a Unitarian from Carmarthen who was the greatest music teacher in south Wales (he is said to have introduced Handel's Messiah into Wales); a Zetetic friend of Zephaniah Williams, he launched his Zetetic eisteddfodau in 1831 and with Morgan Williams, edited Wales's first working-class newspaper, *The Worker/Y Gweithiwr*; he was responsible for the Welsh section: a eulogy of the Tolpuddle Martyrs. Men like these were among the first generation of Chartist leaders; they served their apprenticeship in the crisis of 1830. Those of Merthyr are *visible* because they were concentrated and because their activities have been documented. But they were everywhere in the Valleys, around Llanidloes and Newtown, in Carmarthen and the southwest. Zephaniah Williams in Monmouthshire, William Price in Pontypridd were highly distinctive individuals, but it would be a fundamental error to consider them unrepresentative; they had hosts of brothers, far less visible, but identifiable from their actions and occasional side-comments.

It seems to have been through this cultural milieu, under the dramatic pressures of industrial capitalism (much as the Scotch Cattle grew out of the 'ceffyl pren' world) that the new working class achieved an identity and committed itself to democracy.

Such an outcome, of course, was not inevitable.

Forms of Action

In considering working-class and popular action between the 1790s and the 1840s it is difficult to avoid some sense of a linear and almost inevitable progression towards Chartism. Even if one tries to break free of this teleological prison and to analyse particular and concrete conjunctures, the end-product seems much the same.

The 1790s clearly belong to Edward Thompson's moral

economy of the crowd: mass actions in north Wales against the militia, the Navy Act, enclosures, grain prices; 'traditional' price actions all over Wales during the dreadful years of 1795-96 and 1800-1801; and in those latter years a natural justice insurrection at Merthyr, with the troops in and two men hanged. Even then, however, a political thread of Jacobin democracy runs through everything, weaving in and out of the crowd actions. It is present in the slogans of Swansea colliers in 1793, in the speeches during the great Denbigh riot of 1795, in the crowd protests in Merioneth and Llanbrynmair; it is present above all in the emigrants who voted with their feet and in their free Wales in America drank toasts to the brave sans-culottes and voted for Thomas Jefferson. It finds some kind of institutional base in the Merthyr and Monmouthshire of the 1800s. Moreover, as an epilogue to the Merthyr grain action of 1800-1801, a broadsheet found locally locks at least a militant minority into the nation-wide insurrectionary conspiracies of that year which were to debouch into the abortive Despard affair. How far this represents any interaction between Jacobin villagers and proletarian and populist rebels it is difficult to say; the Jacobins had re-emerged in the petitioning campaigns of 1800. By 1806 the local ones were organised into a Philosophical Society even as friendly societies, often the cover for trade unions and gun clubs, mushroomed in the pubs of that same radical quarter of Merthyr on the lip of what became *China*.

Even more mysterious is what was clearly a decisive conjuncture in 1810-13; in a country so heavily dependent on Atlantic trade, the crisis which precipitated the American War of 1812 in the middle of the Napoleonic blockade was bound to be severe. Yet we know practically nothing about it. What we do know seems significant. These were the years when puddlers formed trade unions and took a Luddite oath, in which tradition places the origin of the Scotch Cattle of Monmouthshire, certainly Luddite in their impenetrable secrecy. The garrison at Brecon was established at the same time. One senses a proletarian rebellion in virtually total autonomy, made manifest by the remarkable south Wales strike of 1816, perhaps the most massive movement on the coalfield throughout the nineteenth century (and trenchantly reconstructed by David Jones). That strike, against the vicious wage reductions of the post-war slump, was an intensely active and sustained movement, ranging back and forth across Monmouthshire and the Merthyr complex, using traditional forms like the marching gangs and attacks on works and masters' houses but also evidently characterised by a high degree of organisation and an apparent independence of any other social grouping. In the aftermath, once more, a leaflet unmistakably linking at least some militants to national insurrectionary movements, such as the Pentrich Rising hints at. How far was this totally independent? Speeches by Hunt and Cobbett came down in Welsh translation immediately afterwards and from 1811 there had been a harsh government crackdown on itinerant preachers (driving Welsh Methodism to seek the protection of the Toleration Act) which radicalised Dissent. The anti-war campaign of the Ricardo-influenced bourgeoisie certainly mobilised radicals and the Merthyr Jacobins made their first organised entry into parliamentary reform in 1815. We just do not know. What *is* clear, however, is that working-class and popular protest on the whole seems to have taken a familiar form, essentially a defensive protest, expressing a consumer mentality, including that of wage-earners as consumers.

There is a qualitative change in the 1820s, mysterious in Merthyr—which nevertheless seems to have shared in the 'silent insurrection' of those years, to judge from responses after 1829 and suggestions of a leftward lurch in the eisteddfod world (there was also a Mechanics Institute at Dowlais by 1829)—most vivid in Monmouthshire. It is at this point that the Monmouthshire colliers take the initiative, wrest it from the skilled iron-men. The colliers' strike of 1822 was a highly sophisticated exercise and running alongside the mass actions, often violent, always highly intelligent, of the troubles of the 1820s are the Scotch Cattle. A highly effective underground movement, with its own Scotch Law and code of honour, its regular rhythmic practice of warning notes, summons by horn, midnight meetings, intimidatory visits by a Herd (from a different valley) under its Bull to blacklegs, profiteers, aliens, offenders against community, this was rooted in the colliery villages which were to be strongholds of the physical force Chartists, but subjected much of the ironworks belt to its moral authority. The 'primitiveness' of this movement (again brilliantly analysed by David Jones) has been grossly overstated. It was in fact a sophisticated, well ordered exercise in solidarity (necessarily terrorist in the circumstances of Monmouthshire). It looks like a wholly proletarian exercise moreover and noticeable is the stress on *control*. This, however, is no less apparent, strikingly so, in the great strikes of 1830 when the colliers, trying to impose production quotas on shifty and arrogant employers, were in fact elaborating a complicated mechanism in defence of their trades, their communities and their standard of living, and moreover did not hesitate to call in a local surgeon to help them. By 1832 the Bull's warning notes were carrying the slogan *Reform*.

This rising significance of ideas of workers' control, running into congruence with the explosion of self-consciously *working-class* politics in the early stages of the crucial Reform crisis, is also visible in Merthyr, where of course the outcome was dramatic. The slump of 1829 generated a severe debt crisis. The new stipendiary's court together with the local debtors' court co-operated to hold the working class together during the slump. Inevitably this imprisoned much of the working class in debt (Merthyr at one time ran out of funds for poor relief) and thrust the shopocracy into crisis. Distraints for debt and a campaign against petty criminals subjected a whole sector of the population to misery and repression, began to mark off a 'working class' negatively defined *against* the rest of the population at the very moment when the great tide of radical and working-class propaganda of 1830 came flooding into a Merthyr, whose Unitarian radicals were organising political unions, preaching them to workers, striking for local power in alliance with William Crawshay, a radical ironmaster who did not hesitate to deploy his own men in the cause.

The trigger was the arrival of delegates from the new colliers' union affiliated to the National Association for the Protection of Labour. The latter had made its first penetration into Wales at Newtown; the colliers' union swept north-eastern Wales over the winter of 1830-31, provoking riots and a millenarian response. The coming of the delegates to the great working-class Reform meeting in Merthyr at the annual Waun Fair (last of three such held by independent working-class initiative) precipitated an explosion, in which Owenite unions were engulfed in a classical (but highly organised) natural justice action against the shopocracy, led by Lewsyn yr Heliwr; a direct attack on soldiers marched in from Brecon, again led by Lewsyn, with the loss of two dozen dead and seventy wounded, was itself followed by a communal insurrection which held the town for four days, defeated regulars and yeomanry twice, mobilised (too late) a force of 12,000-20,000 from Monmouthshire and was beaten only after anything from 800 to 1,000 troops had converged on the town and after sustained efforts by masters, using some of the town radicals, to divide and disorganise the rebels. Melbourne played the whole incident cool; a dozen or so scapegoats were punished; Lewsyn was reprieved and only Richard Lewis went to the gallows, as Dic Penderyn, to become (and to remain) the first martyr of the Welsh working class.

More significant in many ways than the Rising itself (and generally ignored by historians) was the massive union campaign and the ghastly, hard-fought lockout which followed, as dour and grim as anything in the black history of the coalfield. In this lockout, the men of Dowlais and Plymouth works acted as a conscious vanguard for the whole working class of south Wales. Support came from as far away as Maesteg; at the last moment, as the Plymouth men were caving in, men marched to try to stiffen them, not only from Cyfarthfa but from Nant-y-Glo. In this struggle, when the men were left isolated, even by Unitarian Jacobins and radical Baptists, the emphasis was wholly on working-class independence and, as among the Monmouthshire colliers, on *control*. By the November when the men were finally beaten, they were rallying to the simultaneous meetings called for by the National Union of the Working Classes (NUWC) in London and committing themselves to the radical, self-consciously working-class wing of the movement at the crisis point—the people Francis Place and the Birmingham crew were organising to defeat. In this cause moreover, the Merthyr men sent delegates to Carmarthen.

The movement was patchy. Of course it was. Dowlais was often out of step with Cyfarthfa; there was great difficulty in co-ordinating with Monmouthshire and such difficulties often led to recrimination and disunity. The men of the Swansea and Neath valleys acted independently. This kind of phenomenon is normal and customary in working-class action; it reflects some rooted realities; Merthyr was never a stronghold of the Scotch Cattle, for example, probably because of its more complex mix of trades and much more visible democratic organisations. But what is really significant is that in both Merthyr and Monmouthshire, as men's minds concentrated on the idea of control (central to the new colliers' union) in a context of almost millenarian political crisis, what can only be called a working-class consciousness emerged. It was defeated, as the NUWC and their kin were defeated in the nation. It had to live in a South Wales where there were garrisons in the five major towns and in which the middle class had been armed against them. That consciousness could not immediately act in independence; it had to operate under other people's hegemony.

But its existence was real enough. Patchy and incompletely autonomous though it was (the Merthyr men of 1831 were committed to Free Trade, for example), it persisted and billowed up in strong waves of feeling and action through the 1830s; in the massive Owenite union movement of 1834, when its first newspaper appeared; in the last great movement of the Scotch Cattle in support, in the intervention in the Merthyr election of 1835 and the power which buttressed the Unitarians as they took over Merthyr from 1836, above all, of course in the unforgettable experience of Chartism, that Chartism which yoked Scotch Cattle and Unitarians, the eisteddfod world and *China*, which united the Valleys with the not-so-very-different world of Llanidloes, Newtown and their villages (where the differences are really those of scale and concentration) and the distinctly more sans-culotte milieux of Carmarthen and its villages; that Chartism which was so much more than the march on Newport, significant though *that* is, the Chartism with its coveys of girls in white dresses and green flags, its men marching blue uniformed into the churches, its ritual and colour and ceremony, its endless debating clubs and hidden arms clubs, its Chartist caves and Chartist churches, its massive and all-pervading working-class culture, which lived on in South Wales long after the climacteric moment of 1838-42 and the upsurge of 1848, which so registered on the minds of Marx and Engels and which indulged in its last ghost campaign as its former militants moved on to councils and library committees and sat on the platforms of Nonconformist radicals (including Henry Richard).

The strength and reality of working-class consciousness in the 1830s and early 1840s is best measured by the response of its enemies. Official and respectable reaction to the Merthyr Rising, at the height of the Reform Bill crisis of course, had been hesitant, unsure, careful. Ironmasters were divided over the unions; the Home Secretary of an alarmed government, recognising it eight years later as 'the nearest thing to a fight' they had ever had, trod very carefully indeed. As soon as the Act passed and the great wave of anti-working class legislation began to surge through the Commons, as soon as necessary if rather rowdy allies had become

Destructives, all that changes. In 1834 the masters presented a uniform face of brass to the unions and broke them without mercy; troops, police, spies, propaganda, the pulpits were turned massively against the Scotch Cattle to stamp them into the ground. After the Newport march, the Cabinet were hell-bent on hanging Frost. Williams and Jones and were stopped only by a liberal Chief Justice, while the working-class people of the Valleys were drenched in the respectable spittle of ferocious class hatred. Not until the later 1840s, with the education commissions and others coming down to 'solve' the problems of Wales, did that virulent tone slacken.

But by that time, of course, Chartist militants were already on their long march into the radical wing of Liberalism.

Memory

The realignment and the absorption of much working-class enterprise into a liberal consensus, the 'disappearance' of militancy, of autonomy, are, of course, as familiar in Wales as in Britain as a whole. They remain unexplained, peculiarly so in Wales.

Some of the central features are symptoms rather than causes. There is the creation of county constabularies and the battle for *China*; the Temperance movement with its great choirs which wrenched the eisteddfod out of the pub; the preoccupation with education and the renewed Nonconformist drive against the Anglican counter-attack, the increasing mobilisation of working-class leadership by Dissent. Can there be a more structural explanation along the lines advocated, in varying terms, by Lenin, Eric Hobsbawm and John Foster, the articulation of a labour aristocracy in a new imperialism? Certainly, from the 1850s, there was another pulse of growth which made South Wales into yet more of an Atlantic economy, in the world-wide and massive railway empire of its iron industry; coal begins its thrust into world power. Sub-contracting dies out rapidly. But, to put it bluntly, we do not yet know enough to be able to give even a tentative answer.

What is clear is that with the rise of South Wales into an imperial metropolis of British world hegemony, the Dissent of rural Wales moves over to the offensive. From 1843 dates the first aggressive Nonconformist press of rural west and north; reaction against resurgent Anglicanism and the bilious anti-Welsh racism of an education report of 1847 whipped a species of Welsh nationalism to life. Since it took the form of a 'Nonconformist people', there were here the makings of a powerful synthesis, as the leadership of working-class self-help movements in the industrial areas also moved into the orbit of Dissenting populism. Such a synthesis in fact occurred. It is visible as early as the 1840s in the Aberdare Valley to which initiative in the south had been shifting; it registers dramatically in the shock election of Henry Richard at Merthyr in 1868. The seeds had been germinating earlier of course. Popular and working-class radicalism through the frontier years had been a dialectic between attitudes and actions which later commentators could and did label 'middle class' and 'working class'; in its later phases the Chartist movement itself seems to have acted as a force for integration. By the late nineteenth century, the Nonconformist people had become the hegemonic power in Welsh popular life; the un-persons were not to acquire historical existence, and then a Socialist one, until the 1890s.

The most striking consequence for a historian is that, in this process, the Welsh working class lost its memory.

Industrial capitalism seems to destroy the popular memory; perhaps it needs to. The circumstances of its rise in Wales, its cultural expression in the pseudo-nation of Welsh Dissent, were even more inimical to working-class memory and therefore of identity. When the history of Wales came to be written. it was the new organic intellectuals of that pseudo-nation who wrote it, spitting the Anglican gentry out of it. Within it, the Welsh working class figured as 'hearers' in a Nonconformist service or as incomprehensible hooligans outside. On no people do the corpses of the dead generations weigh with quite so peculiar and particular a heaviness as on the working class of Wales. It is time to remove them.

We have one, rather melancholy, consolation. There is evidence that *some* memory of the frontier years *did* survive into the later years of the century. Characteristically it was a martyr, not a leader they chose to remember. My great-grandmother, Sarah Herbert, came from a Tredegar family of long radical tradition. A pillar of the chapel in Dowlais, she was the sister of a Chartist. She was an indefatigable worker for Henry Richard and on behalf of the 'working classes' of the Nonconformist people. But she was prepared to spend the not inconsiderable sum of 4d to see what was alleged to be Dic Penderyn's ear on display in Dowlais market. Some kind of Dic Penderyn was alive, then, in people's memory. What those people chose to remember from the frontier years was the condition which Dic himself had denounced in his last cry from the scaffold: *injustice*.

Bibliographical note

I assume that you've just read the essay to which this note is an appendage. If you want to follow up this early period and you're a newcomer to the history of Wales, the first thing to do is to read the essays in this volume. Then get back to the 1920s and the organic intellectuals of the Welsh working class. Read Ness Edwards, *The Industrial Revolution in South Wales*, brought out by the Labour Publishing Company in 1924 complete with foreword by A.J. Cook and a bibliography which includes *The Times (Bloody Old)*.

The first serious history of Wales, serious in the sense that it (a) took cognisance of the Welsh as they actually existed on the ground, rather than in an instrumental ideology which bordered on theology, i.e. took cognisance of a 'proletariat' as well as a 'people' and (b) was theoretically aware at a high level of intensity, worked to a 'problematic' without losing its grip on the essential *human* character of its discipline, employed the empirical method without succumbing to empiricism, was produced in the 1920s *by* organic intellectuals of the Welsh working class. Classic examples themselves of that Gramscian Hero, they dedicated themselves to the no less Gramscian objective of achieving the *historical autonomy* of their class.

Inevitably at that stage they were obsessed with their own experience, in industrial south Wales; only recently, of course, have 'peasants' ceased to be 'sacks of potatoes' in Marxist thinking. Their enterprise did not outlast the 1920s. Nearly two generations later, however, it has been re-engaged, characteristically by a generation of academics whose family roots lie deep in the same seam (soil sounds too folkish). It was such people as these who launched *Llafur*, the Welsh Labour History Society, which now has some 1,200 subscribers, which successfully

assimilates academics and workers and whose journal, published
annually, were it more charged with theoretical awareness, could
be identified, albeit through the refraction of two generations'
dark-glass experience, as the (or perhaps an) inheritor in apostolic
succession of those maimed but creative militants of the Central
Labour College and the Plebs League.

In between lies Dagon's Country, black as night, peopled by
one ambivalent giant and a clutch of industrious and unduly
defensive apprentices. But this is no place for an essay in
historiography. Begin with our onlie true begetters in the twenties.

You can savour something of their calibre (and their sweat)
in the *Position Paper* which the Ruskin History Workshop Students
Collective presented to History Workshop 13 (Oxford, 1979).
They raided the archives of Hywel Francis and the South Wales
Miners Library (50 Sketty Road, Swansea) to print the syllabuses,
notes and other material of D.J. Williams, Glyn Evans and George
Thomas from the CLC of the 1920s. Their project was stunning in
its sweep, its rigour, its ambition, with a literally ferocious
concentration on *totality*, conceptual precision, theory of
knowledge and *process*. Not until our own day, as our bookshelves
and journals have slithered into that acid-bath of clinical
scholasticism which leaves the consumer feeling he has just got
drunk on vinegar, have we met people quite so obsessed with
'epistemology' and 'conceptual rupture'. The 1920s brew is more
accessible and congenial. Admittedly, their syllabus left little scope
for *particularity*; this was *inserted* by an act of will or tribal loyalty.
Their enterprise bore all the stigmata of its time and place. We are
uncomfortably aware that some of these militants were to tread
that road, so faithfully followed by the labour movement from its
birth, onward and upward into the huge absorbent sponge of the
bourgeois hegemony in its peculiarly succubus-like, voracious and
glutinous British form. Nevertheless, 'The point was', said George
Thomas (and he had *and has* a point) 'we had the bourgeois
textbooks of course but we knew how to handle them . . . It was
this drilling in Marxism really that put us on our feet, also Marxist
philosophy, they did a lot with Dietzgen in those days, Joseph
Dietzgen, *The Science of Understanding*, as an introduction to
dialectical materialism. So when I left the Labour College I was
equipped, I knew what I was doing and why I was doing it . . .'

And, nevertheless, after a syllabus almost blinding in its
totality and its methodological and epistemological obsessions,

George went on to focus on the history of Dic Penderyn, the first Welsh working-class martyr. And D.J. Williams, in a course of lectures in 1926, after a Long March from the General Strike and Modern Capitalism through a breathtaking vista of medieval heresies, Marxism, Problems of Knowledge, the British Working Class Movement, and Economics, closes with . . . 'No.11. Early Industrial Development in Gwaun-cae-Gurwen . . .'

Out of this world comes Ness Edwards's *Industrial Revolution in South Wales* (sample his own histories of the Miners, too and Mark Starr's *A Worker Looks at History*). Faults it has in plenty and conceptual ruptures by the dozen, no doubt, but there had been nothing like it before and there was to be nothing like it for more than a generation. It is a remarkable achievement, not least in his pioneer use not only of Blue Books and the press but of what became the celebrated Home Office 52 series. We should dig it up like the Republicans of 1830 dug up Tom Paine.

We have no political economy yet in Wales but there are some very useful 'economic-history' introductions, notably A.H. John, *The Industrial Development of South Wales* (Cardiff, 1950) A.H. Dodd, *The Industrial Revolution in North Wales* (Cardiff, reprint 1971) and J. Geraint Jenkins, *The Welsh Woollen Industry* (Cardiff 1969). If you have, or can learn, Welsh, there are brilliant essays by the man who taught David Williams how to walk a country like an historian and was himself the 'organic intellectual' of a whole people, R.T. Jenkins, *Hanes Cymru yn y Ddeunawfed Ganrif* and *yn y Bedwaredd Ganrif ar Bymtheg* (Wales in the eighteenth and first half of nineteenth centuries) (Cardiff, reprints, 1972).

But the only real place to 'begin' is David J.V. Jones, *Before Rebecca: Popular Protest in Wales 1793-1835* (Allen Lane, London, 1973). David Williams, of course, is step-father to the lot of us. He is a small universe in himself. But if we are to boldly go where no man has gone before, it's necessary to get our parameters right. David Williams did an almost incredible job in mapping out the territory; his list of writings is longer than de Gaulle's nose. You can find it in the special number of the *Welsh History Review* (1967) devoted to his work. His master-piece, of course, is his *Rebecca Riots* (Cardiff, 1955) which is a *total* achievement (Art Schoyen, Harney's biographer, exploded into ecstasy over it . . . 'A gem . . . a gem . . . a gem.' and rightly so). David Williams came from Narberth, of course, where they demolished the workhouse. On industrial Wales his work is technically strong, informative

and a starting point. *John Frost* (Cardiff, 1939; reprint, Evelyn,
Adams and Mackay London 1969) was written *in a single year* and
he followed up with his essay on Chartism in Wales in *Chartist
Studies*, ed. Asa Briggs (London, 1959). These badly need to be
corrected and followed through in David J.V. Jones, *Chartism and
the Chartists* (London, 1975), his article in the special Welsh Labour
History number of the *Welsh History Review*, vi (1973), the work of
Angela John, 'The Chartist Endurance: Industrial South Wales
1840-68', *Morgannwg* (journal of Glamorgan History Society) xv
(1971) and her MA (Wales) thesis on the theme, and the work in
progress of Brian Davies.

On industrial militants, David Williams's sympathy faltered;
his favourite adjective for them was 'unsavoury'; his comments on
two of them in Gwent Chartism, *Jones the Watchmaker* and *Mad
Edwards the Baker* would fill an anthology of feline malice. But his
heart was in the right place and he tolerated the vagaries of the
young. So David Jones managed to break through to his thesis and
his fine book *Before Rebecca*. This has quite literally opened up a
world. Particularly effective are the essays on the South Wales
strike of 1816, on riotous Carmarthen and on the Scotch Cattle.
This last is quite brilliant—compare it with the 1920s essay of E.J.
Jones reprinted in *Industrial South Wales 1750-1914* ed. W.
Minchinton (Cass, London, 1969) and even more revealing, with
the section on the Cattle in Eric Wyn Evans's technically sound *The
Miners of South Wales* (Cardiff, 1961).

So, as a quick (well, relatively quick but essentially painless)
initiation into the half-explored years of the emergence of a
'working class' in Wales, start with this book, go back to Ness
Edwards, brief yourselves in A.H. John and A.H. Dodd and
Geraint Jenkins and then get down seriously to David Jones, *Before
Rebecca*. Read his chapters 1 and 2 first, together with chapter 5 on
Carmarthen. Then switch to my *The Search for Beulah Land: the
Welsh and the Atlantic Revolution* (Croom Helm, London, 1980); for
further human material, chapters 5, 6 and 7 of my *Madoc, the
Making of a Myth* (Eyre Methuen, London, 1980). Go back to David
Jones, *Before Rebecca*, for his chapters 3, 4 and 6 and follow up with
my *The Merthyr Rising* (Croom Helm, London, 1978). Then go for
David Williams, *The Rebecca Riots*. Stop for breath before you tackle
Chartism as I've suggested above. To look ahead, read Ieuan
Gwynedd Jones's essay in this book and trace his many articles in
Welsh journals. To get some sense of movement over time in one,

quite important area, sample *Merthyr politics: the Making of a Working-Class Tradition*, ed. Glanmor Williams (Cardiff, 1966)—a series of lectures organised by the W.E.A., you remember, the Other Lot whose heart was better placed than their collective head.

Keep your eyes on the *Welsh History Review*, of course, and see if you can work through the Byzantine labyrinth of the *Bibliography of the History of Wales* (Cardiff, 1962, supplements in the *Bulletin of the Board of Celtic Studies*). After 18 years, I still can't.

Above all, of course, after a reassimilation of Ness Edwards and Mark Starr and the History Workshop Position Paper of 1979, read *Llafur*. Read it constantly. In fact, you'd better subscribe to it; you don't know what you're missing.

Language and Community in Nineteenth Century Wales
Ieuan Gwynedd Jones

My theme is the difficult and puzzling one of the relationship of language to social change in nineteenth century Wales. It is, of course, a very familiar one and for some people, particularly for those who are most sensitive to religious and cultural changes generally, it is a contemporary theme. It has always been felt that somehow these relationships, subtle and tenuous and everchanging as they are, lie at the very heart of our civilisation. This familiarity and contemporaneity, indeed, much of the language that we necessarily use in setting out the terms of the problem, are what make the theme such a difficult one for the historian. It is easy to mistake the language of the present for that of the past and to fall into the trap of believing that the problem is the same for us as for past generations. Such anachronism is common, particularly among those for whom language has become a political issue and a motive for political action. But equally it is the existence of the language now that makes its persistence through time, and particularly through the crises of the past century or so, a question of the highest relevance and importance. What I propose to do is to attempt to study the language in its relation with the major cultural forces with which it was constantly interacting. It is to the social aspects of language, or language as institutionalised and language as an institutionalising agent, that I want to direct my attention. It was Vyrnwy Morgan who said in one of his books, 'All history is difficult but Welsh history particularly so'. Perhaps what follows will be a demonstration of that.

The problem that I want to keep in the forefront is relatively simple to state. It is this. How came it that the Welsh language survived when so many social forces appeared over the generations to be antipathetic to it? For example, there was the relative unimportance of the Welsh people within both the British and a European context. Numerically, there were never more than two millions, and politically they can scarcely be said to have existed. There were serious doubts about their nationhood. They possessed none of the institutions of statehood and it did not appear, except briefly at the end of the century, that they aspired to possess them. Then there was the relative insignificance and inferiority of the Welsh language within the British and European cultural world. As the *Eclectic Review* put it, 'the retention of the language obstructs the progress of the inhabitants of the Principality in all the higher developments of civilisation'. Nor did the language possess a socially acceptable prestige-value, more especially the prestige embodied in an indigenous Welsh-speaking aristocratic and gentry class. Furthermore, in an age which was increasingly 'fact-conscious' there was evidence enough of relative decline. The movements of the language-frontier were observed and the growth of 'Cymru ddi-Gymraeg' (Wales beyond Wales) at the expense of 'Cymru Cymraeg' (Welsh Wales) noted. Finally, there was the virtually unanimous opinion of the Welsh elite—the educational, religious, commercial and political leaders of Victorian Wales—that the disappearance of the language was inevitable and a good thing. Why then did it not die? To look for possible answers we need to examine the relations of the language to the economic, religious and political life of the times, and in particular, we need to look into the new kinds of social relations which were being engendered by the concurrence of changes in these fundamental areas of human experience.

The first and possibly the most fundamental of the forces that we have to consider in its relations to language is that of economics. There are two factors which we must distinguish, namely, the demographic ones and the creation of surplus capital. Both grew enormously in the course of the century and both, as a consequence, profoundly affected what was happening to the language. In demographic change, there are two related aspects which are of importance in this, as in all other, respects. First, there is the aggregate growth in the crude numbers of the population—that is to say, of the numbers of people who, after taking into account migrations to places outside Wales, remained within the country. In the course of the century population nearly quadrupled, growing from just under 600,000 in 1801 to just over two millions in 1901. It is of the utmost importance to bear in mind that this growth was not evenly spread throughout the century, but on the contrary varied greatly from decade to decade and from year to year. Thus, the rate of population growth was higher in the first half of the century than in the second half, but highest in the first decade of the present century. The differences are quite significant: the rate decade by decade runs like this: 15 per cent, 18 per cent, 13 per cent, 17 per cent; then 11 per cent, 11 per cent, 10 per cent, 11 per cent and 19 per cent.

Obviously, this growth and its uneven occurrence over time affected the language. One simple but very important fact is that there were more people who could speak Welsh in 1901 than in 1801. J. E. Southall estimated that there were probably a total of about 1,060,000 Welsh speakers in Wales and England, or something in the region of 54 per cent of the population within Wales, in 1891. He and other commentators pointed out that even with the massive immigration of non-Welsh speakers the proportion was still 50 per cent in 1901 and 44 per cent in 1911. It is important to stress these apparently simple facts and not to lose sight of the point that until well into the present century a large—though declining—population was Welsh-speaking. Later we shall have to ask more qualitative questions about levels of literacy and the state of the language: but it is sufficient at this point to stress that this was an undoubted consequence of population increase within the country and that the highest sustained rate of growth had taken place in the first rather than in the second half of the century.

More important than this absolute growth in numbers was the redistribution of population that was constantly taking place. The population of Wales was a highly mobile one and the movement was from rural to industrial areas and, therefore, a largely internal migration of Welsh-speaking Welshmen. It was as if, to all intents and purposes, the unpopulated, unexploited parts of the country where mineral wealth had been discovered were being colonised by the Welsh people themselves. This was apparently so even though the strategy of that colonisation, its character and its speed, seemed to be entirely beyond the control of the Welsh people themselves. In the case of migrants from regions which had long since been anglicised in speech it was a migration of people who could readily reabsorb Welsh culture and be reincorporated into Welsh language communities. While, therefore, it was true that linguistically Wales was becoming a divided country and that the boundaries between 'Cymru Cymraeg' and 'Cymru ddi-Gymraeg' were constantly changing and zones of effective bilingualism or zones of linguistic neutrality being set up, it is still necessary to emphasise that not until the beginning of this century had these movements fundamentally altered the linguistic balance or that it had become evident to contemporaries that, although its demise would probably be slow, the death of the language was now inevitable.

Clearly, in all this the nature of the industrialising process was crucial. In the first stages of industrialisation migration from outside Wales was negligible and, throughout the coal era until the last two decades before the first world war, migration was still predominantly from Welsh Wales. It is necessary to emphasise the continuing Welshness of the new urban regions, those concentrations of people that had grown up in the hitherto unpopulated moorland on the coal measures and in the expanding industrial towns of the south-west and north-west. Even at the height of the invasion from England at the beginning of this century, there is evidence to show that the preference shown by these migrants for coastal towns rather than upland valleys helped to preserve relatively undiluted the essential Welsh language basis of the new culture.

Certainly, there were plenty of evidences of change, but we can understand what these were only when we observe them in the context of a kind of 'pura Wallia' which un-self-consciously survived.

The second economic factor is the creation of surplus wealth in quantities sufficient to maintain the necessary cultural overheads. Language—that is to say, the people who speak a language—creates its own characteristic institutions. This is particularly the case in bilingual or multi-lingual situations where there is inequality as between the languages and in which the majority language lacks prestige or feels itself to be deprived or is regarded as culturally inferior. These institutions—the 'cultural overheads'—have to be financed and they can be paid for only out of the surplus wealth being produced by the community. These institutions in Wales fell into several groups. First, there were the eisteddfodau. These—strange as it might sound when we think of the colossal sums required to run the National Eisteddfod today—were largely self-financing and required but very little capital and that little required was spread, even in small localities, over so wide a contributory area as to be scarcely detectable. Even that essential concomitant of the eisteddfod, the publishing of transactions and adjudications, could be done for virtually nothing in newspapers and magazines. The financial aspects of the eisteddfod in general merit separate study: here it is sufficient to point out that they were devised in such a way as to avoid capital outlay and to recover costs immediately. The second of these overheads were buildings—halls, pubs, meeting places (other than religious ones). In the nineteenth century these could be financed only by co-operative means, friendly societies, temperance movements, clubs and so on, or by local capitalists or individual firms, such as ironmasters and coalowners, or by democratic local government initiative (after 1886 and 1894) and working-class initiative. Finally, and most typically attached to the language, were the means in communications—the 'media'—which meant the printing press for the publication of newspapers, magazines, pamphlets, books and advertising. Now, it is probably impossible to cost the capital outlay in these cultural overheads, but it is clear that in terms relative to the amount of wealth being created by industry it was trivial. The eisteddfod was not costly as we have seen: amenity buildings were extremely rare both in old and new towns, especially the latter; and the press in Wales, with some notable exceptions, was characterised by the fragility and insecurity of its financial base. Whatever happened to the profits of industry, very little of it was ploughed back into the institutions in which the language could hope to thrive. But if this investment was trivial in relation to productivity, it was enormous in relation to earnings. That is to say, the institutionalising of language under the conditions of a maturing capitalism, depended upon the surplus increment in the earning capacity of the common people, and not on the surplus profits of capitalists. Hence the importance (often ignored in discussions like this one) of numbers of people. Lacking state finance, having few capitalists or landed proprietors who were prepared to be munificent in their patronage of the indigenous culture, the language had to depend upon the individually minute contributions of large numbers of ordinary people.

There is one other economic force which we must mention, namely, improved physical communications—railways, roads and better, more reliable faster transport all round. This enormously eased the movement of people and made possible the rapid distribution of ideas. Obviously, these improved forms of transport could have deleterious effects likewise: if it speeded up the internal movement of people it also facilitated immigration into and migration out of Wales. But there is no denying the impact of the railways and the means these placed at the disposal of the main cultural organisations for the rapid dissemination of ideas and thus for the growth of a sense of cultural unity. Macadam, Brunel, David Davies—the sense of achievement and of national cultural maturity which is present in Victorian Wales depended as much on these men, perhaps, as on the bards and, as we shall see and as contemporaries recognised, even the powers of religious enterprise depended in large measure upon the effectiveness of the business entrepreneur and the engineer. But capital is essentially unattached to any culture and is not essentially based in any particular language. From the beginning, economic change had deleterious effects upon the Welsh language and culture, in particular by associating the idea of progress with the English language. Economics tended to reinforce the prestige-value of English and to lower the esteem of Welsh among the classes most sensitive to the possibilities of social change and mobility.

The second of the major forces is that of religion. That there has always been a close relation between the Welsh language and organised religion in Wales has been commonplace since the Protestant Reformation. After all, this is the essence of the Protestant Reformation, the substitution of a formal ecclesiastical language by a vernacular. The relationship is not a simple one, however, and always there have appeared to be elements of equivocation and ambiguity. For example, in theology there have always been quite fundamental differences of view. Many theologians have believed that the relationship between the language and religion is providentially ordered. Such a belief can be the basis of both a conservative and a liberal point of view, and go along with quite contrary ideas as to the social and political implications or the consequences of such a belief. For example, Charles Edwards, the seventeenth century divine and historian, author of *Y Ffydd Ddi-ffuant* (1667), which has been one of the most influential books in the formation of Welsh culture, quite unequivocally believed that the union of Wales with England under Henry VIII was an act of God designed to make it possible for the true religion to be given to the people in their own language. The prerequisite, in other words, for the reception of an official form of Protestantism (though not of unofficial forms) was the loss of independence or what vestiges of it remained at that time. Or, put in another way, Charles Edwards appeared to accept that political absorption by an alien people was the prerequisite to the reception of the written essentials of Christianity in the Welsh language. Some of our contemporary theologians as une-quivocally reject that view and argue that it is the mind of God that since religion and language are undissolubly linked, political independence becomes a prerequisite for the survival of either or both.

There are also those who believe that the Welshness of the revelation vouchsafed to the people of Wales is unique, and by definition different in important respects from that revealed in other languages to other peoples. Hence the belief that the Welsh language already possessed the core and kernel of Protestantism in the history of the Church in Wales—that the religious revolution was by definition conservative since it harked back to the purity of the Celtic Church. From this there follows the religious obligation to preserve the language, for, *mutatis mutandis*, to preserve the language is to preserve the uniqueness of the revelation. This is contested by others who hold that the medium of communication should not determine the message, that it is the substance of the revelation which must be proclaimed whatever the language and that the true faith is not diluted when it is anglicised.

It is not my purpose to develop these arguments either one way or the other. It suffices to point out that such questions could arise only in a bilingual society or in a society experiencing linguistic change. Hence, to mark the emergence of such questions into public debate is to mark a point of transition or of change in the religious sensibilities of the people concerned. Language in this sense is an indicator of religious ideology and of the value systems generated by religious organisations.

Looking at the nineteenth century as a whole there is no doubt that whatever may have been generally assumed by religious leaders about the uniqueness of the Christian revelation in the Welsh language they were unanimous in believing that there were special features belonging to the religious organisations which had been developed in Wales over the generations. For example, it was confidently held that Wales was the most religious part of Great Britain. And judged by the external standards of religios-ity—numbers of places of worship and of attendants at places of worship—this was certainly true. Probably this state had been reached as early as the mid-1830s, and it was confirmed by the mid-century census and by unofficial counts at various subsequent dates. It was also recognised as a unique feature and of immense significance that the appeal of religion in Wales by mid-century was universal and its success not delimited, determined or otherwise circumscribed by class considerations. The working classes of Wales, observed Edward Miall, were a cheering exception to the religious apathy (at best) and antipathy (at worst) of their English fellows. Welsh commentators, such as Dr Thomas Rees of Beaufort and Swansea, went even further and claimed that nine-tenths of the working population were formally or informally attached to religious organisations. Factually, there is no doubt that Rees and the others were exaggerating: as we shall see there was a strong class element in the chapels as well as in the established church, apathy was constantly complained of and infidelity was by no means unknown. But it is the belief that is interesting and significant, the quality of myth which it generated, and which was typified as early as 1859, for example, by the question 'A ellid dychwelyd holl drigolion Cymru at Grefydd?' ('Can all the inhabitants of Wales be brought back to Religion?') as if this had been the norm at some point in the past. Welsh religious leaders emphasised yet another organisational difference, namely, the fact that, unlike England, religion was equally successful in town and country. Here again there was a fatal lack of precision in their thinking, for they failed to recognise the fact that though the differences in Wales were less pronounced than in England, the town/country disjunction was present in Wales as well and that already it boded ill for the future. Finally, they took immense pride in the fact that the purity of the Protestant faith was nowhere more secure than in Wales. All in all, there would have seemed justification enough for the astonished and heart-felt delight of the eloquent commentators of 1850, 'O Gymru, pa le y mae dy debyg wlad dan y nef? A pha genedl dan haul a chymaint o ôl crefydd arni, ag sydd ar genedl y Cymry'—adding in true prophetic fashion 'Nac anghofia doniau Duw'.[1] ('O Wales, where is thy like under heaven? What nation under the sun possesses more of the marks of religion than the Welsh? . . . Forget not the gifts of God'.) Notice that this has nothing to do with denominationalism. In this context the jealous denominational competition so characteristic of Victorian Wales was not a sign of weakness but an indication of vitality, an essential element in the development and maintenance of popular forms of religious organisation.

We return to our central problem of the relation of language to religious experience when we examine the arguments used to explain this achievement. First of all, there was the historical argument. This was an argument of great persuasiveness and potency and one which, we might add, is still an essential element in the Welsh consciousness however much contemporary historians might decry it. It was the equivalent of the 'Whig interpretation of history' and very similar in the well-nigh universality of its acceptance and its readiness to find in the past only what happens to be of importance in the present. It was first elaborated in the sixteenth century and had received its classical expression in Charles Edwards's *Y Ffydd Ddi-ffuant*. The core of the argument was that the justification of the union of the two countries and the guarantee of its permanence was the production of the Scriptures in Welsh. To this was added a further dimension, the essence of which was the failure of the established Church to fulfill its proper evangelical missionising function. In explanation of this critics from within the Church itself, like Erasmus Saunders, tended to stress the malign effects of bureaucratic deficiencies, such as pluralities and absenteeism stemming from poverty, while critics from within the Methodist movement concentrated on its spiritual, doctrinal failures, its lack of vision, of zeal, of warmth and of a hunger for souls (this became the orthodox Methodist view very quickly and has remained an essential ingredient of Methodist historiography). What both had in common was the accusation that the Church neglected the language of the people and, counterwise, that the success of Methodism was primarily due to its unquestioning acceptance of the need to preach and to teach in the Welsh language, and ironically and tragically for the Anglicans this was the statutory law of the Church. Gruffydd Jones and some of his predecessors had realised that only by using the language of the people could the people be saved. There are elements in this total argument from history—for example, the claim that the Church was sunk in apathy and indifference and worldliness, that it was 'anglicised', or that the Methodists were self-consciously 'Welsh' in attitude—which historians would no longer accept. It was not an age as depicted by William Williams Pantycelyn shrouded in night and heavy with sleep, but rather an age of gestation and slow change in which forces which would secure the future of the language were at work precisely at the time when its rejection seemed most imminent and inevitable.

In addition to this historical argument there was associated with it what we might call a sociological argument. In this also language played a critical part. It concerned the nature of the ministry and its role in bringing about those typically Welsh features in organised religion to which we have already alluded. It was pointed out, firstly, that the method of recruitment to the ministry ensured that it was in large measure socially identified with the chapel membership. The method of recruitment was the same in all the denominations though, of course, there were fundamental differences in the methods of ordaining to the ministry which reflected differences concerning the nature of authority in the different churches. The important element in the recruitment was the emergence of spiritually and intellectually superior men out of, or rather from within, the individual congregations. In all denominations, therefore, the congregations established norms of spirituality and intellect, and in dissenting congregations these norms were absolute and beyond interference by any other sovereign body, while the modified presbyterianism of the Calvinistic Methodists was a way of formalising and of enforcing the opinion of the churches at large. Within nonconformity these norms changed with time and from place to place and from congregation to congregation. For example, formal learning was not held to be a *sine qua non* in the early decades of the century but became a primary *desideratum* in the second half of the century. In the silver age of religious growth it was the congregations which established the norms.

Secondly, it was emphasised that the Welsh ministry was not a settled ministry, but on the contrary, a very mobile or peripatetic one. It was pointed out that this was a priceless blessing alike to the churches, to the country at large and to the ministers themselves. Dr Thomas Rees, for example, or Dr Abel J. Parry, Rhyl, the one a scholar and the other a preacher of peculiar power, both emphasised that they would have remained buried in their home villages or lost in the anonymity of towns had the system of perambulating ministers not been in operation. As it was, the system helped to maintain agreed standards of excellence within the denominations by ensuring that the most gifted should be universally known and acknowledged, and, of course, that these leaders should be suitably rewarded in terms of prestige and social class.

Thirdly, it was a missionising ministry. It was this which

justified and stimulated the mobility. Economics come into it as well. Many Independent chapels, for instance, for whom the settled ministry was important, just could not afford to maintain a minister. It is not until towards the middle of the century that the 'missioner', as distinct from the minister, comes into his own in Wales and it is interesting to note that these missioners, including those employed by the Calvinistic Methodists, were felt to be most needed in the poorer parts of the country rather than in the rich towns—in South Pembroke and Radnorshire rather than in Nantyglo or Bethesda—in 'English Wales' rather than in 'Welsh Wales'.

Fourthly, it was necessarily a Welsh language ministry. This was so despite the fact that the education which almost all of them received, once the idea of an educated ministry had become commonplace, was in English. But even then—from the mid-century onwards—a minister could carry out his duties properly only with the Welsh language. It was only later that individuals would go to great trouble to acquire the English language as a *spoken* language.

Finally, it was therefore, for all these reasons, a ministry which mediated between the native population and the dominant and dominating culture over the border. As Christmas Evans explained in about 1837, the Welsh ministry undertook the obligation of making available the richest and most health-giving of English theological thought to their congregations.

> Ni adawsent hwy . . . neb llyfrau duwinyddol yng nghuddfeydd yr iaeth Saesneg heb ddwyn eu mêr a'u brasder i bwlpudau Cymru, gyda'u golygiadau cynenid ac athrylythgar eu hunain. Fel hyn fe gyhoeddwyd â thafodau Cymreig bethau mawrion Duw. Dygwyd allan bethau newydd a hen fel teisenau bob wythnos ar y bwrdd aur ger bron yr Arglwydd i borthi eglwysi Cymru.[2]
>
> They allowed no works of theology to lie hidden in the caves of the English language without bringing the marrow and fat to the pulpits of Wales, adding their own original and exalted observations. In this way the great things of God were given utterance in the Welsh tongue. Each week new things and old were brought like sweetmeats and placed on the golden table before the Lord to feed the churches of Wales.

In addition to the spoken word, there was the written word. The vast efflorescence of publishing in the Welsh language which had originated at the end of the seventeenth and beginning of the eighteenth century (before the Methodist revival) was so closely associated with religion as to be, as it was to remain, virtually a function of religion. This was the case even where as, for instance, in historical scholarship, the subject of discourse did not formally come within the ambit of religion. It may be a mistaken idea, but it is not far from the truth, that the printing press became an extension of the pulpit and the ministry to have educative functions which in other societies would have been regarded as secular.

Clearly then language was of cardinal importance and in the context of subsequent history one can see that what these early Victorian commentators were claiming was that they had succeeded in bringing to completion what government had attempted at the time of the Reformation but which their chosen instrument for this purpose, the Established Church, had conspicuously failed to do. They saw that the failure of the Church had been consistently a failure to use the language of the people. This certainly ignores the enormous contribution of churchmen as writers, scholars, thinkers, patrons and saints to the development of Welsh-language culture. It probably exaggerates the extent to which the Church at the level of the parish church has become anglicised. But the fact remains that a cardinal plan in the strategy of revival and renewal which was being worked out and applied in the Church of England from the mid 1840s onwards was the rehabilitation of its Welsh language heritage.

But the testing times came when the impact of economic change began to alter the language composition of the country in an unmistakable manner. This, as we have seen, occurred massively in the last decade of the century though, of course, the process had begun earlier. It is arguable that so powerful was the alliance of language with religion that it was able to contain the challenge of English culture up to and even beyond the first world war, and that it was not prosperity but depression which ultimately broke the organic connection. That it was able to do so becomes clear when we examine some of the relations of language to politics.

Earlier we noted that there were elements of ambiguity or of equivocation in the relation of language to religion and we can understand that this was probably inevitable among a people who were constantly being reminded by circumstances of the linguistic diversity in their culture. We get glimpses of this in, for example, the increasing admiration of ministers for English culture. At first, as the quotation from John Elias showed and as we know to have been the case with the leading figures of Methodism. this was confined to theology and works of piety, all of which (to the satisfaction of the leaders) were made available in Welsh. But a generation later John Williams, Brynsiencyn, was claiming 'that it was necessary to advise the present generation of Welsh preachers to read Welsh books. They read English books galore, but many of them ignore their own vernacular'. Notice too the enormous efforts which young men, aspirants to the ministry, put into learning English. Dr Abel Parry thought it required at least six months in an English school to learn the language, and what was so painfully acquired was likely to be used on all possible occasions with pride. For these, English became an additional code, an indicator of social class, which is why they enjoyed using English when writing privately to each other and why they multiplied the social and public occasions in which its use might seem to be prescribed. We note also that the colleges and academies and eventually the University were all, with the exception of Michael D. Jones's academy at Llanuwchlyn, entirely and exclusively English institutions. Kilsby Jones points out that the venerable Dr Phillips used the Welsh Not (or its equivalent) in his school at Neuaddlwyd, the resultant fund being used to provide the good doctor with his weekly ration of tobacco. Some of the colleges were aggressively English in tone and culture. Pontypool Academy under Dr Thomas Thomas, for example, was certainly so and we know that the great Dr Lewis Edwards thought of the new college at Bala as preparing young men linguistically for the inevitable flood-tide of English culture.

This attitude to the two languages—the acceptance of the prestige-giving English language and the superiority of its cultural possibilities to that of Welsh even though the latter was still the language of primary communication—must be taken as one symptom among others of a very profound change taking place within organised religion. We might mention the new consciousness of architectural style in chapel building: it now enters its mahogany phase: new chapels are described as Neo-gothic, or Classic with Ionian pediments, and so on, or in the Byzantine style, while the old original chapels are regarded as crude and vulgar.

> Un o arwyddion daionus ein cyfnod . . . Boddlonwyd yn rhy hir ar
> yr hen gapelau cyffredin, diaddurn, ysguboriaid eu dullwedd, fel pe

> buasai raid i harddwch sancteiddrwydd oddimewn gymryd un
> gydymaeth anharddwch ymddangosiad oddiallan.[3]

> One of the good signs of the time . . . For too long have we
> been satisfied with the old, ordinary, undecorated, barn-like
> chapels, as if it were necessary that the beauty of holiness internally
> should be related externally to ugliness.

It was said that ministers tended to ape the manners of English
ministers in style of dress and mode of living. No less an acute
observer than Professor Sir John Rhys in 1905 thought that even
as English sacerdotalism was interpenetrating the Established
Church, so 'in outward appearance the religious leaders among
the Nonconformist bodies assimilate themselves now more and
more to the clergy of the Church of England and the white tie has
invaded distant dingles where so much vision was formerly seen.'
More serious than that and much earlier in time was the readiness
of ministers who knew little English—like Dr John Thomas in
Bwlchnewydd, his first chapel in 1842, who used to switch to
English for the sake of the one monoglot English schoolmaster
whom he (of all people) had been instrumental in appointing.
Here we might remark that criticism of Anglican clergy in Welsh
parishes for providing occasional services for the sake of gentry
families came strange from the lips of such as John Thomas. More
revealing of the true situation and symptomatic of the social
changes was the movement to build chapels for the English
resident in Welsh towns. David Rees, Capel Als, Llanelli was doing
this virtually in anticipation of an English invasion (which scarcely
ever materialised on the scale imagined by him) and even
encouraged Welsh speaking members of the various Independent
chapels to migrate to the new English centres in order to help out.
Thomas Rees, Beaufort and Swansea, who certainly mastered the
English language sufficiently to write the kind of inflated prose
that was so typical of the worst Victorian pietistic style, had an
almost pathological urge to provide English chapels in Welsh
towns. Nor were the Calvinistic Methodists behind-hand in this
suicidal enterprise. 'It would be wilful blindness on the part of the
Welsh Calvinistic Methodists if they refused to acknowledge the
fact that the Welsh were adopting the English language' said the
Cymdeithasfa meeting at Wrexham in 1871. But this movement
had started much earlier, in the 1850s. 'The jealousy with which
the English language was once regarded, as a means of setting

forth the truths of the gospel, has passed away,' declared the *Welsh Calvinistic Methodist Record* in 1852 and it advocated a diversion of capital from Welsh Wales to English Wales, from building Welsh chapels to building English chapels.

Nothing is more symptomatic of this ambiguity and of the cultural shift that it signifies than the readiness to think of language in functional terms only and by implication to create a hierarchy of values with consequential language attachments. It was common by the mid-century to accept that while English was the language of science, business and commerce, philosophy and the arts, Welsh was the language of religion. One can understand the psychology and, indeed, some of the reasons why such judgements should have become general. For one thing, they were empirical judgements, certainly so far as business and commerce, government and administration, law and philosophy were concerned. For another, the Welsh were becoming conditioned by the mid-century to the idea that Welsh was an inferior language. This had not been the case during the lifetime of, say, the Reverend Henry Rees, Carnhuanawc, who believed in 1834 that it was highly probable that English would go the way of Latin 'and be known only in musty parchments and old records, and that the ancient language of this island will again be the universal language of its inhabitants.' There were also the contemporary anthropological notions which equated language with race: primitive peoples have primitive languages: compared with English Welsh is a primitive language, *ergo* . . . Sir John Rhys was one of those who rejected such notions: skulls, he said, are stronger than consonants and race lurks when language slinks away. Arthur James Johnes was one of those who deduced racial characteristics from language. But above all the Welsh were accustomed to being distinguished as a religious people, predisposed to awe and wonder. 'They are mystics. They dwell in the realms of imagination'—and what mystic has ever understood the second law of thermodynamics?

So it is not to be wondered at that this notion of the restricted value of Welsh should have become so general. What is strange is that the religious leaders themselves, like Dr Lewis Edwards, should have agreed and, indeed, assisted in propagating it. For the implications of such a notion were very serious. Firstly, religion was being degraded in comparison with other mental and social activities and, secondly, religion was being defined in exclusive terms. Both of these were destructive of religion itself and made possible a total secularisation of culture. For the Reformers of the sixteenth century and the fathers of Methodism, religion was all-inclusive and theology the queen of the sciences. And one can see how this philosophy led to the pernicious education system by which Welsh was excluded from all schools—National, British, industrial, private, school-board. In 1852 only one industrial school in South Wales used Welsh as a normal medium of instruction and that was Sir Benjamin Hall's Abercarn Colliery School. Twenty years later the social scientist, Ravenstein, failed to find a single Welsh school in Glamorgan.

The obverse of this coin, of course, was the image of what English was good for. Briefly, the advantages of the English language were what Lord Powys at the 1850 Rhuddlan Eisteddfod referred to as 'the highest objects of ambition,' and since he was supported in this delphic remark by Sir Watkin Williams Wynn, Mr Mostyn and other gentlemen of rank and station he was probably referring to material well-being. This, in fact, is what English was good for and it is ironic that at almost precisely the time when Matthew Arnold was extolling the virtues of Celtic literature to the philistines of his own country, the philistines of Wales should have been sacrificing that selfsame language, as one bard put it, 'on the alter of utilitarianism' and material welfare. 'Os ydych am barhau i fwyta bara tywyll a gorwedd ar wely gwellt, gwaeddwch chwi eich gorau, "Oes y byd i'r iaith Gymraeg": ond os ydych chwi yn chwennych bwyta bara gwyn a chig eidon rhost, mae yn rhaid i chwi ddysgu Saesneg.'[4] ('If you wish to continue to eat black bread and to lie in straw beds carry on shouting "Long life to the Welsh language". But if you wish to eat white bread and roast beef you must learn English.') Thus David Davies of Llandinam, the exemplar of the self-made man. More of an image-maker, perhaps, was the Unitarian minister turned banker, Lewis Lloyd, the father of Lord Overstone. As *Y Geninen* put it,

Nis gwyddom am gymaint ag un Cymro uniaith a gasglodd gyfoeth heb wybod Saesneg . . . Er fod Cymru yn un o rannau cyfoethocaf Prydain Fawr, a'i thrysorau cuddiedig dan ei drwyn a'i draed, eto, trwy ei anwybodaeth, ni wnaeth ddim ohonynt hyd nes i'r Saes llygad-graf, profiadol ac anturiaethus brynu llawer maes ar gyfer y trysor cuddiedig.[5]

We do not know of a single instance of a monoglot Welshman who has gathered wealth without knowing English . . . Even though Wales is one of the richest regions in Great Britain, and her riches hidden under his (i.e. the Welshman's) nose and feet, yet by his ignorance, he made nothing of them until the keen-eyed, experienced and enterprising Englishman came and bought the fields for the sake of their hidden treasure.

That is the authentic voice of Welsh philistinism and it goes on to deplore the fact that there is no Welsh Samuel Smiles to guide the footsteps of incipient child entrepreneurs into the rich paths of self-help.

> Ond y mae ein llyfrgelloedd Cymraeg yn ddiffygiol iawn mewn llyfrau fel rhai Dr Smiles, ac eraill, a ddangosent i'r ieuanc yr hyn sydd bosib mewn bywyd drwy benderfyniad, addysg, diwylliant, gonestrwydd, sobrwydd, darbodaeth, a dyfalbarhad. Y mae llawer Cymro, wedi dyfod i gyffyrddiad a llenyddiaeth y Saeson, wedi dymuno mewn ing—'O, na chawn i fyned yn ôl i ailgychwyn fy mywyd eto; mi fynwn wneuthur rhywbeth iawn ohono'.[6]
>
> But our Welsh libraries are very deficient in books such as those of Dr Smiles and others, which show to the young what is possible through determination, education, culture, honesty, sobriety, prudence and perseverence. Many a Welshman, after coming to know this English literature, has agonisingly sighed, "O that I might not return to begin my life over again: I would be sure to make something of it."

It is difficult to imagine the stresses that such doctrines placed upon the intelligent Welshman who was being taught at the same time to think of his language as his most precious possession. Or how was he to react when repeatedly told in his own language that his lack of cleanliness, his readiness to tolerate dirty houses, women who lacked pride in manners and appearance and, above all, his lack of common honesty was attributable to his ignorance of the English language? (When did you last beat your mother?).

But having said that such was the general attitude we have immediately to qualify and to turn to quite contrary attitudes which were as widely held and could often coexist in the same person. For if it was universally recognised that English was essential for a number of prudential and utilitarian reasons it was also for moral reasons a language to be feared and kept if possible on the other side of Offa's Dyke, (or at any rate wherever the language boundary happened to run).[7]

> [The English] . . . reveal more infidelity and beastliness in a week
> than many a part of Wales ever experienced; drunkenness,
> lewdness and all other curses of the English will flood our dear
> country unless we are prepared to withstand the attack and turn
> back the flood by raising the banner in the name of our God.

English was the language of infidelity and atheism, of secularism,
of the higher criticism, of extreme liberality in theology. Dr
Thomas Charles Edwards, surveying the religious scene in 1892,
saw scepticism and agnosticism spreading through Wales—in the
villages, quarry towns, coal regions and even among the
peasantry. 'Y mae y fath lyfrau anffyddiol a Robert Ingersoll yn
cael eu darllen, nid gan ysgolheigion ond gan bobl gyffredin.'[8]
('Such infidel books as Robert Ingersoll's are being read, not by
scholars, but by the common people.') He believed that it was not
impossible that Wales could become irreligious yet again. 'Wedi ei
dyrchafu hyd y nef, hi a dynir i lawr hyd uffern.'[9] ('Having been
raised to heaven she will be dragged down to hell.') It was certainly
the language of Tractarianism, of High Churchmanship, Anglo-
Catholicism and sacerdotalism. English corrupted the 'natural'
and pure political views of Welshmen. It was the language of
socialism, of co-operation, of trade unions and of all political
ideologies antipathetic to the official Liberalism of virtually all
nonconformist establishments. What must have been meant by
this was that such ideas originated in and were mediated to Wales
by the English language: for it is clear that these ideas, or
moderate forms of them were not long in taking on a Welsh dress.
It was also the language of the quite opposite tendency to the
levelling ideals of socialism, namely, the language of ostentation
in dress and style of living, and the English railway was the
corrupter-in-chief. 'Ni fedr yr agerbeiriant fwy o Gymraeg na
thywysog cyntaf Cymru, yr hwn a anwyd yng Nghastell
Caernarfon.'[10] ('The steam-engine knows no more Welsh than the
first prince of Wales, who was born in Caernarfon Castle.')

   The Welsh language was a defence against these evils. There
seem to have been two reasons for this. First, the very simple
reason that the ideas did not exist in the Welsh language, and
second, the fact that the Welsh language media were such as to
lend themselves to control from above. The first raises interesting
problems in socio-linguistics and it is probably to the second that
one should look for an explanation. The virtual monopoly of
power in the cultural sphere which was exercised by organised

religion involved, in effect, the exercise of a kind of censorship. It was not always thus: there had been a time in the first decade of Chartism, for example, when newspapers, such as *Utgorn Cymru* managed to exist—albeit briefly—outside the magic circle of denominational indulgence or acquiescence. As late as 1849 Thomas Stephens, chemist and literateur of Merthyr Tydfil, was expressing satisfaction on seeing the cause of 'Cambrian literature' being divorced from the tavern and entering into alliance with the chapel. But it entered into alliance with the chapel on the terms of the chapel, and one of the major principles demanded was a return to the psychology and general attitude (if not precisely in the same terms) of the Calvinistic Methodists in the period of political revolution in the first three or four decades of the century. 'It is not, gentlemen, in my estimation', said the president of the 1828 Gwyneddigion Eisteddfod in Denbigh, 'the least valuable feature in the advantages of the Welsh language, that it has been the means of preserving the Welsh peasantry . . . from the pestilent contaminations of such writers as *Paine, Hone, Carlile,* and I will even add *Cobbett* . . . Wales has ever remained in a state of peacable subordination'. Control of the Welsh press, even though only a partial control, ensured the perpetuation of that philosophy. Thomas Gee had to be very careful what went into the *Gwyddoniadur*, and Christmas Evans and John Jones, Talsarn, were deeply perturbed when it became known that a Welsh version of *Chambers Penny Encyclopaedia*—under the title *Addysg Chambers i'r Bobl* (1851)—was being prepared for publication. It is clear that John Jones and John Elias were familiar with volume I, in which they would have read the article on *Iaeth* (Language), and found that it was based on the philological theories of Horne Tooke, the radical of the previous generation, whose name was anathema to Welsh nonconformist leaders. They may also have known that one of the Chambers brothers (probably Robert) was very likely the author of the controversial and rather scandalous *Vestiges of the Natural History of Creation* (1844). Note also the dismay with which John Elias regarded the inclusion of articles on politics in *Cronicl yr Oes* (established 1835 as *Y Newyddiadur Hanesyddol*), edited by Reverend Roger Edwards who was a founder editor of *Y Traethodydd* (with Lewis Edwards). This is why Welsh effectively failed to become a language of political discussion in the widest sense, why its vocabulary remained restricted, and why English therefore became the language for what it scorned or feared to express. This explains the kind of schizophrenic phobia of so many Welsh leaders: 'Learn English, my boy, to get on; but learn English and risk being damned and, what is more, risk bringing about the dissolution of the society we have created,' might nicely sum up the attitude.

I have only hinted at the complexity of this situation and these cultural developments, but it is clear to me that it is this that gives to Welsh politics in the last century its unique character. When one considers the social impact of the changes in the economic bases of civilisation with which I started, the marvel is that Wales in fact remained the quietest, best governed, most law-abiding part of the United Kingdom. When one thinks of the appalling living conditions, the food and housing in the rural districts from which people tried to escape in their hundreds of thousands; of the impact of the new industry on the old towns; of the creation of frontier settlements, 'condensations of people' in the iron and coal districts; how sewers overflowed and water supplies gave out; how housing deteriorated and disease raged among the poor; of the vacuity and hopelessness of the poverty of the unfortunate in society; of the harshness of social controls disguised as social services—do we not wonder? After the late 1830s and the final outbreak of violent forms of protest the people who were the victims of these changes suffered virtually without demonstrable revolt. They developed no mature trade unions, and almost the only politics they knew were those which could be discussed in the language of morals and middle-class values.

Why? It is not that the working classes were not aware of their situation and critical of it. The magazines are filled with articles on 'Cyflwr y Gweithiwr' (The Condition of the Worker') and such like. But the analysis is in terms of the vocabulary made familiar to them in religious discourse and handed down to them by the ministerial class. 'Boddlonrwydd yng ngwyneb caledi yr amseroedd: rhaid i bawb ymfoddloni i'r gwahanol sefyllfaoedd ac ymdawelu tan alluog law Rhagluniaeth'. ('Resignation in the face of hardship: all must accept their diverse stations and be silent under the powerful hand of Providence'.) That is *Yr Haul*, the Church of England monthly, in 1851, but it was the commonly accepted philosophy.

Y mae gwahanol raddau cymdeithas wedi eu trefnu gan yr Hwn sydd a'i Frenhiniaeth yn llywodraethu ar bob peth. Nid yw y

gweithiwr yn weithiwr o ddamwain ac nid yw y cyfoethog yn
gyfoethog o ddamwain . . . Na, cofied y gweithiwr, er ei les ei hun,
mai nid da rhyfela yn erbyn cyfreithiau gosodedig cymdeithas.

The various gradations of society have been arranged by Him
whose Sovereignty governs all things. The worker is not a worker
by chance, nor is the wealthy wealthy by accident . . . No, let the
worker be reminded, for his own benefit, that it is not fitting to
rebel against the fixed laws of society.

That was written by a worker and is taken from an eisteddfodic
essay in 1852 in Merthyr. It shows to what an extent the working
classes had been socialised in accordance with the norms of the
middle classes. Hence, the relative weakness of class attitudes as
reflected in institutions of a militant kind.

Yet it is clear that it was these selfsame people that for their
own reasons and of their own volition clung to a language which
seemed to give them no hope for the future beyond a com-
pensatory heaven beyond earth, and a doctrine of self-
improvement and competition which effectively condemned them
to perpetual injustice. Why should they have reacted thus? The
explanation, I believe, must be sought in the deep consciousness
of the people themselves and we might consider some of the more
obvious expressions of this. Firstly, let us not forget that the Welsh
language was *their* language, the language of the common people
more so than it was the language of *savants* and the *literati*. For the
latter it worked in only well-defined social networks: for the former it worked through all networks—work, religion, politics,
friendship. If there had been, or was in the process of taking place,
a betrayal, it was a betrayal of the clerisy, not of the laity, and if
there was a crisis of conscience concerning the language it was a
crisis only for the *savant*.

Secondly, it was the language of the common people in the
sense that it was incorporated into their own institutions. The
chapels had originated as their institutions: it was they had
provided the elite, and for nearly a century there had been har-
monious understanding and an implicit realisation that they—the
common people— could exert some kind of control. After all, this
was why they were nonconformists and not anglicans.

Thirdly, the language had become a way of expressing social
difference: in particular, it marked them off from the English
aristocracy and the anglicising middle-classes. Closely associated

67

with this was the function which language had for them of expressing national differences: it was a symbol and more than a symbol, for only in this language was the heroic past encapsulated, and only this language could bind the present in an organic continuum with the past. This led on, finally, to the function of language as establishing class differences, or, put in another way, of stimulating the growth of class consciousness. The Welsh language was a precious and singular possession of the masses of workers at a time when the inhuman, dehumanising and brutalising forces of industrialism were alienating them from nature and from society. All this is to say that the language survived at the levels where it was most important that it should survive. It heightened the consciousness of the people, gave them self-confidence and pride in themselves precisely at the time when all else seems to conspire to reduce them to the level of slaves.

This is why language is so crucial in politics. In my thesis language becomes the touchstone of both politics and religion, the certain indicator of profound spiritual change. Consider what happened when, by 1898 in South Wales and by 1900-03 in Gwynedd, it had become crystal clear to all that the workers were an exploited class, that the basic inequalities in society were widening year by year. One effect was a marked movement away from religion, especially from the chapels. Large numbers of men became disillusioned with a religion which failed to speak out clearly on social issues of real relevance to ordinary men and which could organise only on political issues, such as disestablishment, which had become meaningless. Some turned to the new-fangled Labour Churches, others tried to reform the chapels by liberalising its teaching in socialist directions, as by R. J. Campbell and Gomer Harris and the *English* branches of the Calvinistic Methodists. In essence this was an attempt to re-use the language for their own felt social needs. Maybe 1904-05 was the last attempt by ordinary Welshmen to make of religion what it had once been—popular, nonclerical, unlearned, unsophisticated, enthusiastic, organic in the community, and Welsh in language. The Revival failed in these objects, the first sign of failure, perhaps, being Evan Roberts' instinctive feeling that to try to give the Revival an English dress or to take it outside Wales would be to betray the newly gathered faithful.

Inevitably, the next movement would be in the direction of socialism. and by the years just before the War, from 1911 onwards, socialism and the new miners' union were becoming the new religion. The language of socialism was English. Of the first 130 Fabian Tracts, for example, only two were translated into Welsh, and only two of the pamphlets of the Social Democratic Federation were available in the Welsh language. To abandon Welsh became not only a valuational but also a symbolic gesture of rejection and of affirmation—the rejection of the political philosophy and the sham combination of Lib-Labism and the affirmation of new solidarities and new idealisms based upon a secular and anti-religious philosophy. Fifty years earlier the new unions of the coalfield had issued their pamphlets, transacted their business and organised themselves politically in Welsh. *The Miners' Next Step* was written in English and never translated. What some thinkers had consistently feared had come about: the language and the religion which had grown together would decline together.

I have tried to show that the causes lie deep in the consciousness of the nation and can be seen powerfully at work in the experience of only a few generations. Institutionally, these years saw the decline into a kind of impotence and irrelevance of organisations which for generations had contained and shaped the highest and noblest aspirations of the people as a whole, and which had provided explanations of existence in terms of a distinctive theology and history that had been sufficient for the times. Now, with the popular withdrawal from them, counter institutions, expressive of alternative cultures, came rapidly to the fore. Not necessarily antagonistic at first, and often existing institutionally side by side in the same industrial villages and towns, even as complementary beliefs and attitudes in the same individuals, it was the new that proved to be the most adaptable and which came finally to express the newfound confidence of a genuine proletariat.

1. *Yr Adolygydd*, III (1850).
2. *Y Traethodydd*, I (1846).
3. *Y Traethodydd*, (1864),pp. 384 ff.
4. Quoted in *Y Geninen*, I (1883), p. 19.
5. *ibid.*, p. 20.
6. *ibid.*
7. *Y Diwygiwr*, (1851), p. 64.
8. *Liverpool Courier*, 7 January 1892.
9. *Y Geninen*, Hydref 1896.
10. *Y Geninen*, I (1883), p. 20.

Bibliographical Note

The scientific study of the history of the Welsh language during the successive phases of industrialisation is still in its infancy. Until the Census of 1891 it lacks the essential statistical data. J.E. Southall, *The Welsh Language Census of 1891* (Cardiff, 1894) is the most interesting of contemporary attempts to interpret the new body of information which then became available. Subsequent population censuses have all collected data on the language, and all have been studied by geographers, such as Professor E.G. Bowen, Professor Harold Carter and Dr. R. Gareth Thomas, whose works will be found listed in *A Bibliography of the History of Wales* (2nd. edn. 1962 and Supplements). For the pre-1891 period data is difficult to find and hazardous to interpret when found. Official papers, parliamentary investigations, committees and commissions of the Victorian period contain a great deal of information, as do the records of religious bodies, friendly societies and the other cultural institutions of the coalfield. The most important pioneering work of the century was E.G. Ravenstein's 'On the Celtic Languages in the British Isles; a statistical survey', *Journal of the Royal Statistical Society*, 42 (1879). Contemporary scholarship owes a great deal to the economic historians and to the geographers. Pre-eminent among the first are the essays of Professor Brinley Thomas, especially 'The Migration of Labour into the Glamorganshire Coalfield 1861-1911', *Economica*, X (1930) (reprinted in W.E. Minchinton (ed.), *Industrial south Wales 1750-1914* (Newton Abbot, 1969)). Among the latter see the essays of W.T.R. Pryce, especially 'Industrialism, urbanisation and the maintenance of cultural areas', *Welsh History Review*, 7 (1975), P.N. Jones, 'Some Aspects of immigration into the Glamorgan coalfield between 1881 and 1911', *Trans. Hon. Soc. Cymmrodorion* (1969) and his 'Baptist Chapels as an index of cultural transition', *Journal of Historical Geography*, II (1976).

The most wide-ranging and perceptive essays on the cultural background are by Professor Glanmor Williams in his *Religion, Language and Nationality in Wales* (Cardiff, 1979). The title essay and 'Religion and Education in Wales: an Historical Survey' are essential reading. My essay is interpretive and is based mainly on literary sources in the Welsh language, including periodicals and newspapers. It scarcely needs to be pointed out that the essential key to the understanding of the social history of the Welsh language is the Welsh language itself.

In addition to the periodicals mentioned above I have made extensive use of contemporary denominational and chapel histories, biographies and memoirs, the most important of which are listed in the *Bibliography of Welsh History* (and its Supplements) referred to above. Finally, I have used newspapers including the *Monmouthshire Merlin*, the *Cardiff and Merthyr Guardian*, the *Liverpool Courrier*, the *Welshman, Baner ac Amserau Cymru, Seren Cymru* and *Tarian y Gweithiwr*.

Empire and Identity: the 'Case' of Dr William Price

Brian Davies

In the last quarter of the nineteenth century Cardiff had become the 'coal metropolis' of Wales, Britain, and the world. In the summer of 1896 the city, convinced of its self-importance, organised its own grand Victorian extravaganza—the Cardiff Fine Art, Industrial and Maritime Exhibition. In Cathays Park the triumph of Empire was celebrated; inside the Indian-style exhibition pavilion the visitors found the places of honour occupied by symbols of Britain's industrial supremacy—a model South African gold mine, a model coal mine, railway locomotives and coaches, hydraulic pumps, printing machinery, a collection of ship, dock and harbour models, weaving machinery . . . From the main hall, dominated by Sir William Armstrong and Mitchell's display of artillery and ammunition, an arched doorway led into a different world, that of the 'Old Cardiff' exhibition. Here, amidst a motley collection of minor relics, the curious could see 'the right foot of Dr William Price of Llantrisant', the programme explaining that it was 'said by scientists that the whole nature of his body must have dropped to his foot, which is on view.' Of course it was not really William Price's foot. Price had been cremated, very thoroughly, on top of two tons of coal, three years previously. But this bizarre and fraudulent display, in the middle of a demonstration of imperial prosperity, confidence, and respectability, was a singularly appropriate way of marking the death of the most remarkable individualist in Welsh history.

It has been customary to treat Dr William Price merely as an amusing eccentric, but his activities and beliefs, and his impact on Welsh popular memory, should make us ask some important questions about the society which shaped him.

William Price's life almost spanned the nineteenth century. He was born in 1800, the fifth of seven children of the Reverend William Price and his wife Mary, and descended, on his father's side, from Nicholas Pryce, an ironmaster of Pentyrch, Glamorgan.

William aroused a certain amount of curiosity in the neighbour-
hood by his early practice of nudism, but otherwise his childhood
appears to have been fairly uneventful. Welsh was the language of
his home, so William did not learn English until he went to
school, at the age of ten. He left at thirteen and a half, sure that he
had absorbed all that his master could teach him, served his
apprenticeship with an apothecary in Caerphilly for five years,
then went to London where he qualified as a member of the Royal
College of Surgeons in 1821. In 1823 he returned to South Wales
and became medical officer at Ynysangharad works, Pontypridd, a
post which he held for many years. He later claimed that by this
time he had acquired some knowledge of most European
languages, and was becoming interested in Hindu literature and
religion.

Price makes his first distinctive appearance in public life in
the late 1830s. By this time he had become familiar with Druidic
legend, and in March 1838 he issued an appeal for funds to erect
at the Rocking Stone on Pontypridd Common a stone tower, 100ft
high, which would be a museum, scientific institution, and school
for the children of the poor, with a house nearby for the bard of
the Cymreigyddion Society of Newbridge. His appeal was
addressed to all those 'interested in the preservation of the Ancient
Institutions and Antiquities of Britain' and explained that his
purpose was to enable future generations 'to learn the music, the
language, and institutions of the Britons.' Price was promised sub-
scriptions totalling £130, with Francis Crawshay the Treforest
ironmaster heading the list, but this amount was hopelessly
insufficient so the tower was never built.

William Price does not seem to have been involved in the
Merthyr Rising of 1831, but he did support Josiah John Guest, the
ironmaster of Dowlais, during the Merthyr election of 1834, when
Guest, the nominee of the Radicals, fought off a challenge from
the town's Tories. This activity must have brought Price into contact with the future leaders of Merthyr Chartism, and when, in
1839, Chartism grew into a mass movement in South Wales, Price
soon became enthusiastically involved. He took the chair at
Blackwood on 22 April when Henry Vincent, the Chartist orator
and publicist who won great popularity in the valleys, spoke to a
meeting of two to three thousand. He was soon recognised as the
leader of the Chartists in the Pontypridd area, and at the meeting
which elected him to this position he is said to have concluded his

speech with the words 'I will repeat that we have tolerated the tyranny of those who oppress us—landlords, coalowners and the clergy—too long. We must strike with all our might and power and strike immediately.'

During the next few weeks Price was reported conducting political agitation among the colliers in Llanfabon and Blackwood, and around Nantgarw. In August a request from the Cardiff Reform Association to help them in the registration of voters brought from Price the sharp reply that 'The Battle of the Country for equal laws and fair play is to be fought in the brains—for I am well assured they have brains—of the Working Classes; and not in the Registration Courts, as the Whigs and Tories would make them believe.' This letter, which the Swansea *Cambrian* refused to print, is a strongly argued statement of Price's political position. He advised the people to 'have nothing to do with Whig or Tory', and likened the two parties to players at a card game. Just as players throw away a pack of cards when it gets old and dirty, so these parties condemned people to the workhouse when they could no longer work or fight for their masters. Both parties were parasites, living on the industry of the people, and inciting nations against each other. Price advocated a boycott of unsympathetic ministers, and a general policy of 'exclusion' towards all those hostile to the Charter, and he anticipated a popular victory before the next general election.

Following the arrest of Henry Vincent on 7 May, and his trial on 2 August, Dr Price was again the chairman at the great protest meeting at Dukestown, Sirhowy, on 12 August. According to one source Price spent some time in September on a political tour of Staffordshire and the North of England.

His role during the rising of 3/4 November 1839 is not quite clear, but neither is it as mysterious as is sometimes assumed. His own account centres on his distrust of John Frost. Price says that he attended a clandestine meeting at Twyn y Star some six weeks before the rising. Frost, chairing the meeting, was interrupted by a delegate from Abersychan, David Davies, an ex-soldier, who announced 'I have been sent here to tell you that we shall not rise until you give us a list of those we are to remove—to kill. I know what the English army is, and I know how to fight them, and the only way to succeed is to attack and remove those who command them—the officers and those who administer the law. We must be led as the children of Israel were led from Egypt through the Red

Sea.' According to Price, Frost could not go through with this. A week before the rising Frost sent for Price, who suspected that a spy was listening in on the conversation. The prospect of conflict with the troops reduced Frost to tears. Price cursed him—'You shall not put a sword in my hand and a rope around my neck at the same time'—and left. Price was seen outside the Coach and Horses public house at Blackwood, on Friday, 1 November, when the final delegate meeting was held, and spoke to Frost there, but he doesn't seem to have taken part in the meeting. The rising took place on 3/4 November but although one contingent from Glamorgan 'consisting of over three hundred colliers from Llanfabon and Gelligaer' joined the Monmouthshire men very few from Merthyr, Aberdare or the Pontypridd area were involved. Price's explanation, given many years later, is that his distrust of Frost led him to anticipate the failure of the rising, so he made sure that no-one from his area took part, and then, disguised as a woman, he escaped to France.

His story can be partly corroborated by other evidence. On the Wednesday before the rising David Lewis, a shoemaker and beerhouse-keeper from Brynmawr, told a meeting at the Royal Oak, Blaina, to aim at the magistrates and officers because then the soldiers would join them. As the crowd moved down the Eastern Valley on the night of 3 November, William Woods, the manager of Abersychan Ironworks narrowly escaped capture, and rumours spread of intentions to seize the magistrates at Newport and Hanbury Leigh the Lord Lieutenant. These and other details make Price's account of David Davies' speech at the Twyn y Star meeting several weeks earlier quite plausible. Captain Howells, Chief Constable at Cardiff, had written to the Marquis of Bute on the 1st of November, reporting that he had 'written to Mr Price of Porth-y-glo to remove his cannon.' Another statement confirms that William Jones, leader of the Pontypool contingent, was expecting Price to arrive with cannon. Price's claim that John Frost had told him that the Chartists' plan of organisation was in Samuel Etheridge's printing office in Newport also rings true. After the rising the police found in Etheridge's office a paper drafted by Richard Rorke—an 82-year-old veteran of the Irish Rebellion—which outlined the 'cell' structure of the United Irishmen. Etheridge claimed that this was part of Rorke's manuscript autobiography, but there is clear evidence that some of the Monmouthshire lodges were adopting this form of organisation in late October, and Rorke's paper seemed sufficiently incriminating to Feargus O'Connor and William Geach for them to burn the original as soon as they saw it. So Price's account, given nearly half a century later, cannot be far from the truth.

Other parts of his story are less likely. It is not clear exactly when Price fled the country; one report has him still at Pontypridd on the day of the rising, escorted by four 'very notorious fellows,' each carrying a double-barrelled gun; but he had definitely gone within a few weeks. His claim that there was a reward on his head appears to be untrue, because as late as the beginning of December no reward had been offered for lack of sufficient evidence to convict. Particularly unlikely is his story that during his stay in Paris he frequently visited Louis Phillippe, and became associated with a Captain Phelps, supposedly Louis' brother-in-law. This acquaintance is said to have ended when Phelps discovered that Price was in the habit of undressing his 16-year-old daughter.

Whatever Price did in Paris, within six months he was back at Pontypridd, working again for Crawshay, and resuming his involvement in Chartism. In June 1840 an attempt was made to assassinate the queen. Meetings all over the country responded by declaring their loyalty and congratulating Victoria upon her survival. Not in Pontypridd. When the local gentlemen and clergy arrived at the hall, William Price and his friends were already in occupation. The 'respectables' proposed that the chair should be taken by the Reverend David Williams of Glyntaff. Price proposed William Williams, landlord of the 'Prince of Wales' beerhouse. Price won the vote, and the 'respectables' adjourned to another room to vote their loyalty without interference.

During the autumn of 1840 Price was holding meetings at several places in the Pontypridd area. In the 'Commonwealth Society Hall of the Industrious People of Great Britain'—an unlicensed beer-house just out of Pontypridd, Price held regular Sunday morning Welsh classes which the police suspected to be a cover for an arms club. He now began to clothe political activity in Druidic symbolism—'his "scholars" walk openly with a stick in their hand, about four feet in length, shaped like a bayonet, three-sided, with figures and letters on them; but not an iota of their instructions or discipline is yet known' as each member took an oath of secrecy. In mid-October the Pontypridd Chartists, having concluded that all the shopkeepers were against giving the people the vote, decided, under Price's leadership, to form a co-operative (the first in Wales) which they called the 'Pontypridd Provision Company'.

During the general election of the summer of 1841 significant political divisions developed in the Chartist movement, both nationally and locally. The Monmouthshire Chartists were divided over the question of what attitude to adopt towards the two parties—the Whigs and the Tories. One group, led by William Townsend, the son of a wine merchant, opposed the Whigs—then in power—for having promised reform but failed to deliver the goods, and emotionally argued that the return of the Tories was preferable, because at least they were open and honest enemies. The other group, including William Edwards, the baker, a founder of the Newport Working Men's Association, and John Dickinson, a butcher, took a more favourable view of Whig promises of reform, and advocated giving them a second chance. On the day of the nomination William Edwards was nominated as the Chartist candidate, but the meeting was then thrown into confusion by the entrance of William Price, who was also proposed as a candidate. Price's nomination was not accepted. Edwards won the show of hands by the non-electors but then withdrew from the poll in favour of Blewitt, the Whig. This caused uproar among the Chartists, most of whom regarded Edwards' withdrawal as a betrayal. That afternoon a crowd carried effigies of Edwards and Dickinson through the streets of Newport, and later in the night, with a drummer at their head, they wrecked the houses of the two leaders who had been seen to compromise with the Whigs.

Price continued to be involved in the Chartist movement for some time after this election. Although he complained of a wholesalers' boycott of the Pontypridd co-operative in 1841, the store seems to have survived this crisis, for when the Newbridge chain-workers struck against a reduction in wages in April 1842 Price was able to supply them with a large amount of provisions, and during the following weeks Chartism gained ground considerably in the area. When a government spy penetrated the Merthyr Chartist organisation in early September 1842, following the defeat of the political general strike in August, he sent back information about arming, and gave details of a system of organisation, resembling that of '39, which was said to have been invented by a Dr Price. This seems to be the last piece of evidence connecting the Doctor with Chartism.

From the mid 1840s onwards William Price turned much of his energies to litigation. He had already been involved in legal proceedings on several occasions, but these had been relatively humdrum affairs. In 1847-8 Price was involved in a succession of cases in the Small Debts Court, as well as making two appearances at the Glamorgan Summer Assizes. In the second of these, in which he was a witness, his style of dress seems to have been of more interest than his testimony. Price had become such a familiar figure in the courts of South Wales during these years that the local press affected an air of boredom; 'we . . . are accustomed to Mr Price's appearance' on these occasions, wrote the *Merthyr Guardian* laconically. Nevertheless, possibly for the benefit of new readers interested in the Doctor's latest and most ambitious legal enterprise to date, then being heard in Bristol, the paper a few weeks later described carefully what Price himself explained was 'the dress of the Ancient Court of Glamorgan.'—

> This eccentric gentleman, who is a son of a deceased clergyman, wears a beard flowing to his waist, and his hair, which has evidently not been cut for many years, descends to as great a length, but is tied up with sundry long tails, *à la Chinoise*. His dress consists of a jacket and trousers of emerald green, fancifully knotched and scolloped, lined and pointed with bright scarlet, and adorned with numerous small gilt buttons bearing devices. His cap is of sable, of singularly quaint form, and has attached to it three pendant tails of the same fur, one falling over each shoulder of the wearer, and the third coming down to the centre of his back.

This Bristol hearing in August 1848, of the case of 'Fothergill v. Price', turned around the question of whether Prices's father had been sane in 1809, when he had sold 85 acres of land at Rudry, Glamorgan, which William and his brother Charles were now trying to reclaim. The testimony of several witnesses proved that the Reverend Price had unquestionably been insane for at least the last forty years of his life; indeed, on this particular occasion the signing of the necessary documents had had to be postponed for a day because the Reverend had escaped by jumping out of a window. With such evidence the Price brothers won their case, but not before William had incurred the wrath of the nonconformist establishment in South Wales by performing a post-mortem on his father's body to prove that he had been *non compos mentis*.

In 1850 the Doctor was back in the Cardiff Small Debts Court, and this time we get an indication of what was happening to the man's mind. Price had refused to vacate a piece of land rented from a Maria Price. He had employed ingenious delaying tactics to get the case transferred from one court to another, and sent to Maria Price's solicitor a letter which attempted to change the issue completely by arguing that she had usurped the legitimate claims of her half-brother James to some of her late father's property, and claiming that James had entrusted his interests to the Doctor. This letter is written in an extraordinary style which gives a foretaste of what is to come. The relatively lucid exposition of Price's argument is coolly interrupted by the observation—'I presume that wonders will never cease in the confusion of ideas till the day of judgement, whence *everything* will move *in order* in all directions to the sound of music.' The court wisely ignored this, and the argument about Maria's half-brother James, but William got off the hook after all, because the piece of land in question had in fact been held by his brother Charles, so Maria had prosecuted the wrong man.

The Doctor's next notable appearance in court in 1859 began in a fairly ordinary way. Price was called to the Glamorgan County Court in March to give evidence in a case in which an Ann Millward had used improper means to recover unpaid rent from her brother William. The Doctor gave his evidence, but within a few days found himself charged with perjury, and in July appeared before the Glamorgan Summer Assizes accused of having prompted Ann Millward to take illegal action against her brother. Price conducted his own defence, with his seventeen year old daughter Gwenhiolen 'Countess of Glamorgan' acting as his legal counsel and provided with a seat at the barristers' table. The Clerk to the Court began by recalling Price's behaviour at the first hearing. When offered a Testament on which to take the oath, Price had objected because it contained a map of Judea, to the accuracy of which he said he could not swear. The second Bible was objectionable to him because it had someone's name in it; but the third proved acceptable. After a few preliminary questions the July hearing became hopelessly confused, for Price accused both the Clerk and the Assistant Bailiff to the County Court of extortion. This was the outcome of a series of minor proceedings dating back to the previous August, as a result of which the Doctor had lost two cases and fallen behind in his payment of court fees. Langley,

Clerk to the County Court, had overcharged Price, who now claimed that the action for perjury was a frame-up by the court officials in revenge for his charge of extortion against them. Price at this point submitted a lengthy statement which began dramatically—'As my brain has been ploughed and harrowed for the last five months, and sown by the conspirators, with the seeds of villainy and malice, I beg you will hear me patiently, and with all the indulgence you can afford, to an innocent victim of persecution, to mow down their Harvest of Perjury.' He accused the Judge and officers of the Small Debts Court of bringing this charge against him 'for the express purpose of taking away my liberty, destroying my reputation, and arresting my right course, because I have repeatedly refused to prostrate my senses in this Court, and other places, to his dictation, and their threatenings of prosecution.' Price obviously saw the Court officials as agents acting against him on behalf of the government, and went on to express this in a characteristically bizarre manner—

> What. Cannot her Majesty, as the Mighty Huntress, in her day, before the Lord, go out like the Sun, to find beasts of prey enough for her bloodhounds, *without* hounding them to sacrifice the liberty and the life of an inocent man, upon her criminal altars, with the bloody hands of her Law Priesthood?

In spite of this outburst the Doctor was able to present the factual matter relating to his case clearly, and to conduct a lengthy and perfectly coherent cross-examination of one of the witnesses. The Judge agreed that the conduct of the officers of the Small Debts Court had been irregular, and the jury declared Price 'Not Guilty' of perjury. This verdict, reacned at 1.15 in the morning when the court had been sitting for over sixteen hours, brought 'enthusiastic cheering' from the large crowd inside the hall and outside in the street. The press compared the response to the 'unanimous approval' of a great public meeting. William Price had won his greatest legal battle to date.

For several years prior to this case litigation had seemed to be the Doctor's main pursuit, but from 1853 onwards his legal skirmishes became less frequent, and they are of interest mainly because they illustrate his withdrawal into a world of his own fantastic creation. In 1861 Price was again involved in a dispute relating to his possession of a piece of land. He found it necessary to retreat for a time to Boulogne, and from there wrote a number of remarkable letters to different parties involved in the case. The first, dated 24 December 1861, is addressed to the auctioneers of the property. In it Price identifies himself and his daughter Gwenhiolen as children of the Lord Ris (Rhys ap Gruffydd, 1132-1197, lord of Deheubarth, and leader of the rising of 1164-5) and asserts that the security of his claim to his 'father's' estate and title was the reason for the indecent haste of 'these Pretending Attorney Mortgagees . . . [and] . . . their Golden Geese, Their Capitalists, who are obliged to hire their Brains' in taking action against him. According to Price there could be no solution other than the recognition of his rights by the Lord Mayor of London, to whom he had written six weeks earlier. This letter had contained the warning that 'on the First Second of time, in the morning of the ninth day of November Instant, one thousand eight hundred and sixty one, the present Foreign Government of Great Britain, geared into office by you, as my Father's Steward . . . shall cease to be, and shall die out.' In his letter to the auctioneers Price expanded upon this with the announcement—

> Capitalists are Hereby informed that There is no Title to hold Land now, and has not been since The ninth of November 1861, but The Title of the Goat of our Father the Lord Ris . . . Marriage Settlements are voidable now, in The Court of Law and Equity. A Divorce Court to separate husband and wife, now, is an useless Court to the Public. The woman, as well as the man, is Freed now, and liberated, henceforth, to enjoy themselves in this respect, as they will, in The Light of the Sun and Moon!!!

He concluded by advising capitalists 'at This Period of Revolution in The Title to Real Estate' to consult the Latin Breviarum (the book which contains the daily service of the Roman Catholic Church).

A few days later Price elaborated his fantasy in a letter requesting a printer named Jones to produce several hundred copies of the following notice:

> All the Greek Books are The Works of the Primitive Bards, in our own Language!!!!!! There is a Discovery for the Cymmerian Race!!!!! Discovered by me in 1839!!!! No man living can form an opinion, or imagine, The consequence of my Discovery Before He shall be taught, *by me*, to read Homer, The Greek New Testament,

81

> or any and all The Greek Classics, which I can do, perfectly, in less
> than six days!!!!! Homer was born in The Hamlet of E Van near
> Caerphilli. He built Caerphilli Castle . . . The oldest *Books of the
> Chinese* confess The Fact!! This looks more like a Dream than a
> Reality in The absence of Light.

A day later he wrote again, insisting that this was 'the most
Important Manuscript Notice that has ever been *sent* to *any Press*,
for The Public!!!,' and instructing the printer to put the words
'Plant Ywein Lawgoch' in red ink at the top of the notice. The
reference here is again to a historical figure, Owain Llawgoch
(Owen of the Red Hand), who fought with the French against
Edward III, and passed into Welsh legend as a hero who would
one day return and rule over Britain.

This use of historical figures as the basis for a bizarre
mythology centred upon an idiosyncratic interpretation of
Druidism absorbed Price's energies for the rest of his life. In addition to his imagined relationship with Rhys and Owain, he
claimed that Dr Coch, who was supposed to have carried the Red
Dragon at the battle of Bosworth in 1485, was his ancestor. A few
incidents in his later life stand out. In March 1881 William Price
appeared in the streets of Treforest, wearing a white robe, red
trousers, fox-skin headdress, and carrying a large red silk flag. He
marched to the Rocking Stone on the hill overlooking Pontypridd,
mounted it at noon, and proceeded to address the sun. Three
years later he gave an astonishing performance at the Cardiff Art
Exhibition.

> In a manner which had about it a touch of the occult, the lecturer
> connected his early ancestry with the contents of the Goose's Egg,
> and declared, . . . that 3,700 years ago his birth was
> registered . . . Subsequently the doctor struck up a Welsh song, in
> the course of chanting which, and with his face to the ladies and
> gentlemen, he removed his tunic . . . disclosing what appeared to
> be a red flannel shirt beneath . . . The audience laughed at the
> coolness and singular simplicity which marked the lecturer's
> conduct as he thus divested himself of a part of his curious
> costume, but they were altogether unprepared for what was to
> follow. In the next place Dr Price deliberately kicked off his boots,
> and then, with an apparent unconsciousness which the alarmed
> looks of the audience did nothing to dispel, he removed the green-
> coloured trousers. The various habiliments were taken off, one

after the other, with a slow deliberation. A number of ladies left the room . . .

Price stood on the stage in a skin-tight red outfit covered with green lettering.

The Doctor's defiance of convention culminated in the act for which he has become famous. On 18 January 1884 the faithful nonconformists of Llantrisant, coming out of chapel on Sunday evening, saw a fire burning on the hillside. William Price, at the age of 83, was illegally cremating the body of his five month old illegitimate son, Jesus Christ Price, Son of God. Price's victory in the court proceedings which followed established the legality of cremation. The old man fathered a second son, also named Jesus Christ, and another daughter, before finally expiring at the age of 92.

Welsh historians have tended to treat William Price simply as a crank. And if the generally accepted image of nineteenth century Wales is correct, then they are right. In a Wales which was steadfastly nonconformist, honestly radical—but not revolutionary—and at the popular level culturally Welsh to the core, Price's behaviour would indeed be an inexplicable aberration. So it has been fashionable to repeat the verdict of a contemporary representative of the establishment that William Price was 'a fit subject, in the opinion of most, for a lunatic asylum' and to leave the matter there. Recently a more sophisticated explanation diagnoses Price as a kind of schizophrenic—a paraphrenic, to be exact. But this more 'scientific' analysis is no more useful as an explanation than the earlier simple-minded verdict of Henry Scale. Price's eccentricity, even madness, must be understood in historical context.

Before William Price began his exceptional contribution to Welsh mythology, there was already a pretty substantial foundation of falsification and fantasy to build upon. Although Price later ranged far and wide in his search for material which could be turned to his purpose his inventive intelligence had plenty to begin with in the *Myvyrian Archaeology of Wales* or Rowland Jones' *The Circles of Gomer*. Price was, after all, only the most colourful of a number of individuals who tended in the same direction—towards a pyrotechnic combination of political radicalism, historical forgery, and Druidic mythology. The most obvious other example is Iolo Morgannwg, but there are many more. If we dispose of

Price we still have to deal with lesser figures like Morien and his inventive 'history' of Pontypridd.

Now, after all, there is no *a priori* reason why Wales should produce more cranks per square mile than any other part of the world, so what is behind all this?

In order to see Price in perspective it is necessary to consider a broad context, namely the expansion of Britain as an imperial power and the economic and social consequences of this for Welsh society in the nineteenth century. Frederick Engels summed up the results, with an evident note of disgust, in a comment made in 1858—

> the English proletariat is actually becoming more and more bourgeois, so that this most bourgeois of all nations is apparently aiming ultimately at the possession of a bourgeois aristocracy and a bourgeois proletariat *as well as* a bourgeoisie. For a nation which exploits the whole world this is of course to a certain extent justifiable.

Twenty five years later he repeated this argument—

> Participation in the domination of the world market was and is the economic basis of the political nullity of the British workers. The tail of the bourgeoisie in the economic exploitation of this monopoly but nevertheless sharing in its advantages, they are, of course politically the tail of the 'Great Liberal Party'.

The key factor in creating political stability, he believed, was 'the improved position of a more or less privileged minority' of the working class. The strength of Engels' explanation has recently been proved by studies of several English and Scottish towns during the industrial revolution. These same general features of political adjustment and accommodation, of incorporation of the working class into a comparatively stable economic and political system, can also be seen in Wales in the mid-nineteenth century.

In the years immediately following the defeat of the Newport rising Chartism in South Wales remained stronger than has sometimes been assumed, and in the summer of 1842 the movement again posed a real threat to the establishment. In a serious economic recession which brought a reduction of wages at the ironworks the crisis broke in August. The ironworkers of Merthyr

struck for the restoration of the wage levels of 1840, then resolved
not to return to work until the People's Charter became the law of
the land. Within twenty-four hours the town was under military
occupation, and the strike was swiftly broken. Nevertheless the
following year was equally turbulent, and the authorities were pre-
occupied with the possibility that Chartism, Rebecca, and 'combinations' among colliers and coppermen might fuse into one
massive popular movement. They did not, but at the end of 1843
arms clubs were again being organised, and the resources of
Merthyr Chartism were channelled into an attempt to establish a
local organisation of the Miners' Association.

Six years later we are in a different world. The major
industrial disputes of the mid century in the area were the colliers'
strikes in the Aberdare valley and Monmouthshire during the
winter of 1849-50. None of the speakers at the strike meetings can
be connected with the Chartist movement. In Merthyr the
Chartists were not even meeting regularly, and Wilkins 'the
workmen's bookseller' who supplied the markets at Merthyr and
Dowlais was selling only 12 copies per week of the Chartist
Northern Star compared with 189 of the *News of the World*. Chartism
in South Wales was effectively dead.

The economic changes that caused its early demise took
place in the mid-1840s with great speed. Within two years of the
strike of 1842 the growing demand for rails lifted the iron industry
out of the slump and began a period of rapid expansion which was
not interrupted for half a decade. Dowlais, given stability by a
large Russian order for rails, removed a long-standing grievance
by changing over to regular payment of weekly wages; and by mid
1845 ironworkers' wages generally had increased by around 25 per
cent in little over twelve months: differentials within the industry
began to open up. The economic upturn brought a new emphasis
on leisure: Friendly Societies celebrated in style; the organised
day-trip now began to become a regular feature of working class
life; the Taff Vale Railway introduced cheap excursions on
Sundays, liberating Merthyr and intimidating Cardiff. Enjoying
the gratitude of their now-loyal workforce, ironmasters founded
Mechanics' Institutes to educate the sober and steady.

The boom could not last forever, but the fluctuations in the
iron trade in the late forties and fifties never threw the industry
back to the conditions of the early forties. As a result the fragile
unity between colliers and ironworkers which had been achieved

during the heyday of Chartism was never recreated. Indeed, in the strikes of 1849-50, commented upon bitterly by Ernest Jones, there was much less cohesion among the colliers themselves than there had been in 1843. When trade unions emerged in the skilled trades in the early fifties their behaviour was typical of the craft unionism of the period—generally cautious, narrow and exclusive.

A handful of Chartist activists kept the flag flying, but their popular support had gone. As the organisation disintegrated even the individuals who remained active tended to shift their political position. Morgan Williams, leader of Merthyr Chartism in its early years, disappeared from the political scene after 1842 and became a respected figure of Merthyr society. Henry Thomas, J.W. James, George Morgan and William Gould, who all remained Chartists to the end, had become Liberals by 1868.

Britain's domination of the world economy soon led to the development of attitudes expressing the conviction of cultural, even racial superiority. This can be illustrated in Wales just as in England; a few examples will suffice. A Mr Aldridge, who called himself 'The African Roscius', amused the 'gentry' of Neath in the summer of 1845 with his rendering of 'Lubly Rosa' and 'Oppossum up a gum-tree'. When 'Templeton's African Troupe' of 'Negro melodists' performed at Dowlais in 1861 the chief attraction was an intentionally ludicrous presentation of a 'niggerised' version of Italian opera—'as laughable a conception of Italian art as ever entered the head of a darkey'. Touring the coalfield at about the same time was Wombwell's Menagerie's 'far-famed collection of wild beasts', which also exhibited Zulus who begged from the audience. These are typical of the popular entertainment of the 1850s and 1860s as recorded in detail in the local press.

The extension of imperialist culture, however, has another aspect. The methods through which an imperialist ruling class strives to control the cultural expression of a subordinate nationality in order to maintain social order are extremely complex. In the case of nineteenth century Wales the emphasis of ruling class policy seems to change from heavy-handed suppression in the early decades, through assimilation/anglicisation in mid-century, to an encouragement at the end of the century of an acceptable, docile Welshness in which the Welsh language and culture became a respectable badge of identification for people who were as loyal to the Empire as any other section of the British establishment.

According to the orthodox version, the history of Wales in the second half of the nineteenth century is the story of the steady, almost inevitable, rise of Liberal nonconformity and the growth of a national consciousness, in part as a response to that monumental insult the Blue Books of 1847. From this point of view the National Eisteddfod, especially after its reorganisation in 1858, played a crucial role in this consolidation of a Welsh identity.

Reality is more awkward. In 1865 the National Eisteddfod was held at Aberystwyth. The opening speech was given by the Rector of Neath. All the mythology is there: 'Before foreign foe ever trod upon Albion's soil, before even the missionary planted the standard of the cross upon these territories, the national Eisteddfod had a place, exercised an influence, and wielded a mighty power over the people.' But the competitions do not fit the usual picture. The principal prize was a hundred guineas for an 'Essay on the Origin of the English Nation', the entries to be written in order to illustrate especially the connection between the English Nation and the Ancient Britons. The entries could be written in English, French, German or Welsh (although some commentators forgot to mention the last of the four alternatives). The adjudicator was Prince Lucien Bonaparte, who did not think any of the entries worth the prize, and commented that they were all rather weak in their argument—a weakness understandable when one remembers that they were trying to demonstrate a connection between the English nation and the Ancient Britons. The whole atmosphere of the Eisteddfod was that of Victorian 'improvement'. Two new sections were added—a social science section and an industrial exhibition; and Dr Nicholas read a paper advocating the establishment of public schools for the Welsh middle classes. A few years later a prize was actually given for an essay on 'The efficacy of eisteddfodau as a means of disseminating the English language.' A local eisteddfod at Tredegar rewarded efforts to domonstrate 'The consistency of the Volunteer Rifle movement with Christianity.' Engels again makes the point quite neatly—'The English know how to reconcile people of the most diverse races with their rule; the Welsh, who fought tenaciously for their language and culture, have become entirely reconciled with the British Empire.' So it is not surprising that it was also in 1865 that the most consistent advocates of Welsh cultural nationalism settled in Patagonia, or that projects to create Welsh utopias inevitably involved physical removal from Wales as the first step.

So perhaps William Price becomes comprehensible. His mind was not weakened by the study of Welsh literature as the 'Modern English Biography' arrogantly claimed. The direction of his schizophrenia was determined by the triumph of Victorian imperialism.

Consider his early enterprises. At a local eisteddfod held by the Cymreigyddion Society of Pontypridd in 1837 Dr Price offered £10 in prizes, £1 each for the best essay on the following subjects—Love, Pride, Belief, Faith, Superstition, Prejudice, Fame, Opinion, Profit and Truth. Quite sane. His first failure came in 1839—the attempt to found an educational institution at Pontypridd. He wrote an angry letter to the *Merthyr Guardian*:

> . . . I imagined, *like a child*, there would be no difficulty in inspiring *in the whole length and breadth of Britain*, a thousand ladies and gentlemen . . . to subscribe a sovereign each . . . But to my great astonishment, I have found that they were either ignorant—*some with a net income of £1000 a year*.—of the rationale of their *creation* and *civilised existence*, or that they were biased to think or suspect that some *sinister* motive or passion inspired the projector to plan the institution . . . I see a vote in the House of Commons, granting £70,000 for repairing the Queen's stables for a few horses, and *but* £30,000 of the people's own money, for educating a whole nation of 26 million, *laughing me* in the face . . .

Still, on the whole, clear.

In the next few years Price experienced several defeats in rapid succession—the Newport rising, the Newport election in 1841, and the Chartist-inspired strike in Merthyr in 1842. The fragmentary evidence of Price's activity as a Chartist indicate that he had a firm grasp of reality. His speeches were competent, if colourful, political statements, showing, for example, a typical reliance on the works of Thomas Paine. He accepted the implications of considering 'physical force' when others hesitated. The defeat of the movement was not only a severe setback for the aspirations of the working class; for Price it signalled a victory for forces whose offensive against his people was gaining momentum on other fronts as well. One aspect of the Chartist threat had been the impenetrability of a movement whose proceedings were frequently conducted in a language which was incomprehensible to the great majority of the local ruling class. The authorities soon dealt with this difficulty by ensuring the rapid translation of any potentially subversive publications. To those without this facility the idea that their workers could hold meetings whose proceedings they could not understand was itself seditious. A Chartist meeting at Cefn Cribwr in August 1839 was interrupted by several 'gentlemen' who insisted that the speakers should use 'English, the Queen's English'. The majority of those present could only understand Welsh, so the meeting continued in that language. This so incensed the 'gentlemen' protesters that one of them attempted to assault the chairman, and was only prevented from doing so by William Price. The incident symbolises the attitude of the ruling class at this time. Welsh was seen as the subversive language of a rebellious proletariat. In the years immediately following the defeat of Chartism the majority of establishment spokesmen saw the extirpation of the Welsh language as a necessary mopping-up operation.

With a working-class movement in disarray and a popular national culture initially under heavy attack, and later assimilated and at important levels anglicised, William Price, the Welsh rebel, turned to individualistic protest and Celtic fantasy on the grand scale. Faced with a situation in which he saw the culture of his people under attack and their history denied, he reacted by reaffirming, through invention, their existence.

Price was in this respect in direct line of descent from Iolo Morgannwg. That is not to say that he made a contribution to Welsh culture in the way that Iolo—in spite of his tendency to create material when he could not find it—undoubtedly did. Iolo's invention had been motivated by the aim of forging a national consciousness. The resulting tangle of texts of doubtful provenance may well exasperate the more pedantic historian, but Iolo's literary creations were produced at a moment when a radical and national consciousness did seem to be developing in Wales. Iolo was quite closely in touch with the political reality of the Wales of the 1790s and early 1800s: he was frequently regarded as eccentric, but never as insane. William Price's purpose was the same, but by the middle years of his life the gap between reality and possibility was far wider. In spite of this he retained an instinctive sense of allegiance, supporting the miners during the strike of 1871 and denouncing the coalowners as Welsh Pharoahs. He also participated in quite ordinary cultural activities, chairing a Baptist eisteddfod in Tabernacl, Merthyr, in 1870, and patronising a production of Othello in Pontypridd in 1874.

But although he never completely lost touch with reality his Druidic fantasies became progressively more extravagant. In 1844 he attempted to organise an eisteddfod at Pontypridd. This time the material included much of his own creation as well as the more traditional bardic references. It was a dismal failure: no-one entered the competitions: the only event of note seems to have been the initiation of Price's two year old daughter, Gwenhiolen, Iarlles Morgannwg (Countess of Glamorgan).

In the following years Price's activities became more and more bizarre. Nevertheless his explanation of his beliefs is sometimes quite lucid. He rejected orthodox religion on several grounds—'I have not seen anybody or anything greater than Nature to worship . . . Man is greater than God, for man created God in his own image . . .' Preachers, he maintained 'are paid to teach that the world of thieves and oppressors, of landlords and coalowners, is a just world'. Their theology is always that of the doctrine that 'the powers that be are ordained by God.' But remarks like this are frequently interspersed, particularly in his later years, with the most outlandish propositions, such as that 'It is clear to me that Abraham was a cannibal, and it was with the view of destroying that trait in the nature of his descendants, and to raise tame animals, that the first pyramid in Egypt was built.' Obviously the author of such a statement cannot avoid a charge of spectacular mental instability, but in spite of these outbursts Price seems to have retained a remarkable ability as a doctor. No less remarkable were his beliefs regarding his profession. Doctors, he argued, should be paid according to their efficiency in keeping people healthy rather than by a system under which they found it economically advantageous to have people ill as long as possible. People should only pay the doctor when they were well; when they were ill the doctor should pay. Price's medicine rejected 'pills and potions and poisons' and concentrated on nature cures and vegetarianism. Over many years he held the reputation of being a very skilful surgeon.

Even as he retreated into Druidism William Price found himself at odds with the establishment. By now 'mainstream' Druidism had become respectable—just another manifestation of the attempt to establish a genuine British pedigree for England and her Empire. At the lowest level it was indeed a sorry spectacle of conformity. To the 'regular druids' Price was a heretic, while to him one suspects they must have seemed just a bit square. In July 1880 the enraged elders protested at Price introducing his 'vile' singing into the proceedings of the Gorsedd, and warned him of the terrible penalty awaiting him for such 'unholy' innovations. Nine months later the *Western Mail* carried an account of these gentlemen celebrating 'the feast of the Vernal Equinox . . . in the Zodiacal circle of Hu the Mighty, and within the folds of the Holy Dragon on the Pontypridd Common' which leaves the sceptical reader wondering whether there is much distinction to be made in terms of 'eccentricity' between the 'orthodox' elders on the one hand and Price on the other, except that Price's appearance in Treforest the following year shows a far better sense of dramatic style.

In 1871 William Price systematised his fantasies in a document entitled *The Will of My Father*. On its cover is his crest, a red goat, surrounded by a green serpent with its tail in its mouth. The text is rambling and confused, but the direction of Price's concern is fairly clear. He emphasises that he is addressing the Welsh people in correct Welsh in order to reveal 'The Song of the Wand of the Lettered Lore of the Welsh' which he has rediscovered after 2,600 years. The will of his father, he says 'has been kept in secret during the (time of) the foreign kings for their own advantage to mis-rule the nations of the earth.' He repeats the instruction—'. . . Remember that the living God himself is born a Welshman in his natural memory.' Price makes it clear that he is not here referring to the Christian God, and insofar as it is possible to unravel his meaning this 'living God' appears to manifest himself through the transmission of an ethnic identity from generation to generation. Price continues—'In the way in which you hear, they have conquered the memory, the hearing and the Welsh speech of the living God himself by bringing him up from his birth quite safely, dumb and deaf in the cradle of the learning of the foreign language books of the priests, the lawyers and the doctors of the God of the Father of Baptism . . .' (i.e. the Christian God). The second half of the *Will of My Father* contains Price's greatest fantasy—an eisteddfod of a million Welsh men and women, on the slopes of Snowdon, with himself at the centre repeating in the form of a catechism questions intended to show the Welsh origin of all things. Price includes a poem which he says is a translation of the strange symbols on his red tights, and sums up his claim—'I have proof positive that I am the son of the Welsh Primitive Bard and I am equally certain that this second child of mine, whom I have called Iesu Grist [Jesus Christ], will reign on earth, and that in him the ancient Druidical system will be restored.'

His fantasies, in a sense, formed a system. Towards the end of his life he claimed that his first major discovery had been made during his stay in France after the defeat of the Newport rising. There, in the Louvre, he had found 'a precious stone, on which was inscribed the portrait of the primitive bard in the act of addressing the moon.' On it were inscriptions and hieroglyphics which only he had been able to decipher. Later he claimed to have drawn up 120 'proofs' to support his claim to 'the authority that the Primitive Bard had to govern the world'. Price had become, in his own mind, the embodiment of an unbroken Druidic tradition originating in the distant past. At the moment which would appear to be that of his death he would exchange his body for that of his son, and would continue to exist in him.

Such a system of ideas would not normally be a subject for 'serious' commentary. Whether we choose to use the terms 'mad', or 'eccentric' or 'schizophrenic' William Price was unquestionably not sane. But there is a logic to his 'madness'. Christopher Caudwell once argued that

> Madmen are men whose theory has got out of gear with reality as
> evidenced by their practice—their action. This reality can only be a
> social reality because this is the only reality known to society.
> Madmen are men whose theory of reality differs markedly from
> that of society. They are socially maladapted. In them there is a
> conflict—a conflict between their social experience—their life in
> society—and their phantastic theory of life.

So an individual is seen to be 'mad' because he is out of step with everyone else. But it is always possible that a longer view will reveal that he was the only one in step. To say this of William Price would be taking special pleading too far. What can, and must, be said is that an imperialist society at the zenith of its power is a mad world, and that a sympathetic examination of William Price's reaction to it can help us to appreciate the extent of the cultural damage and the number of human casualties involved. Price defended his people to the best of his ability. He summoned the champions of the Welsh past to fight the enemy of the present—the capitalist class. But he fought at a time when the battle could not be won. His mind could not withstand the terrible pressures of defeat. But he stayed at his post when few others did. That is why he is remembered with affection and respect.

Bibliographical note

The best known work on William Price is undoubtedly Islwyn ap Nicholas's pamphlet, republished by the Ffynon Press in 1973 as *A Welsh Heretic, Dr William Price, Llantrisant*. For anyone who wishes to follow the subject further John Cule's thesis 'Dr William Price, Llantrisant. A Study of an Eccentric and a Biography of a Pioneer of Cremation' is the only recent (though perhaps too 'scientific') study. The thesis is summarised in an article in *Morgannwg* vol. VII. Cule has most of the known biographical details about Price and gives a full bibliography, but there is additional information concerning his Chartist activity in the *Cardiff and Merthyr Guardian*, the *Western Vindicator* and the *Northern Star* as well as in the basic manuscript sources in the Home Office Papers, the Bute Papers in Cardiff and the Special Commission Papers in Newport.

On Chartism in Wales the standard works are of course David Williams's *John Frost, a study in Chartism* (Cardiff, 1939) and his chapter in Asa Briggs (ed,) *Chartist Studies* (London, 1959). Angela John's article in *Morgannwg* vol. XV and the thesis upon which it is based contain much useful biographical detail on South Wales Chartists.

The standard histories referred to are David Williams' *History of Modern Wales* (London, 1950; reprint 1977) and Kenneth O. Morgan's *Wales in British Politics, 1868-1922* (Cardiff, 1963).

For the argument about the rise of a 'labour aristocracy' see Marx and Engels *On Britain*, and John Foster *Class Struggle and the Industrial Revolution (London, 1974)*. My sketch of economic developments in South Wales relies on the local press and various Parliamentary and Board of Trade papers.

Anyone wishing to penetrate further into the mysteries of Druidism should begin with Stuart Piggott's *The Druids* (London, 1968).

The quotation from Christopher Caudwell is from *Illusion and Reality*.

The Coalowners
L J Williams

The concept of labour history has changed substantially over the
last decade or two. In particular it has been opened out from a
central concern with (at its widest) the development of the labour
movement and, more usually, a concentration upon a small range
of institutions dominated by the trade unions. The change has
been very evident in Welsh labour history where *Llafur* (both the
journal and the society) has been an innovating influence. The
nature of the shift is too broad to be easily itemised and
catalogued. However, perhaps something of its flavour can be
indicated by suggesting that labour historians now take as their
province the general social history of the (widely-defined) working
class. It may be that the result has been to make the subject too
amorphous for coherence, that in breaking out from the earlier
tight institutional constraints it has overflowed into excessively
broad pastures. Time will tell whether this intellectual imperialism
can or should be maintained. But at present the subject seems
comfortably able to span the elucidation of movements in the
patterns of popular culture and recreation; the search into the
particular processes and rhythm of work; and the effects of education (or religion or whatever) on the working class or—more
usually perhaps—some particular group of workers or the working community. All this and much else is, of course, in addition to
a continuing commitment to the traditional interest in strikes and
unions and political activity.

Despite all this current permissiveness an essay on the
coalowners may seem incongruous, seem to be stretching matters
too far. Even in the present atmosphere the elasticity of the subject
is not infinite. There are still topics, even in the mainstream concern with industrial strife, which are not tackled—perhaps because
of some inherent feeling for the rightness of things. It might seem,
for example, that the tendency to want to look at the full range of
labour response and thus to reduce the emphasis on the history of

union leaders and the sacrifices of the rank and file, would have given rise to some sympathetic accounts of blackleg labour. Sympathy, after all, need not imply approval. It is a matter of fact that most strikes of any consequence threw up a rash of blacklegs. And it is a demonstrably inadequate and false response to imply that these were only the dregs of the community, that they were all motivated by only the most sordid of considerations. It needs little imagination to see that, in some situations and at some times, the role of blackleg demanded substantial courage; nor to see that this courage could as well be fuelled by religious belief or moral principle or individualistic ideology as by simple greed. But it remains a theme without a literature.

At all events, it is concluded here that coalowners are a fit subject for labour history, and that the time is right at least to begin a reassessment. We are now into the second generation in South Wales which is growing up with only the NCB as coalowner, more anonymous even than Amalgamated Anthracite but perhaps—though perhaps inadvertently—no less lethal. Of course, not even a contemporary child of the valleys—even of valleys where the soft-shoed and civil assassins of the NCB have killed off all the pits—can escape the myth which surrounds the old coalowners and be unaware of their pride of place in the demonology of the region. Nor is it intended to dislodge them from the high depths of this position or to tear aside the myth—whatever the 'objective' findings there will remain a sense in which the myth incorporates the essential truth.

The possibilities for upward social mobility within South Wales before 1914 were generally constrained. They were constrained everywhere, of course. But—although the assertion at present rests only on impressionistic grounds and could not be convincingly substantiated—it seems reasonable to state that the difficulty of workers moving up the social ladder were greater in South Wales than in Britain as a whole. Indeed, it is likely that this was one of the contributory factors making for the extraordinarily strong development of working-class consciousness in the region: the more able and gifted amongst the workers were not siphoned off.

In part the limited opportunities for social mobility simply reflected the occupational structure of the region. In 1911, 40 per cent of the occupied males in Glamorgan were engaged in mines and quarries. The dominance of mining meant the dominance of a heavily labour-intensive industry with over 150,000 workers in this single county before 1914 and it also meant that, proportionately, the outlets for a shift of social class were meagre: in 1911 less than three per cent of the occupied male population of Glamorgan was classed as professional. It would be a mistake, however, to suggest too rigid a framework. There was bound to be substantial fluidity in a region as buoyant and expansive as was South Wales in the decades before the first world war. It is not difficult to find examples of Nonconformist ministers who started life as working miners or the sons of working miners—S.O. Davies would have fallen into this category if his basic radicalism had not been so pugnacious: Nonconformity demanded a high degree of conformity. But although the celebration of such social shifts serves as eloquent testimony of the values of the society, they were statistically insignificant. The recruitment of teachers from working-class backgrounds took place on a larger scale but it was still relatively unusual and, in 1914, still a relatively recent phenomenon. A more general experience was to become one of the clerks servicing the growing labour-intensive commercial sector of the region. And a still more natural progression was for a worker to move upwards within his own industry. In mining some few made the eventual jump to become managers, but the most normal progression was towards the positions of the lesser officials in the pit, the deputies and overmen who were generally recruited from the rank and file. It was this sector which, in terms of talent at least, perhaps most directly competed with the unions looking for their lodge secretaries, checkweighers, agents and delegates—and perhaps this element of competition has been too easily passed over in labour histories.

Thus although there was a fair degree of mobility most of it was severely constrained in social terms. In particular, it was over-whelmingly occupational mobility rather than social mobility, a shift of job rather than of class. Given the status and prestige which they carried with the general community a miner who became a preacher or a teacher had certainly altered his social standing, and if he became a manager his economic standing also shifted. But the more characteristic change was much more ambiguous. To become a low-level clerk represented a definite occupational shift but—though it might (and was often meant to) distance a man from manual work—it was hardly a decisive class change: and those who joined the ranks of the minor colliery officials often found themselves uncomfortably straddled across the social fence.

An even more constricted channel for social progress was that offered by becoming a coalowner. It was *not* the case that every miner carried in his jack-tin the keys of the board room any more than field marshal's batons realistically resided in knapsacks. There were cases, of course, and enthusiastic Victorian propagandists made an enormous milage out of them. David Williams of Ynyscynon, who played an important part in the early development of the Aberdare valley, probably best fitted this mould. He had certainly been a working collier at one stage, as had William Thomas of Brynawel who had been a child working underground at the time of the 1842 report on the employment of women and children in mines. George Elliot would be a similar case, although his days as a pit-laddie were already well behind him before he came to South Wales in the early 1860s. Naturally none of them made a direct leap from collier to coalowner: they followed some variation on a progression up the colliery hierarchy—colliery clerk, surveyor, manager was the particular path of William Thomas, for example. Two broad features stand out: the cases which occurred were rare and they were early. Not many could thrust themselves along this path and those who did so successfully seem mostly to be confined to the pioneering days of the industry.

It needs to be noted that these comments about social mobility really refer only to a conception of coalowners as being confined to the leading group of men in the industry. If the definition was widened, some—indeterminate—modification would be required. By the end of the nineteenth century when most of the larger enterprises had become public companies it would probably be the case that amongst the list of shareholders—now occasionally numbering several hundred—would be found men holding five or ten pounds who were, or had been, working colliers. The point is of some importance simply because it highlights the basic problem of knowing who, at any time, were the coalowners. At the one extreme it could be plausibly argued that every shareholder in a coal-mining company was a coalowner. But this seems too wide. At the other extreme the term can denote just the handful of the most dominant—the David Davieses and the D. A. Thomases. But this seems too restrictive. In general this essay relates more nearly to the second group. That is, it has in mind the major proprietors in the various firms—not necessarily just one for each firm, but certainly not including all shareholders. The imprecision of this approach needs to be constantly borne in mind. It has a number of obvious immediate consequences. Thus it would be difficult—even for a particular moment of time—to attach a precise number to the group, still less to list their names. It makes even more difficult any effort to indicate the changing composition of the owners as a group. Moreover, it rests on an embarrassing dearth of detail about most aspects even of this limited group. On some of their personal characteristics—social and religious backgrounds—there is tolerable information; on others—their education—there is very little. On some aspects of their public activities—like involvement in politics—there is sporadic knowledge: but on others—particularly on the vital issue of how they conducted their businesses—these are still the dark ages.

The remainder of this essay aims to consider two aspects of the functions and activities of the coalowners. The first concerns the coalowners as economic actors: what economic function did they perform and how did they and others perceive their role? The second concerns their relation to the society around them.

In general views about coalowners have not been given anything more than ritualistic airings for over a generation, at which time they were rigidly and simplisticly polarised. On the one hand, the owners were viewed as men of vision, energy and enterprise. This was the broad line taken by such books as Elizabeth Phillip's *Pioneers of the Welsh Coalfield*, a work first published in 1925 and which had, tellingly, previously appeared as a series of articles in the *Western Mail* then still looked upon as the organ of the South Wales coalowners. It was written in a generally eulogistic vein the overall flavour of which can be conveyed by a brief and reasonable typical quotation: 'one who had spent a life full of work and good deeds, and was well beloved as only a good and kind master could be'. On the other hand, the owners were portrayed as greedy and grasping individuals who appropriated an excessive proportion of the wealth created by the labour of the miners. What these conflicting judgements have in common is a tendency to concentrate upon the personal characters, the moral traits, of the coalowners. It is an approach which is un-fruitful, unpromising and unsatisfactory: not just—or even mainly—because it is necessarily subjective, but because it is uninformative on the functions and relationships of the coal-owners as a social group.

The economic characteristics and attitudes of the coalowners reflected and were conditioned by—amongst other things—two broad factors, the one relating to industry in general the other to a particular feature of the coal industry. Most businessmen right up to 1914 simply accepted the broad economic orthodoxies of the age. They accepted the inherent superiority of an economic system based on competitive private enterprise operating through a general market system which fixed the 'proper' price for all commodities (including labour) and which provided the signals on which owners of capital could base their decisions. It is true, of course, that few businessmen interpreted this model in too literal a sense: none the less, in so far as they consciously thought of general economic principles as opposed to the pragmatic problems of running their own concern, most businessmen from the mid-nineteenth century to the first world war subscribed to the liberal competitive model. Indeed, so dominant was this view of the way in which the economy did and should operate that it is difficult to imagine what else nineteenth century businessmen could turn to. It is, therefore, reasonable to presume that this view of the economy was part of the more or less unconscious attitudes of the South Wales coalowners—and, indeed, of most other groups in the region. (D. A. Thomas was certainly exceptional in his more explicit acceptance of the theory acquired by some reading of economics, and especially J. S. Mill, during his Cambridge days in the late 1870s.) All of which is obvious enough, but if it is kept in mind as a background factor it helps towards an understanding of the actions and policies of coalowners over such fundamental aspects as wages, prices and output. The attachment to the presumed inherently beneficial nature of the competitive market economy, however, went deeper than this: it provided the material basis and justification for the bourgeois social order based on property. We'll return to this point in a less generalised way later.

The second broad factor arose from the extent to which luck was an essential feature determining the degree of success obtained by any particular firm in the industry. The element of fortune does, of course, enter into all business enterprise but the contention here is that it was, for reasons inherent in the industry, likely to be a more marked and more significant factor in coal mining (and, indeed, most extractive industry) than it was for industrial and manufacturing undertakings in general. As time passed and the coalfield became more comprehensively worked the accumulation of detailed geological knowledge did, of course, reduce the area of uncertainty. None the less large doubts still remained, especially in a coalfield as geologically disturbed and varied as that of South Wales. It is in this sense that coal mining was to some degree a 'bingo' industry.

Against these two general conditioning factors—the operation of the competitive private enterprise system and the heightened significance of good fortune in the industry—what did the coalowners contribute as providers of capital, managers, entrepreneurs and potential monopolists?

They certainly provided the capital: that was, indeed, the only function which defined them as a group. It was fortunate (or was it?) that in the early years the amounts of capital required were not vast and could often be raised by local men such as the more successful of the shopocracy spawned by the growing iron industry. Thus the Merthyr and Aberdare draper David Davis was able to embark first on the tiny Rhigos level, which led eventually to the vast Ferndale taking; whilst the Cambrian Combine's foundations were laid when the Merthyr grocer, Samuel Thomas, opened a pit at Ysguborwen with his brother-in-law Thomas Joseph. Few undertakings were financed by a single man, although one man might come to dominate or symbolise the firm. David Davies of Llandinam bestrode the Ocean Coal Company in this way but the capital for sinking the initial pits at Parc and Maendy in 1865-66 was also provided by Thomas Webb, John Riches, Morgan Joseph, Abraham Howell and Ezra Roberts. The smallness of the group was typical. In most companies throughout the pre-1914 period the majority of shares were held by about half a dozen main owners and often several of these belonged to the same family.

The process of capital formation need not be pursued in detail: in general there was little that was particularly distinctive about the experience of the South Wales coal industry in the second half of the nineteenth century. The banks played a relatively modest role, the expansion of the limited liability principle helped to widen the sources from which capital could be mobilised (though there were very few cases where money was raised by direct public subscription), and existing firms grew largely by ploughing back profits. There are, however, two aspects—related to what we have called the 'bingo' principle—which perhaps merit mention and would repay investigation. The first relates to the rate of return on capital. Recent work suggests that the level of profits before 1914 was relatively modest at around ten per cent. Given the nature of the evidence it would be easy enough to quibble about this finding, but its general validity seems well-founded. But it blurs the extent to which some companies fared much better than others. The differences seem unlikely to be explained simply by better management. More favourable conditions also played a part. Moreover, it was this possibility of much higher earnings which served to attract capital. On the whole people did not enter a high-risk industry like coal mining on the basis of earning a steady five per cent or so on their capital: they were lured by the possibility of much higher gains. The fluctuations were reinforced by wide variations over time. In the years of very high activity—the early 1870s, 1889-91, 1900-01—it was impossible to rapidly increase supply to meet the greater demand. As a result prices and profits soared. For the well placed firms this was a lucrative bonus, but for many of the more marginal undertakings it was their life-blood. This, too, was in the nature of the industry. If a pit was sunk and did not turn out well, abandonment entailed the more or less total loss of the capital. Thus a firm might rationally carry on even if, in normal years, it barely covered costs in the expectation of making high returns in the occasional boom years. The second aspect is that many of the firms which expanded most vigorously—like the Ocean, Ferndale and Cambrian undertakings—were those whose coal take was recognised to be unusually good.

The situation was in some respects like the eighteenth century slave trade. The new economic historians may indicate that the average rate of return was relatively modest: but most contemporaries (and historians) were more aware that some adventurers extracted substantial fortunes from the business. Similarly in South Wales before 1914 the ghostly ranks of failed or faded capitalists were barely perceived. The million pounds left by John Nixon seemed more substantial (and perhaps also raises some reservations about how far distributed profits were a reliable indicator: in 1893 Nixon had stated—as a boast so it was unlikely to be an underestimate—that the total amount distributed by the company over the previous thirty years had been £1.8m). Nixon was, at his own wish, buried at Mountain Ash despite his North Country origins, and despite the fact that he had, at the time of his death, hardly visited South Wales for a quarter of a century. In his case the withdrawal was largely a function of age (he was 60 in 1875), but it underlined the fact that being a coalowner did not necessarily carry with it active participation in management.

None the less, the characteristic pattern before 1914 was for one or more of the major shareholders to be involved in management. Partly for reasons indicated below, the trend was away from the proprietor directly managing the process of coal production. He was more likely to be found in the Cardiff or Swansea or Newport office and be concerned with general administration and coal sales. Did they, as owners, bring any special features—apart from self-interest—to the tasks of management, and was it an especially crucial function in the coal industry? In the present state of the game any answers to such questions are bound to be both tentative and subjective: my judgement would be to give a qualified negative to each.

Of course, skills in management were essential and important but there is no reason to suppose that these skills were necessarily best provided by the owners. Indeed there are some good reasons for considering that the significance of the owners' contribution to management was severely constrained by the nature of the industry. The obviously dangerous nature of the industry produced pressure for legislation on matters of safety. The slow accumulation of such legislation in itself encouraged the emergence of a profession of colliery managers. The Act of 1872 gave this trend a more explicit push by requiring, in all but the smaller collieries, that managers needed to be certified. Such a development necessarily meant that at the production end control was increasingly in the hands of salaried professional managers. Of course, managers could be made partners, and proprietors—like W. W. Hood of the Glamorgan collieries or John Nixon's nephews (H. E. Gray at Merthyr Vale and C. J. Gray at Navigation)—could acquire the necessary qualifications, but the general drift was clear enough.

As a result, control over the most crucial aspect of coal production—dealing with labour and restraining wage costs on a day to day basis—was not normally in the immediate hands of the owners. The nature of colliery working made the day to day aspect particularly important and also imposed its own constraints on the normal processes of management. In the often narrow, often dimly-lit, often shifting underground passages supervision as it was understood in workshops and factories was hardly possible. A mine could not, for example, be laid out as were many factories so a foreman could instantly and constantly view the workers. And yet a colliery because of its peculiar hazards demanded a more disciplined work-force—Mackworth, the pioneer mines inspector in South Wales, was fond of remarking that mines safety required the miners to observe discipline as scrupulously as a good regiment. The basic instrument of control was the piece-rate method of payment to the coal-cutters since it was their output and rhythm of work which dominated the entire pit.

Moreover, the range of management decisions was, in several crucial respects, restricted. Once a mine was sunk or acquired, the location of the enterprise was fixed with a rigidity greater than in most other industries. The basic product was also determined: coal mines produced coal. Nor could managerial decisions do much to alter or effect the particular product of a particular mine. It could be washed or sized or double-screened at the point of shipment but these were all minor adjustments compared to the range of choices normally facing managers in manufacturing industry. The basic point being made here was, moreover, reinforced by lack of significant technical change before 1914 in the basic process of coal-getting in South Wales.

There is a tendency to see in the lack of change in the basic system of coal-getting a proof of the coalowners' failure to innovate, and more particularly to treat the substantially lower proportion of coal which was machine-mined in South Wales before 1914 as substantive proof of the especial backwardness of the owners of South Wales. And it may be so. But an impressionistic and unsystematic survey of the evidence suggests that much if not all the difference can be accounted for by the peculiar geological conditions of South Wales. It is at least uncertain that a lack of technological initiative has to be added to the coalowners' sins.

Their significant entrepreneurial failure lay elsewhere. The possible sources of industrial capital in and around the coalfield were still limited in the second half of the nineteenth century. The coalowners were a major group amongst these limited sources. A vast labour force had been attracted to South Wales to meet their needs. It was in the nature of the industry that its size would eventually diminish. Yet the coalowners as a whole contributed very little towards diversification by investing to establish subsidiary, ancillary or alternative industries in the region.

Some commentators have seen further shortcomings (or virtues) in the inability of the coalowners to combine together to form a selling cartel. The argument, used at the time, rested on the special qualities of South Wales steam coal which could only be obtained from a relatively small area worked by a relatively small number of producers. The obvious course, instead of driving down the price by competing amongst each other, was to work together to raise prices by restricting output. Yet none of the schemes which were proposed was implemented. The most common explanation suggests that the coalowners as a group were too individualistic to be contained within such combines, an explanation which again places great emphasis on the personal characteristics of the owners. A subsidiary explanation stresses that their belief in the virtues of competition made such monopolistic proposals unattractive. Both these possibilities can be used to show the coalowners in a relatively favourable light: the first depicting them as a bunch of amiable eccentrics unwilling, for mere material gain, to subdue their individualistic traits; the second suggesting a positive philosophical commitment to full competition as an ideological system. Neither seems more than superficially plausible. Of course, personalities played some part: the 1896 scheme, for example, partly foundered on the personal antagonism between W. T. Lewis and D. A. Thomas. And, of course, once it had been decided not to adopt a scheme the decision was imbued with virtue by the rhetoric of free competition. It seems more likely, however, that the supposed advantages of such schemes were less overwhelming than was suggested. And there are good reasons for doubting whether the main, much less the only, constraint on the price of South Wales steam coal was the intensity of the competition amongst producers. Cardiff steam coal did have special qualities which did enable it to command a higher price, but before these facts could be easily transformed into a secure basis for cartelisation there were several major qualifications to be added. South Wales was, and always had been, a high cost producer so some ability to command a higher price was necessary before it could compete at all. The special qualities, moreover, only conferred a limited price advantage. In addition the market for South Wales steam coal was overwhelmingly over-seas: there was not a large home demand where a degree of natural protection from outside competition might exist in the form of high transport costs. And the coalowners were acutely aware that the price they could obtain overseas was—whatever the degree of internal competition—largely determined by the price of alternative coals from whatever source. They had to accept the prices at the given markets and these prices were only partially determined by the amounts of Welsh coal available. The possibility of monopoly gains was thus likely to be generally limited.

In any event, the stress on individualism and the attachment to the abstract concept of price competition is given some perspec-tive by observing the behaviour of coalowners in another sphere, that of their relations with the miners. Labour costs normally represented about 70 per cent of total production costs so the con-trol of these costs was a matter of crucial concern for all coalow-ners. In this area, where their interest was clearly and directly involved, they could and did work together: the Coalowners' Association from its early beginnings in the 1860s was overwhelm-ingly concerned with matters of industrial relations. There was a fierce resistance to wage claims, safety legislation, reduction in hours, union organisation—anything that was likely to add to the labour cost whether at a general level or at the level of the individual colliery. The resultant antagonism between owners and men was not the product of the personal characteristics on either side—though these could exacerbate any particular situation: it was embedded in the economic realities which made labour-cost the most important consideration for everybody and thus con-tinually underlined the inherent conflict of interest between owners and miners. But even for those who do not attribute everything to the wickedness of the coalowners but acknowledge a degree of objective reality making for a clash between labour and capital, the intensity of the pressure exerted by the owners on wage-levels is still surprising. They are, even in the generally expansionary market before 1914, continually trying to curtail or abolish established customs, cut back on allowances and press legal rights to an astonishing degree. Between the wars, in a less favourable economic climate, all these pressures on the miners, their wages and their working conditions were sharply intensified into a naked antagonism.

The nature, extend and significance of the contribution made by the coalowners to the wider life of the coalfield was full of ambiguities. Did they, for example, provide some justification for their incomes by using the money for further development rather than for personal consumption? At the impressionistic level, which is all that is currently available, the evidence suggests a cautious affirmative. On investment, for example, it has already been suggested that a significant proportion of the capital for coal mining was obtained by ploughing back profits, and parts of the essential infrastructure—the building of the Barry railway and docks would be the outstanding example—was largely financed by coalowners: but it was also noted that they provided little capital for the industrial diversification of the region. Similarly, they moved into or built substantial houses, often in or around Cardiff or Swansea, they sent their sons away to school, they bought land (some like the Davies family of the Ocean Coal Company or D.A. Thomas of the Cambrian Combine, deliberately buying up land near their ancestral origins at Llandinam and Llanwern); but the overall impression is not one of ostentatious living. Holidays seem to have been more characteristically spent at Tenby than at Nice; they were more likely to cultivate flowers than to breed race-horses; and there is an extraordinary, almost unnatural, absence of scandal. These impressions chime in with the deeply-held Nonconformity of many of them.

More positively, there is considerable evidence that the coalowners (not necessarily all of them, of course) made financial contributions towards the social capital and institutions of the coalfield communities. Chapels and churches seem to have been the commonest beneficiaries, but assistance was also given to schools, libraries, hospitals and workmen's institutes. Porth Intermediate School was provided by the County Council, but it charged weekly fees. At the ceremony to lay the foundation stone it was revealed that Edward Davies of Llandinam had given £2,000 towards a fund for scholarships and amongst several others—mostly landowners—who had each given £100 were F.L. Davis, Ferndale and Cory Bros. Councillor Clifford J. Cory had provided Ystrad-Rhondda with a library costing over £2,000. Sir W.T. Lewis presented Merthyr hospital with an accident-receiving ward which was then equipped by the Dowlais and Cyfarthfa companies. Workmen's Institutes, although mostly dependent on deductions from the pay of the miners, were often given a lump sum assistance from the local colliery owner—as in the case of T.W. Powell's contribution at Abertillery or that of Thomas Griffiths at Cymmer.

An even more direct form of activity was that of sitting on public bodies. Until somewhere around the 1880s this type of involvement by the owners was very frequent both for representative bodies like the Boards of Guardians and for nominated functions like the Justices of the Peace. There was, indeed, almost a prescriptive right about the process epitomised perhaps by the youthful D. A. Thomas who in 1881 at the age of 25, just down from Cambridge and learning the trade at the family's collieries in Clydach Vale was elected top of the poll from a score of candidates for the Ystradyfodwg Local Board of Health and also appointed as Justice of the Peace (at a time, before the Local Government Act of 1888, when the counties were governed by the JPs sitting at Quarter Sessions). The close participation of the coalowners in local administration and government declined both relatively and absolutely from the 1880s. This was partly because many moved away from the collieries to the ports (or beyond); partly because the 'natural right' to such positions was being challenged (although the extent of this challenge before 1914 should not be exaggerated); and partly because the legislative changes substantially increased the democratic nature of local government (although again it is important to remember the limitations of this process—the effective franchise, for example, was still severely restricted). Part of the decline was, in any case, deceptive. The owners simply delegated this representative function to their professional managerial staff at the collieries.

It is not at all clear that the involvement of the coalowners in community affairs amounted to a conscious attempt to exercise social control. Other considerations apart, such deliberate manipulation of the community was frequently otiose. Many colliery villages were essentially one-company communities. They were established in areas which had previously been relatively empty and barren so that there was little in the way of an established, traditional authority structure: they were frontier settlements in an almost American sense. They were economically dependent on a single enterprise to a degree which was rarer in most urban industrial areas. In such a situation it was clear enough where the ultimate power lay. Indeed, the basic power relationships (who could do what to whom) were so clearly defined in the South Wales coalfield before 1914 that a plausible case could be made for turning the whole 'social control' thesis on its head: the financial assistance given by coalowners to community activities were intended to disguise the degree of control they already possessed.

In addition emphasis upon concepts like social control fail to do justice to the complexity of the motivation which was involved. Given the nature of the time and place, and given what we know of the character and beliefs of some of the coalowners, an act of some historical violence is required to stress that they were only, and consciously, concerned with the manipulation of their workforce. Some gave funds and joined in community activities because they were aware of, and wished to maintain, cultural values and links; many more were doubtless moved by a variety of religious considerations (the need to do 'good works'; missionary zeal; to glorify God; to undermine the established church); others were concerned with moral elevation—and were more likely to be concerned with deflecting workmen from drink than from revolutionary thoughts; and there was some simple benevolence as well as the provision of conscience money.

Such moral justifications were certainly important to the coalowners themselves. They naturally saw their riches as a reasonable reward for their own individual virtues: they were not likely to consider that they were merely active as the agents of abstract forces like capitalism when they were—like all the other actors on the historical stage—all too conscious of their own personal feelings and thoughts. In one of his novels (*A Time to Laugh*) set in South Wales around the beginning of the twentieth century, Rhys Davies presents three contrasting coalowners. There was the self-made C.P. Meredith, who had:

> an intrinsic sympathy with the men. He was one of them. And even now he wanted to be a democratic employer, knit into the same texture of thought as his men . . . [But] . . . they had struck in violation of their agreements ... They had burnt down his house, though last year he had built for them a meeting-hall complete with library and billiard-room. Something had gone seriously wrong with the bond that existed between him and his men: *they* had soured. He blamed the secret trading of a pernicious doctrine brought to the valley by elusive outsiders. A respectable trade unionism, kept by temperate men, was to be welcomed..

In contrast Sir Rufus Morgan 'would not recognise a Trade Union, except to fight it with bitter and intolerant wrath'. Sir Rufus 'tried to imitate God'. and the novel also contains independent, pragmatic John Johns:

> He was solid as a bank safe, as impregnable and full of riches. People never knew whether to admire and like him or to roundly abuse his apparent soullessness. He paid his men a better average than other employers—remaining outside the Association of Owners, whose men he had encouraged to fight for the abolition of the Sliding Scale. In fact, he had inflamed them to strike once, declaring that the Scale ought to be abolished. When this strike had happened five years ago, his own pits at Nant Vale did very well indeed: a fortune had been made. For this he had been attacked and reviled at the time: he remained unaffected.

In the novel, when John Johns' own men struck he considered himself to have been deserted and betrayed. 'I shall cease to think of you as men in my care and honest men with a respect for their word...we will fight to the bitter end, the last ditch. You need not send your Federation to us with offers. *We* will dictate terms, when *we* think fit..'* Such a situation could be depicted as a fictional illustration of the breaking down of the methods of social control developed by the coalowners. And the actual parallels are obvious enough (they have to be there because the novel is modelled on them). The six month stoppage of 1898 and the nearly year-long Cambrian Combine confrontation of 1910-11 can be interpreted as major break-downs in social control with the inference that such control had previously been successfully implemented. There would certainly be grounds for such an inference. For at least a generation before 1898 the miners seemed to have adopted attitudes that mostly embodied the values of the coalowners. In particular, they accepted the sliding-scale system of wage regulation which in its apparent automaticity emphasised the mutuality of interests between owners and miners, and played down strife and conflict. It is, however, still not established that such action by

---

*Compare the statement of D. A. Thomas to *The Times* (5 September, 1919) at outset of the Cambrian stoppage: 'Since the Cambrian men have taken matters into their own hands I am off for a holiday . . . I am certainly not going to beg the men to return to work I shall certainly not go out of my way on the present occasion to secure a peace which seems impossible of any permanancy . . .'

the men mostly reflected manipulation by the owners. It could as easily be explained by the extent to which the incipient unions were effectively crushed in the long stoppage of 1875.

The discussion of the nature or existence of social control should not, however, be allowed to get out of perspective. There is a prior point. So far as most people were concerned, in most places, for most of the time, the relationship with the owners was one of (not necessarily malevolent) neglect. In looking at the evidence of the coalfield before 1914 it is difficult to view it as an area with a high provision of social needs. And much of what did exist stemmed not directly from the owners but from the new local government structure set up around 1890. In areas like education, for example, there is no doubting the acceleration of the pace of development about this time, though again caution is needed. The local government bodies were mostly very wary spenders and not just because the effectively limited franchise helped to sustain a significant representation of owner interest: even where miners were in a clear majority (despite a restricted franchise) those who were voters were as interested in keeping down the level of rates as were the colliery owners.

There is much, therefore, to suggest that the coalowners' constructive impact on the social institutions and infrastructure was relatively muted. There is even more to suggest that their direct social influence in any functional sense was waning before 1914. By then most of the largest coalowners had moved away from the actual collieries, they were much more likely to be found in the Vale than in the valleys. Cultural leadership or involvement, especially in terms of Welsh cultural activities, had not disappeared but had become a less prominent characteristic of the coalowners. Political leadership, especially at the parliamentary level, was still a reality. D. A. Thomas persistently polled more votes in Merthyr than did Keir Hardie who was arguably only carried in as the second member for the constituency on the Liberal coalowner's coat-tails. The hold was, however, becoming more tenuous. The nature of the tensions was, for example, clearly indicated in the Gower campaign in 1900, won—just—by the coalowner Aeron Thomas standing as a Liberal against John Hodge the secretary of the Steel Smelters' union standing as a Labour candidate. The resultant splits and ambiguities pointed up the difficulties of the Liberals hanging on to the labour vote. The men of Bwllfa colliery roundly condemned the miners' leaders,

Mabon and John Williams, 'for supporting the candidature of Mr J. Aeron Thomas, a capitalist . . . against Mr John Hodge, a Trade Unionist candidate..' But Aeron Thomas's own workmen gave him a dinner at the Mackworth Hotel in Swansea at which Thomas declared himself totally unrepentant about being a capitalist, but more defensively said he would have stood down if the miners had had a candidate and even thought about stepping aside for a Labour candidate but felt the district should be represented by a Welsh-speaker who 'knew and sympathised with Welsh aspirations.'

After 1898 there is a shift of emphasis in the relations between owners and miners, a shift which is no less decisive for being intangible, gradual and difficult to pin down. Previously the necessary co-operation between capital and labour in the productive process had been predominant and had encouraged a notion of an inherent mutuality of interest. After the crucial conflict of 1898 it was the equally necessary distribution of the proceeds of production which was stressed carrying with it the notion of an inherent antagonism of interest. It was a change which gave force and impetus to the other developments tending to constrain the social influence of the owners. In the atmosphere of gathering suspicion and conflict the functional possibilities of owners' exerting any substantial social influence based on consent receded.

All these trends increased in the inter-war years. Up to 1914 the positive role of the coalowners was, implicitly or explicitly, generally accepted. The acceptance was partly based on very general considerations affecting society as a whole—the nature of the dominant (liberal) economic and political ideas, and the general atmosphere of deference in social relationships. But, in the South Wales coalfield, the acceptance was difficult to combat and withhold in a region which was so obviously expansionary and buoyant. The growth depended upon capital investment which involved very real risks (there were many examples of failed colliery enterprises). The coalowners were the risk-takers. They were men of some enterprise and much energy, energy perhaps being the characteristic which the most successful had in common. The acceptance, moreover, was essential if they were to play any positive social role. None the less even before 1914 there were important qualifications to be attached to the functional significance of the coalowners. The nature of the industry severely constrained the range of decision making; success—especially big success—was likely to owe more to fortune than to skill; and social control was less a matter of winning the consent of the community by manipulation than a simple reflection of the power realities in single-enterprise communities. And once the cushion of growth was removed the limited function of the owners was more exposed. Their one undisputed role as providers of capital was vastly demoted in significance. Managerial skills became more important in the face of falling markets and ageing collieries, but even if the skill was provided it was not likely to command much admiration or acceptance when its exercise required—or, at any rate, received—much ruthlessness. The end of growth also saw the clash between owners and men emerging stark and strong. Any social role by the owners would have been difficult: but in general there is little evidence that they sought one.

It is now the 1980s. A whole generation, more than a generation, has grown up without there being any coalowners. And, indeed, it is as if they had never been. It is difficult to find many permanent legacies. There is no great architecture, no school of literature or art. The Misses Davies of Gregynog seem to have been alone in using their money from Ocean coal to build a significant art collection (now at the National Museum), and unique in their direct patronage of music and of the Gregynog Press. There were no model colliery villages, no hopeful experiments in industrial or social relations. There are a few undistinguished statues of themselves. When the coalowners went in 1947 there was—and perhaps this is the most damning indictment—no sense of anything missing. They left the slag heaps, of course, and they lived on in the bitter, sour, angry memories of miners. Most of these—coal tips and collieries—now have a decent covering of grass.

> 'You should forget all that. Banish hatred,' said Willie zealously.
> 'You cannot forget things that have been your entire life for many years. The insult of a moment, Willie, is hard enough to forget but when men have to endure the insult of being idle, degraded and useless for years on end, not only is it impossible to forget that, it becomes an act of faith to cherish the memory of it every moment one lives, because one's duty as a human being from that time on is to fight against the possibility of that insult being levied against oneself or against others again. You're young, Willie. You only caught a glimpse of the knife that went right through our bodies.' (Gwyn Thomas, *The Sky of our Lives: The Dark philosophers*)

Bibliographical Note

A large literature, mostly American, now exists on entrepreneurs and entrepreneurship. The present essay has, however, made little direct use of these works partly because they still do not provide a generally accepted conceptual apparatus and partly because, even if they did, the existing knowledge on Welsh entrepreneurs is too fragmentary to make good use of such general frameworks. A recent work of this broad type, excellent of its kind and in an historical setting, is A.D. Chandler, *The Visible Hand: the Managerial Revolution in American Business* (1977).

Nor was extensive direct use made of most of the existing biographies of the coalowners of South Wales which tend to be highly uncritical like the biography of Lewis Davis of Ferndale—David Young, *A Noble Life*; or that of David Davies of Llandinam—Ivor Thomas, *Top Sawyer* (1938). In any event, there are not many such biographies. Lord Rhondda is exceptional (in this as in other respects: he was himself, for example, a serious writer on the coal industry) in that he is the subject of more than one full length biography (Rhondda, Margaret, Viscountess (ed.), *D.A. Thomas, Viscount Rhondda* (1921); J. Vyrnwy Morgan, *Life of Viscount Rhondda* (1918)). The biographical gaps are, moreover, significant as well as numerous—there is, for example, no full published biography of Lord Merthyr (W. T. Lewis). Smaller-scale treatments suffer from the same problem of lack of criticism and poor coverage so such works as Elizabeth Phillips, *A History of the pioneers of the Welsh coalfield* (1925) are of limited use. Where possible it is still better to go back to Charles Wilkins's books on *The South Wales Coal Trade* (1888) and *History of the Iron, Steel, Tinplate and other trades of Wales* (1903). The numerous books of the Eminent Welshmen type cover surprisingly few industrial figures and the coverage in *The Dictionary of Welsh Biography* is also disappointing.

There is some useful treatment in general works on the Welsh coal industry like H. S. Jevons, *The British Coal Trade* (1915) or J. H. Morris and L. J. Williams, *The South Wales Coal Industry, 1841-75* (1958). It is, however, essential to place a great deal of reliance on the information which can be gained from contemporary newspapers (the *South Wales Daily News* and the *Western Mail* are especially valuable), and from the evidence given by owners and managers to various parliamentary enquiries.

Rural Society Inside Outside
David Jenkins

Once upon a time such a shire as Cardigan was held to be a 'natural community' wherein the inhabitants despite all the differences between them had that in common which made them a community. However strange this may appear today it was by no means incredible until fairly recently. As late as 1901 nine out of every ten of its people had been born within the county or just over the border in Pembrokeshire or Carmarthenshire. And agriculture was far and away the most important single employment: the occupational census (of 1901) shows that four times as many men were engaged in agriculture as in the next largest category of male employment. On the basis of the recorders' notebooks of the census of 1861 it can be said that in purely agricultural areas nine people out of every ten were in one way or another connected with agriculture and were familiar with farm work: it is unlikely that this had changed much by 1901. People shared a community of birth, work and language: in the rural district of Lampeter there were 82 who could not speak Welsh in a total population of 3,783; of Llandysul rural district's 8,175 inhabitants 177 were unable to speak Welsh, while 123 of Tregaron rural district's population of 7,947 were similarly placed. The position in the other rural districts was little different. In this essay I propose to discuss some issues concerning the study of such a rural society. It is a study based on or arising out of some of the terms used by people engaged in agriculture, people who were members of agricultural communities within Wales. These terms are part and parcel of the local idiom of a community and a recently revived interest in anthropological studies gives them a significance they have not always possessed. I shall first present certain of the idioms and then refer to the revived interest which has been mentioned.

Idiomatic speech contains a great wealth of sayings, in particular the speech of those who received nothing but a primary school education. A fat boy is 'fel llo yn sugno dwy fuwch' (like a calf sucking two cows) and a fat man is 'fel pot llath cadw' (a pot of 'kept milk', i.e. kept for butter making). If someone will not work unless he has the limelight, he must be a 'ceffyl blan' (lead horse). If he speaks ceaselessly he is 'fel pwll y môr' (like a sea pool) but if his words lack substance he is either 'fel cachgi mewn stên' (like a bee in an urn) or 'mae'r felin yn malu'n wag' (the mill is grinding empty). If he's a man who passes unnoticed he is 'fel mesen ym mola hwch' (like an acorn in a sow's belly), if he claims a leader's position but lacks a leader's attributes, he is a 'daeacon pren' (a wooden deacon). If he quarrels with one and all he is a 'dafad gornog' (horned sheep); if he suffers from hysteria then he has 'pwle dihangol' (escaping fits), and if he dies suddenly it will be said 'fe aeth rhwng llaw a llawes', (he went between hand and sleeve). And we shall now cap the haycock.

The recently revived interest which lends significance to such terms stems from the fact that they can indicate how people conceptualise their own society. And in this regard it is necessary to mention the following consideration. There is no such thing as a 'mere' description of any society, past or present, consisting of nothing but reportage of what is observed. For this there are at least two reasons. Firstly, and as every student knows, it is in the nature of the case that the investigator must decide what is worth recording about a society and what is not: this is not so solely because it is in practice impossible to note everything. Rather, all things are not (or not equally) significant, meaningful. The investigator needs must decide what is meaningful and this he does according to criteria which are his own rather than those of the community under observation. Which of itself and immediately removes him from the sphere of any 'mere' description. Secondly: there can be no such thing as mere description for in the last resort there can be no final separation between description and understanding. No description of society is possible without a measure of understanding: one cannot describe a kinship system without knowing what kinship is, without knowing what is to count as kinship (this, one suspects, is one of the weaknesses of some studies of kinship in medieval Wales). One cannot describe social class without knowing what is to count as class, and that knowledge is not given in nature.

If there is no final separation between description and understanding one is immediately faced with a problem: in what terms, according to what concepts, does one attempt to comprehend a community? The brief answer is that there are two sets of terms in which one may attempt such an understanding. Either one may attempt to understand a community in the terms in which its members understand it, the terms which inform it for its members, to understand it from the inside as it were, in terms of the concepts and categories of those who constitute it, or, one may attempt an understanding according to the concepts and categories which the investigator devises in order to comprehend the society, to understand it in terms of an external observer's (or investigator's) concepts (such as 'structure' and 'function') rather than according to the participants' concepts. Frequently when we discuss a society which is familiar to us we operate with concepts which are little removed from those of the people we study so that we may unwittingly slide over from one type of concept to another (as readily happens when dealing with concepts of class).

In what follows below we shall be principally concerned with looking at a society from within as it were. Our interest lies in this, that a people's language, the colloquialism of idiomatic speech, provide not a ready-made description of how they see their society and their world, but a lead as to how they do so.

To what has been mentioned above there is a parallel in the study of social class, turning on the manner in which social class is to be conceptualised for purposes of study. Among the many distinctions it would be necessary to make in studies of social class is that between objective class and subjective class. By 'objective class' one means the classification (of members of a society) according to objective criteria (e.g. wealth, income) deemed relevant by an 'external' investigator. The strength of such a notion of social class lies in its general applicability, provided the facts are known. It is applicable independently of any investigator's personal bias, it allows of the comparison of the class structure of different communities and societies. The reverse side of the coin is that it is liable to classify together people who do not acknowledge one another as of the same class, and to separate those who do. It takes no necessary account of people's own perceptions and evaluations though they are the people who belong to the classes distinguished by the investigator.

By 'subjective class' one means a study (of class) in terms of those classes which people themselves distinguish (whether explicitly or otherwise), of how people 'see' themselves to be members of the same or separate classes, that is, in terms of how people 'see' their own society and their place in it. It has the advantage of taking account of people's own evaluations, but it has its weaknesses too. Different individuals may have such different ideas about what constitutes membership of particular classes that it may mean very little that people consider that they belong to the same or to different classes. And comparison of different communities on such a basis is liable to be meaningless.

I wish to consider a slightly different notion, namely classification as indicated in local idiom, as that idiom now is or once was, in rural communities with a relatively stable population and a common base in the work of the land. Such idioms indicate how people conceptualise their own society. They are not of the investigator's devising, they do not refer to categories decided upon by the investigator, they indicate how a society is viewed from within. At the same time and by the same token they are particularistic, specific to individual communities, and they do not allow of the direct comparison of one community with another. We shall look at rural communities in Wales more especially during the nineteenth and early twentieth centuries, and it is our intention to consider south-west Wales as a 'base area', and to indicate comparisons with other regions in Wales.

In south-west Wales and elsewhere people spoke of 'y gwŷr mawr' (the great people), or 'y gwŷr byddigion' (the gentry), one stratum of the society as it were. In south-west Wales they also spoke of 'pobol tai bach' (the people of the little houses), and further east of 'gwŷr tai bach' (the men of the little houses). A 'little house' indicated a house without land, while the 'people of the little houses' inhabited them. That is, they were cottagers. In Merioneth 'pentŷ' indicated the 'tŷ bach' of south-west Wales, their occupants being 'pentyaeth' or 'pobl pentai'. Similarly Kate Roberts speaks in *Y Lôn Wen* (1960) of 'tŷ moel' (a bare house), a house without land. And in south-west Wales one finds the proverb 'Unwaith y flwyddyn mae pobol tai bach yn lladd mochyn' (the people of the little houses kill a pig but once a year). Gentry and cottagers comprised two strata as it were, with 'farmers' constituting the third.

If one turns from the main social divisions indicated by local idiom to the classification of types of holdings of land, one finds that land was subdivided into holdings of all sizes from a field attached to a house, to 'a large farm'.

'Lle buwch' (a cow place) indicated sufficient land to keep one cow; 'Lle dwy fuwch' (the place of two cows), etc; 'lle ceffyl' (a one horse place), 'lle par o geffyle' (a place of a pair of horses), 'lle doubar' (a place of two pairs), etc. In a slightly different classification 'lle bach' (a petty place) was distinguished from 'lle jogel' (a considerable place) and 'lle mawr' (a large place). That is, these were the classes of holdings which people in south-west Wales distinguished as of consequence in the local system as they saw it, in the 'folk model'. The difference between studies in terms of 'folk concepts' on the one hand and of 'observers' ' concepts on the other is to be seen if one compares this classification with that to be found in the work of agricultural economists, such as A.W. Ashby and I.L. Evans' *The Agriculture of Wales and Monmouth* (1944).

None of the holdings classified in the local terminology in the way indicated above could be run as an independent unit before the coming of relatively modern agricultural machinery. For this there were at least two reasons. The main financial returns came from the sale of store cattle and of casked salted butter. But no holding had calves to rear for sale or milk for butter making without the services of a bull. Bulls however are expensive animals to keep, and only on holdings of some 65 acres (or more) could they be kept. Five holdings out of every six were smaller than this, so that every five holdings depended on the sixth for a bull's services. And payment for these services was not in cash but in labour at the hay harvest.

The second reason why no holding could be run as an independent unit concerns seasonal labour needs. This is best presented by taking the example of one farm during the corn harvest. The farm was of 220 acres, having 40 to 45 acres under corn annually. Wheat was grown 'at iws y tŷ' (for the use of the house, i.e. for food), barley and oats were grown chiefly for animal feed. As it was one day's work to cut an acre of standing corn with a scythe, 40 to 45 work days were required to cut the corn which then lay on the ground in swathes and it remained for someone to bind it into sheaves by hand. Wheat was cut when fully ripe and bound by a woman who followed 'wrth gwt' (at the tail of) the scythesman. Thus binding wheat into sheaves required as many work days as were needed to cut it. Barley was cut 'yn grin aeddfed', not fully ripe, and oats when 'lliw'r glomen' (of dove hue), that is, unripe. Both were allowed to lie on the ground 'i gael tan' (to acquire a tan) before being bound. When one enquires about the time necessary to bind oats and barley the answers vary. Some experienced people say that they could be bound in half the time needed to cut them: others claim that both tasks required the same amount of time. This variation is not unexpected as binding corn was affected by one consideration that did not affect the scythesmen, namely the amount of thistle in the crop. If one assumes that binding required three quarters of the time required for cutting one will not err seriously. Thus some 70 to 75 work days were needed to cut and bind the corn crop. The sheaves would then be placed in stook and later the corn would be carried for stacking. The stacks required thatching and some of the crop would be threshed with a flail to provide the thatching straw. Further, some (though not all) of the ropes required for thatching were made of straw, by hand, ('rheffyn pen bys', finger tip rope), so that not less than some 100 work days were necessary to secure the crop.

But this assumes good weather conditions. There were two extremes of adverse weather—stormy harvest weather, and drought during the growing season. During a wet windy harvest the corn lay on the ground and could not be cut with a scythe having a 'cader' (cradle) attached. The art of cutting corn with a scythe was to lay the swathe in a manner convenient for the binder, and to this end a light frame ('cader') was attached to the scythe so that the swathe fell first into the frame and it could then be placed on the ground in a suitable manner. But when the corn lay on the ground it was necessary to use a 'pladur foel' (a bare scythe) or resort to the reaping hook, which was used as late as the harvest of 1951. Needless to say, 100 work days underestimates the labour requirements under such conditions.

On the other hand drought in the growing season resulted in such a short growth of straw that it (the straw) could not be used in order to bind the corn into sheaves. It was then necessary to resort to the stack yard and to make sufficient 'finger tip rope' wherewith to bind the corn. This was the mark of a difficult, though not the most difficult, harvest. Under the worst conditions the growth of straw was so short that the corn could not be cut at all and there was no alternative but to pluck the crop by the roots either over the whole corn area or on the worst affected slopes. (This happened on the driest corn ground in mid Cardiganshire as late as 1921). Such corn was known as 'llafur cito' (stunted corn), and under such conditions the labour requirements were severe.

Yet the total staff of the farm under consideration was eight people, including three women. There were six working days in the week and a number of tasks could not be set aside; milking, collecting eggs, butter making, the care of the animals, the preparation of food. It is quite clear that under the variable weather conditions of south-west Wales the corn crop could not be secured regularly without outside aid. And the corn crop was far too important for this to be left to chance. Wheaten bread was a staple for people while the barley and oats were essential for animal feed.

Labour was secured by what can properly be called a social device, the institution of potato setting, whereby cottagers set rows of potatoes in farm fields and paid a work debt for doing so. This was referred to in a set of expressions: 'dyled gwaith' (work debt), 'dyled tato' (potato debt), 'dyled cynhaeaf' (harvest debt). A known and fixed debt of one day's work at the corn harvest was due per row of potatoes (of standard length). More accurately the work debt was for the load of manure which the farmer provided for each row of potatoes. Thus no debt was owed for a row for which the cottager could provide a load of turf ash, or of pig manure. Hence people in some areas distinguished between 'tatw dom' (manure potatoes) and 'tatw mesure' (measures potatoes), that is, potatoes which entailed no debt as the cottager provided the manure, and those potatoes which did incur a work debt according to the measure of potatoes planted.

Thus attached to each farm there was a group of cottagers collectively known as 'y fedel'. In the strict sense 'medel' refers to those who reap corn. The word is connected with 'medi' (to reap), but it acquired a wider meaning. It was the farm's work group. Twenty four families set out potatoes at the 220 acre farm mentioned above. On average these set four rows of potatoes apiece, involving a work debt of 96 days. Similarly 25 families set out potatoes at a 260 acre farm, 14 families at a 140 acre farm, and 3 families at a farm of 34 acres.

It is worth noting that while this was regarded as an informal arrangement, it in fact constituted legal contract. There are reported cases where cottagers set out potatoes, did not attend the corn harvest, were prevented from harvesting their potatoes, and were sued for damages at the county court. The court found for the farmers in the reported cases, it being an 'implied condition' of setting out potatoes that labour debt would be paid at the corn harvest.

Having described these arrangements in south-west Wales we shall now mention corresponding practices elsewhere and consider one of them in detail. Along the English border (in Radnorshire and Montgomeryshire) people paid in cash for setting out potatoes, but this cash payment had displaced the earlier 'love reaps', that is, harvest labour on a reciprocal basis. In south-east Wales and the Vale of Clwyd, labourers were hired for cash for the corn harvest at least from the early nineteenth century. Meanwhile in the industrial valleys of west Glamorgan and east Carmarthenshire miners set out potatoes on the understanding that they would help with the hay harvest and take half the potato crop (leaving the other half to the farmer), but if their occupation prevented them attending the hay harvest they would leave the entire potato crop to the farmer. In parts of Merioneth there were practices known as 'plannu allan' (planting out) and 'tatw cyd' (co-potatoes). Cottagers set out potatoes, helped at the hay harvest, took half the potato crop, and left the other half to the farmer. There was no fixed labour debt, nor were there terms corresponding to the 'dyled gwaith' (labour debt) of south-west Wales.

The area to be contrasted with south-west Wales in greater detail is that to be found on the slopes of the Berwyn in the district of Penllyn in central Merioneth, where the land rises from the valley floor to open mountain, and it is necessary to refer first of all to the classification of land use as found in local terminology.

a)   'Mynydd' (mountain). This is open treeless uninhabited land providing sheep pastures only.

b)   'Ffridd' (upland). This land had been enclosed, chiefly in the nineteenth century, from 'mynydd'. It was in part divided into fields but the word 'field(s)' was not applied to the 'ffridd'. The surface included heather, rock outcrops, coarse grass, bog, intermingled with areas suitable for improvement and known as 'clytiau' (clouts) of land. These were improved by breast ploughing in the first place ('clytiau gwthio') and once improved were known as 'clwt' (clout) or 'erw' ('acre') which was not a measure of area (e.g. 'Erw Lloie', the 'calves' "acre"). After the initial breast ploughing such land was frequently improved by the practices of 'plannu allan' (setting out) and 'tatw cyd' (co-potatoes). But it was land on which no stable plant community of improved growth had been established, and it would readily revert to its natural state.

(The South Wales' term which corresponds to 'ffridd' is 'lan', the word being used not to indicate vertical direction (as is usual), but as a noun referring to land above the level of long established field cultivation but below the level of open unimproved upper ground with its vegetation still in its natural state. 'Lan' is usually found in conjunction with the name of the farm which contains it, e.g. 'lan Tyhen', 'lan Pennar', and again as an element in a proper name, e.g. 'Lanlas', 'Pen-y-lan'.)

c)   'Caeau' (fields). This is lower land (though not on the valley bottom), subdivided into fields, with a stable plant community and acceptable plant growth by the standards of the day.

d)   'Gweirglodd' (meadow). This is wet valley bottom land, improved sufficiently to grow a good hay crop but unsuitable for cereal cultivation. On this land cereals yielded a strong growth of straw but little grain.

(For completeness it may be added that while 'rhosdir' (moorland) is important in surrounding areas it is relatively unimportant in this particular area).

Three classes of farms are to be recognised in this area:-

a)   Farms with the complete vertical range of the land-use classes. These are usually substantial farms and the only ones on which it was practicable to keep bulls.

b)   Farms which lack 'gweirglodd' (meadow) but with 'fields', 'ffridd', and mountain. They grew a corn crop (usually on the 'ffridd') as well as hay, and thus had both corn and hay harvests. Cattle were kept on such farms as well as sheep on the sheep pastures.

c)   'Lle bach' (petty place): holdings farmed by people who had other full time employment as such holdings were too small to support families or households.

It is necessary to mention two relevant considerations. The first is the steepness of slope which made carting home the harvest laborious and time consuming work. The second is the altitude range which was such that there was a significant difference in the date of harvest on the upper and lower ground even of the one and the same farm.

As an example of the organisation of harvest work a 99 acre farm will be mentioned. This farm has 12 acres of mountain, 65 acres of 'ffridd', and 22 acres of 'caeau' (fields). Altitude above sea level ranges from 900 feet to 1200 feet. Twelve acres of corn were grown annually, not in the 'fields' but on the 'ffridd'. Twelve work days were required to cut the corn and another twelve work days to bind it into sheaves. Four or five milk cattle were kept, but the holding was dependent on a larger farm for a bull's services.

At the corn harvest no labour debt was due to our exemplar from any other farm, nor did farms co-operate on any other basis. On the other hand a labour debt was due to the farm which provided a bull's services, and that farm was paid a labour debt not only by the one farm under consideration but by all the farms for which it provided a bull's services.

If we turn away from the relationship between one farm and another at the corn harvest to the co-operation between farm and 'pobl pentai' it will be seen that there was not on the Berwyn a definite and specific labour debt (as there was in south-west Wales). Rather one found there what was a form of insurance. 'Pobl pentai' did set out potatoes, but their debt consisted of 'plyciau gwaith', 'spells of work', indefinite and unspecific. In south-west Wales farms co-operated at the hay harvest but not at the corn harvest, and 'the people of the little houses' could pay their work debt only at the corn harvest. That is, they paid their work debt during that harvest at which farms did not co-operate. On the Berwyn slopes, farms co-operated neither at the hay harvest nor at the corn harvest and 'pobl pentai' could contribute their 'work spells' at either harvest or both. In other words help was available if it was needed while in the south-west the debt was fixed and definite and independent of the aid required during the harvest of any particular year.

To conclude with the matter under discussion, namely the relationship between farm practice and social structure, it can be said that while the details differed from one region to the other, local idiom (which is closely related to the practice of agriculture) indicates that people saw the society in which they lived in terms of the three main divisions of 'gwŷr mawr' (gentry), farmers, 'pobol tai bach' (south-west Wales) and 'pentyaeth' (Merioneth). Yet while this is true it can be misleading for it raises in simple form a matter of some consequence. Society does not consist of blocks of people (in this case three blocks) which put together form the whole society, on a 'building blocks' analogy of social structure. The only 'concrete' units are individuals who see themselves in one way in one context and in another way in another context. Generally farmers and cottagers stood distinguished from one another (as the idiomatic expressions suggest) but in certain contexts they were both of them 'pobl gyffredin' (ordinary people) vis-à-vis 'y gwŷr mawr', and the threefold division of society seems to become two fold. What the expressions indicate are not simply social strata, but certain major contra-distinctions which the people (rather than any 'external observer') recognised as meaningful. People were distinguished from each other in certain ways meaningful within the society (as gentry, farmers, cottagers), and whether they thought of themselves in a manner which can be presented in terms of a two- or a three-class model depended on which distinction was relevant in a particular situation.

A further comment to make at this juncture is that the threefold or three-class model mentioned above corresponds very closely to the three-class model of landowner, (tenant) farmer, and cottager which has been recognised over wide areas of western Europe. In this the 'folk model' and the 'external observer's model' are much alike. But two things are worth noting about social relationships in the areas which have been described. First, the practices which linked farmer and cottager were operative not only at harvest times but throughout the year, at potato sorting, potato planting, the hay harvest and the corn harvest (both of which could be protracted affairs lasting more than a month apiece), the potato harvest, and other less clearly defined occasions. Second, even when relations between landlords and tenant farmers were at their worst, as when there was agitation during the late nineteenth century for a land court to fix rents, those relations were never ones of bare legal contract. It was a feature of farm life that an incoming tenant was very frequently a relative of an outgoing tenant, which means in practice that a tenant had a voice in the choice of his successor, and this he certainly did not have as a matter of contract or of legal right.

In conclusion it is as well to state that we have above considered the society from one standpoint only, namely according to its relationship to the land. It is in that regard that the differences between the 'folk model' and the 'external observer's model' are least. But people were kinsmen as well as farmers and cottagers, fellow worshippers as well as members of work groups, and in consequence two matters deserve mention. Firstly it would be a mistake to equate the society with any one of its aspects. And secondly it is in the study of kinship and of religion that the differences between the two 'models' are likely to be at their greatest. Clearly no study which takes account of 'folk concept' is possible without a thorough knowledge of the language of the 'folk' concerned. And one wonders what can be the aim or value of any study of a community or society unless it concerns itself with those concepts.

Bibliographical note

The first important anthropological study of a rural society in Britain and Ireland was C. M. Arensberg's study of the countrymen of County Clare. The work was published in both a more technical form (C.M. Arensberg and S.T. Kimball, *Family and Community in Ireland*, Cambridge, Mass., 1940) and a more popular form (C.M. Arensberg, *The Irish Countryman*, London, 1937—a most readable book). Arensberg wrote as a functionalist, aiming to explain customary ways of conducting affairs by their function rather than by tracing their development. His work indicates that a functionalist approach is better suited to dealing with some topics (such as kinship) than with others. Thus *The Irish Countryman* is enlightening and uneven. Alwyn D. Rees rejected functionalist accounts of communities and in *Life in a Welsh Countryside* (Cardiff, 1950) he looked for historical explanations of the phenomena he described. In *Village on the Border* (London, 1957) R. Frankenberg considers the 'processes' of everyday life in a village in north-east Wales, 'processes' similar to those which have been described in other small communities in very different societies elsewhere. J. Emmett discusses a community in Gwynedd (*A North Wales Village*, London, 1964) while the contributors to *Welsh Rural Communities* (E. Davies and A.D. Rees (eds.), Cardiff, 1960) adopt various approaches including one in terms of participants' concepts.

   The debate between proponents of studies in terms of participants' concepts on the one hand and observers' concepts on the other can be traced in P. Winch *The Idea of a Social Science and its Relation to Philosophy* and in E. Gellner 'The New Idealism—Cause and Meaning in the Social Sciences' in *Problems in the Philosophy of Science*, Vol. III, I. Lakatos and A. Musgrove, (eds.) Amsterdam, 1968. A general if technical consideration of kinship study is provided by R. Fox in 'Prologomena to the Study of British

Kinship, in J. Gould, ed., *Penguin Survey of the Social Sciences 1965,* (London, 1965) while those interested in kinship in medieval society could consult the same author's 'Kinship and Land Tenure on Tory Island', *Ulster Folk Life*, Vol. XII, 1966. (Tory Island is a Gaelic speaking island off the coast of Donegal). C. Rosser & C. Harris consider kinship in their *The Family and Social Change* (London, 1965) and south-west Wales is discussed in D. Jenkins *The Agricultural Community in South-west Wales* (Cardiff, 1971). For a discussion in Welsh see D. Jenkins 'Llafar Gwlad a Chymdeithas' in two parts in *Y Traethodydd*, Vol. CXXIX No. 552 (July 1974) and Vol. CXXIX No. 553 (October 1974).

Welsh Nationalism, the French Revolution and the Influence of the French Right 1880-1930

Emlyn Sherrington

In 1927 W. J. Gruffydd of *Y Llenor*, the most influential Welsh literary magazine of the century, launched an uncompromising attack on Saunders Lewis and Ambrose Bebb for their anti-democratic views which, he alleged, were the result of their addiction to the writings of the Catholic right wing ideologues of France, particularly Charles Maurras and *Action Française*. He implied that, by importing wholesale such ideas, they were guilty of introducing altogether unwelcomed and unnatural innovations into Welsh politics. Gruffydd had been distinctly unhappy about the anti-democratic and 'Papist' leanings of nationalist leadership in Wales since the early 1920s. In 1922, he had taken on what he considered to be the ultra-right wing of the then amorphous movement, when, in a review of Lewis' play, *Gwaed yr Uchelwyr*, he had dismissed it as didactic and elitist and had used the occasion to include an attack on all 'the verse of the men of reaction'.

W. J. Gruffydd's criticism of Lewis and Bebb in 1927, although it opened up a continuing debate, must be viewed with circumspection. His inability to distinguish between Catholicism and elitist political ideology, though not difficult to understand at the time, casts doubt on his judgement. He was writing in an atmosphere of hysteria. Nonconformist journals like *Y Tyst* and *Seren Gomer* carried alarmist articles which maintained that particularly after 1929, the Papacy had once more become a temporal power and that there existed a secret papal political offensive which, centred on fascist Italy and with bases in countries like nationalist Ireland, was threatening to subvert the constitution of the United States and was actively taking over the British Empire. This spectre was haunting the Nonconformist mind when he attacked Lewis and Bebb, and Gruffydd believed that Wales was not exempt from the sinister ramifications of this plot.

He was also guilty of an uncritical acceptance of the idea that the speech given by Saunders Lewis at the Llandrindod Wells meeting of the Welsh School of Social Service in 1923 was a turning point in Welsh nationalist thinking in that it promulgated the wholly novel idea of conservative Welsh Nationalism. Such was not in fact the case, for Lewis was the heir of a reactionary Welsh nationalist tradition that was fully formed by the beginning of the Great War. Nor could Lewis and Bebb be accused of innovation by relying on French inspiration, for French political events and ideas had been exerting a powerful influence on Welsh reactionism since the early 1880s when a rival Anglican form of Welsh nationalism was struggling into existence in response to the liberal nationalist obsession with Disestablishment.

There were certain parallels and coincidences in the political history of Wales and France which combined to create circumstances so similar in both countries that they could not possibly have escaped contemporary notice. Seminal political events had occurred within two years in both countries. In 1870 France had seen the restoration of republican government and the banishment of the landed aristocracy and gentry into a sullen aloofness from political affairs. In intellectual life many experienced a growing disillusionment with the Third Republic and its democracy, so that within twenty years writers like Paul Verlaine, Ferdinand Brunetière and Paul Bourget were taking a strongly anti-democratic, and in some cases, narrowly Catholic line. In Wales, the passing of the Reform Act of 1867 and the 1868 general election had had similar effect. The republican spirit and mentality of France was closely paralleled by a liberal upsurge in Wales and the triumph of a Liberal party which not only identified itself with, but at times actually called itself 'the democracy'. During the last three decades of the nineteenth century both countries witnessed the routing of organised conservatism and the virtual disappearance from public life of 'the natural leaders of society' and their replacement by a middle class republican or liberal elite infused by a positivist and progressive spirit.

In Wales and France these events had been followed by a growing demand for the removal of Church influence in education, its disendowment and its separation from the state. The introduction of Watkin Williams' motion to disestablish the Church in Wales had come in the very year that the Third French Republic had come into being. Radical agitation for separation, growing steadily in the 1870s and 1880s, had peaked between 1890 and 1905. A year after the Catholic Church in France had been finally separated from the state in 1905, Wales witnessed a radical landslide that left the Tory party without a single Welsh seat in the Commons and which made Welsh Disestablishment a blue-chip political certainty.

The democratisation and industrialisation of Welsh society led the Anglican reaction to view these events with deep pessimism. They saw in the Liberal Party and in Cymru Fydd (the 'Young Wales' movement of the 1890s) the spearhead of an attack not only upon the Church, but also on traditional social structures, economic relationships and cultural and religious values. In short, they believed themselves to be living in revolutionary times. This was deeply at variance with the Liberal Nonconformist propaganda which poured out of the Welsh press. The remarkably durable legacy they bequeathed to the future was a self-portrait of Nonconformist piety, liberal progress and democracy ranged against the forces of tyranny, and a caricature of an Anglican worldliness and neglect, cynically dependent upon an alien establishment and allied to a reactionary and oppressive landlordism. The clash between these forces was the heroic struggle of the mythical 'gwerin' (Folk) against the oppression of political and religious inequality.

Against this picture of a Welsh national society of democratic and classless hue battling for liberty and equality, the Anglicans presented a vastly different scene. Theirs was the portrait of an age deeply riven by class conflict in which the middle class callously and cynically exploited peasant and working class grievances, for which the middle class themselves were largely responsible, in order to wrest social and political dominance from the hands of the traditional leaders of society, the aristocracy and the Church itself. In contrast to the Liberal version of the 'National Awakening' as a moral crusade of high principle, the Anglicans depicted these events as a naked grab for power by a self-seeking, abrasive middle class revolutionism.

Much history, including the real origins of modern right-wing nationalism in Wales, was obscured when this Anglican picture was consigned to gather dust in the attic of political defeat. In order to understand the emergence of a right-wing, anti-liberal and anti-socialist nationalist ideology in Wales, it has to be realised that many Anglican priests, particularly the Welsh-speaking among them, saw themselves fighting on a broad front.

They viewed their defence of the Church against the backcloth of a crisis of European civilisation and were plunged into apocalyptic gloom. An Anglican nationalist, the Reverend David Jones of Penmaenmawr, the editor of the monthly *Y Cyfaill Eglwysig*, expressed a deep sense of decadence when he wrote in 1904:

> In whatever direction we look the great wide world . . . is full of
> unrest . . . unrest, verily, is one of the characteristics of the
> age . . . It is not unlikely that there are great things at its source. We
> do not know if 'the end' is nigh, but there are many signs that 'the
> last of days' are at hand.

Since the 1880s Anglicans had seen the ethics and habits of the market place invade religious and political life, lying and deceit become the daily norms in politics and commerce, and perjury a commonplace in courts of law. No real evidence was ever produced to support these views, but it was clear in their minds that Christianity and its precepts of social behaviour were in serious decline. An anonymous contributor to *Y Cyfaill Eglwysig* complained in September 1887 that 'kingdom was rising against kingdom, class against class, family against family, party against party, man against man'.

These tendencies of the age could be attributed to two interrelated causes. The first was the spread of democracy which was seen as nothing less than a rebellion against the principle of authority. It encouraged the masses to put their trust in their own judgement and destroyed natural deference. The lowly were thus confused and guided by new, half understood concepts. Democracy, declared John Jenkins, the curate of Pembrey in his book *Moesoldeb Gwleidyddol* in 1896, was based on the foolish notion that 'we must lower the franchise in order to raise the nation's wisdom'.

The position was compounded by the second cause, the growth of urban industrialism. This made the era what the reactionary and nationalist curate of Llanrwst, T. Tudno Jones, in a series of 'Letters to the Welsh Nation' (1906) called 'a revolutionary period which threatens to break the ribs of our social system'. Like the right in the rest of Europe, Anglican reactionaries saw democracy resulting in atomisation, urbanism in deracination and mass industrialism in depersonalisation. Tudno Jones believed that the Welsh had been 'an industrious, satisfied and successful nation up to 1868, but ever since . . . (had) been mesmerised by foreign ideas that border on madness'. The foreign ideas were equality, liberty and fraternity and their origins were clearly French.

Democracy and equality were condemned by *Y Cyfaill Eglwysig* in November 1908 as 'the dreams of diseased minds' and, with their aims of extending democracy, dismantling ecclesiastical establishment and investing the state with control over education, late nineteenth century liberalism and Cymru Fydd were the embodiment of bourgeois revolutionary aspirations and clear signs of moral decadence. Drawing their strength from the false premises of rationalism and the Enlightenment which had resulted in the French Revolution, they were perpetuating a poison which had all but ruined Europe since 1789. *Yr Haul*, the intellectual organ of the Church in Wales, warned Cymru Fydd in July 1894 that it was impossible to break the continuity of history and give society a fresh start. This was a pure Burkian conservatism reinforced by de Maistre and Hippolyte Taine.

Welsh Anglican reactionaries, who were pressing for the defeat of Anglicism in the Church and who eventually demanded the separation of the Welsh Church from Canterbury on what amounted to nationalist grounds, were convinced of a Jacobin plot to dechristianise Wales and saw non-denominational state education as a barely disguised form of secular education, bereft of religion and dependent on compulsion. The element of compulsion which enlightened despotism and the Revolution of 1789 had introduced into the state was just as clear and menacing in the 'New Liberalism' of the late nineteenth and early twentieth centuries. In 1885 *Y Cyfaill Eglwysig* believed the liberals' aim was to use the state 'to keep the Bible out of schools . . . and turn Churchmen out of their Churches'. The passage of time did little to allay their fears.

Like their revolutionary forebears, the Radicals viewed the state as a mechanism rather than an organism, a mechanism which could be used to secure the welfare of its subjects only through coercion and to which the individual inevitably became subjugated. The increasing addiction of the Liberal Party to interventionism and state control was proof that individualism led to the kind of anarchy that could only be curbed by state terrorism. As the Reverend A.S. Thomas put it in *Yr Haul* in 1914, the new liberals had become 'the contemporary Jacobins of

Wales'. The idea was not novel, for in April 1889 none other than Emrys ap Iwan, writing anonymously in *Y Geninen* stated that all of Wales' troubles had started with the enfranchisement of the bourgeoisie and the 'sansculotte' elements of the working class, 'blacksmiths, cobblers, stone-masons and carpenters (who) had usurped the seats of the old learned Welshmen of the Anglican Church and the Church of Rome'.

The more spectacular similarities between the Welsh and French experiences in the last thirty years of the nineteenth century reinforced the conviction among Welsh Anglicans that they were still fighting a war that had started in 1789. Although not too eager to associate their cause with that of French Catholicism, as the political reaction coincided with an upsurge of Anglo-Catholicism in the Welsh Church, awareness of French events took on a deeper significance. By the early years of the twentieth century lowly parish priests like the Rev. T. Llechid Jones were urging Anglicans to learn from the example of well-known converts from republicanism in France like Paul Verlaine, Ferdinand Brunetière, Paul Bourget, J-K Huysmans and Laurent Taihadé. Even lesser known converts like Adolphe Rette did not go unnoticed in *Yr Haul*. On their side, the Liberals and Non-conformists did little to disabuse their enemies. Liberal Non-conformist periodicals of the time showed considerable interest in the affairs of the Third Republic and republican leaders like Gambetta ranked side by side with Garibaldi and Kossuth as heroic figures. In March 1883, *Yr Ymofynnydd* described the death of Gambetta as 'one of the most serious events that seemed to change . . . the history of the world'. Liberal newspapers did not hesitate to use the language of force to intimidate their enemies. *The North Wales Observer and Express* declared in January 1889 that:

> the masses mean to engage in a mighty . . . combat with the privileged class. Liberty, equality and fraternity—these are the potent watchwords of emancipated mankind . . . When defensive war is unavoidable, it is the duty of every patriot to acquit himself like a man . . . the enlightened will of England and Wales is more potent than all the red-coated hirelings of the Queen.

Strong words about a county council election even if it was the first, but such references to the French Revolution were taken seriously by the Anglican press. It is hardly surprising therefore that the response of beleaguered conservatism in both countries had much in common. Maurice Barrès' criticism of French education for its 'unhealthy Kantianism' was offered in much the same spirit as Anglican complaints about the Welsh state education system. They were concerned that its insistence on individualism not only made it an agent of intellectual deracination, but also contributed to contemporary 'anarchy' by failing to exercise the social control and conditioning that was its proper function. All this was the more serious as the confluence of social deprivation and the opportunity to do political mischief in the towns made them the scenes of great social and political instability. 'Foreign' ideas had to be combatted with ideas that were close to and which stemmed from the traditions of old Wales. The answers which Anglican reactionism came up with compare with the European right even in their finer detail and are worth noting. They had little faith in scientism or positivism as an antidote to the problems of feeding the urban masses or stabilising them socially and politically. As A. H. G. Edwards of Caerleon declared in *Yr Haul* in 1897, the towns were 'out of all proportion to the ability of science to satisfy their needs'. The answer rather lay in a reversal of the industrial process and in rootedness both physically and intellectually in the native soil of the nation.

La Retour à la terre was thus as much a theme of Welsh as it was of French politics. Although nothing approaching Albert de Mun's *Cèrcles Ouvriers* or La Tour du Pin's *Société des Agricultures de France* has ever been established in Wales, Anglicans indulged in vague yearnings for a return to the local loyalties and to the ties of rural parishes which were, as Elis Wyn o Wyrfai put it in *Yr Haul* in June 1889, 'the main sources of our Welsh civilisation' and 'centres of the *local* organisation of the inhabitants themselves . . . the first element of local and independent government'. In the early years of the twentieth century one parish priest, T. Meredith Williams, did try to organise agricultural syndicates with the aid of Professor Pickard of the University College at Aberystwyth and the Agricultural Organisation Society. His efforts centred around the Newquay, Cardigan, Llanddyssul, Llanybyther, Lledrod and Swydd Ffynnon areas of Cardiganshire. There is no doubt that he was fully aware not only of the co-operative ventures of Denmark, but also of the *Syndicats Agricoles* of France, the *Boerenbond* of Flanders and the *Bund der Landwirte* in Germany. (See *Yr Haul*, 1907.) These attempts, however, were not widely emulated and foundered on the rocky indifference and hostility of the landed aristocracy and gentry. Some, like the parish priest of Taff's Well in the 1890s and 1900s were impressed by Leo XIII's *Rerum Novarum* and by the fact that 'it has thrown all the resources of the Latin Church behind social reform'. By far the most widespread reaction to this kind of thinking, however, was a popular sentimentalism about the countryside and the idealisation of the peasant as the basis of all industry, culture and social order.

Just as important to the future development of right-wing nationalism in Wales were the ideas and sentiments of the period about education, culture, and the meaning of nationality. Rootedness was seen as far more than the physical re-settlement of the nation on the land, it had to be an intellectual and spiritual condition. Anglican poets like Isfryn saw both the town-dweller and the free-thinking individual as the victims of uncertainty and instability. Educationally this could only be overcome if the people were tied to 'Catholic truths' as the vicar of St. Asaph put it in 1892, and if they were educated to their station in life and steeped in the ancient traditions of the historic nation. James H. Jenkins, the vicar of Taff's Well believed that contemporary man in 1904 was seeking 'the consciousness of security in the historic credoes'. This theory of education which Paul Bourget expounded in his novel *L'Étape* and developed more fully in *Nouvelles Pages de Critique et de Doctrine*, was thus to a great extent anticipated by the Anglican reaction. One thing was certain, few in the Anglican nationalist camp would have denied Bourget's thesis that the full integration of the individual into society depended upon 'le développement de l'homme sur place et d'après son milieu'.

The depression which engulfed Welsh Anglicanism towards the end of the 1880s, although brought on by events at home, coincided with and fed upon the French mood of decadence, whose first theoretical exposition was Bourget's *Essaie de psychologie contemporaine* (1880-83). Those French authors who figure in Anglican writings, like Verlaine, Brunetière and Joris-Karl Huysmans were all deeply impressed by it. Huysmans' novel *A rebours* (1884) became the catechism of the Decadent movement. That such writers should appeal to Welsh Anglicans is hardly surprising, for the republican Raoul Frary's explanation of *la Decadence* in his *Le péril national* (1881) as the creed of 'vieillards moroses' and 'les vaincus de la bataille politique' was just as applicable to them as it was to the French ultra-right.

The Anglican revulsion against middle class politics went far deeper than a mere disillusionment with party politics and parliamentary democracy. There was, in a very real sense, a clash of cultures in Wales in the late nineteenth century—not the collision of English and Welsh so much as a conflict between traditionalism and modernist positivism. On the surface the debate over education might have seemed a purely political one and the lamentation of *Y Cyfaill Eglwysig* in 1906 that the system only ensured that 'wild and dangerous ideas are being fostered and taught on social and political subjects' might appear to be the length, depth and breadth of the issue. Such, however, was far from being the case, for the debate centred basically not around political concepts but rather around cultural origins. The cultural leadership of 'tailors and political cobblers', as Tudno Jones had contemptuously described the Liberal Nonconformist hierarchy, was essentially false in this view. The Liberal Nonconformist condominion in Wales was *arriviste*, and the 'new', 'half-Welshmen' were culturally unfit to lead the nation. They were 'common' and 'ordinary', and although many of them were well educated, few, if any, of them were 'cultured'. Nor could they be when 'their democratic spirit . . . in ecclesiastical and political affairs' was merely a reflection of 'their contemptuous opposition to that which is beautiful and graceful'. Their cultural standards were a reflection of the commercialism and urbanism that had spawned them. This was essentially an aesthetic detachment from a repulsive environment that the middle class positivists took to be permanent. It was a revolt against a mentality that accepted industrial society and which took technology and scientism as the basis of its culture. The Liberal Nonconformist nexus was simply the product of the breakdown of Church universality and the effect of an unapostolic religious puritanism which introduced into religious, cultural and political life the values of Mammon.

The feeling of revulsion against middle class industrial values was one that the eccentric and, at times, abusive Tudno Jones had expressed in the late eighties and early nineties when he had described the middle class elite as 'Cheapjacks' who used the press and the Liberal Party as 'their van to carry their political false goods from place to place'. By far the most dangerous and philistine element of this leadership were the nationalist exiles. These were, *par excellence*, the purveyors of foreign ideals and capitalist cultural and moral values in Wales. Prominent among these were the émigré plutocracies of the London and Liverpool Welsh who were, *Yr Haul* suggested in July 1894, the main driving force behind cultural philistinism and middle class revolutionism. They were 'prosperous men who believe Wales a good place to come from' and who 'live in English towns and urge the Weish to keep their language'.

Yr Haul's criticism of nationalists in exile was an important element in the development of an alternative reactionary Welsh nationalism, for it implied that Wales could only be saved from within Wales itself both geographically and culturally. In terms of Church governance this led to a demand for separation of the Churches of England and Wales, and politically to the idea that only men of culture 'sur place et d'après ses milieux' could save Wales. Elis Wyn o Wyrfai had maintained in 1889 that the locality had been, and still ought to be the centre of Welsh culture. Such a concept could hardly be without political implications for it envisaged a system of close social control. In 1894 Elis Wyn made its political meaning explicit. Leadership, both cultural and political, was indivisible and the new middle class elite was ineligible for the role for the very simple reason that in both respects it looked to the capitalist power house of England for its sustenance and was consequently not genuinely Welsh. In the January number of *Yr Haul* he made the issue clear:

> it is true that it was from the old Welsh mounting block . . . that many of them rose to the saddle; but it was towards England that they rode, and it was the English language that gave them their influence . . .

The alternative, both politically and culturally lay not in party, but in the efforts of men of letters who worked among the Welsh people themselves. David Jones summed it up in his *The Welsh Church and Welsh Nationality* (1893) when he expressed his conviction that,

> The great need of Wales today is for men of 'light and learning', whose vision is clear enough to discern the magnitude of the interests that are at stake (the survival of the nation, its language and ancient religion), and whose voice is authoritative enough to restore to the nation the calmness of belief—strength and stability of conviction.

The interaction of Paul Bourget and Friedrich Nietzsche upon one another was to create out of the isolated artist of the decadence and the 'superman' a new concept of the artist as a leader that was to form such a vital part both of French traditionalism and symbolism. The appearance of the man of letters as leader in Wales as early as 1893 suggests that the atmosphere of the time was ripe for such a marriage. In Wales, however, this new concept of a *non-political* or even *anti-political* nationalism, was to have significance only in the future. In the 1890s it remained simply a longing for the example of men like Bishop Morgan, the Vicar Pritchard, Griffith Jones, Llanddowror, and the recently deceased Dean H. T. Edwards. When the patriotic Canon John Owen formed the Guild of St. Davids in 1894 its objectives were educational, literary and religious, but *Yr Haul* expected of it 'beneficial things . . . Magnanimous, elevated, sacred things, something above all the fickle political parties'. The excitement was short-lived, however, and the Anglican patriots remained so isolated from one another that A. W. Wade-Evans lamented in 1911 in the journal *Wales* that they had no 'organisation, and know not who is for us or against us'.

Example and inspiration, when it came, arrived once more from France, this time in the guise of a provincial movement—the Félibres of Provence. Itself a product of a deep sense of Latin decadence, the Félibrist movement suggested to the Anglican right a possible model for alternative action. In May 1914, *Yr Haul* carried an article which held up the work of the provençal writers Frédéric Minstral, Anselme Mathieu and Joseph Roumanille as a glowing example to the Welsh.

> The society aims to form an idealistic union of all the Latin peoples in order to counter the tendencies of the age to centralisation, not indeed through political opposition to Governments . . . but by enlivening the racial life and consciousness . . .

Yr Haul believed there were two lessons which Wales could learn from this. The first was that the efforts of cultured men were far more efficacious than the political antics of party leaders, and the second was that 'centralisation, which is but another name for bureaucracy, is nothing but an unmixed evil for the nation's welfare.' As René Rémond points out in his *La Droite en France*, it was an admiration of the Félibres which led to the contradictory dualism in *Action Française* between its authoritarianism and its regionalism. This dualism was always present in the emerging reactionary nationalism of Wales itself. The Anglican reaction, reflecting a tendency which first manifested itself in Montesquieu's

L'Esprit des Lois and in Adam Müller's *Die Elemente der Staatskunst* (1809) moved towards anti-statism in response to the centralism which they saw as the hallmark of Jacobinism. Yet at the same time, they were convinced that an organic and hierarchical authority was essential if society was to be saved from the effects of untrammelled individualism. This was a cleft stick in which the proto-Fascist right throughout Europe found itself. Such uncomfortable paradoxes, however, held no terrors for anti-rationalist and irrationalists like the French Decadents and Traditionalists and the Welsh right wing. The Decadent movement in France had produced Henri Bergson whose radical and mystical anti-rationalism was to be a deliverance from the tyranny of deterministic science. He and Maurice Barrès, whose nationalism sprang from his sense of decadence and from an overwhelming feeling of weakness, were faithfully reflected in Wales by J. Arthur Price, A. W. Wade-Evans and J. E. de Hirsch-Davies. While Wade-Evans' historical writings were shot through with irrationalism, Price's *élan vital* came straight from Bergson and Barrès. J. E. de Hirsch-Davies, who, with the others, exerted such a profound influence on the nationalist right in the 1920s, never tired of stressing the fact that even if man was capable of *a priori* reasoning, it was relatively unimportant compared with his deeper irrational nature. Whereas he never quite succumbed to Barrès' blood and soil fantasies, just as surely as Barrès, and other Traditionalists like Jacques Bainville, Jules Lemaître, and Charles Maurras, he was the heir of a reactionary inheritance which stretched back as far as Joseph de Maistre's insistence on the primacy of prejudice over reason and Hippolyte Taine's distinction between *raison raisonnante* and *raison qui s'ignore*. This inheritance could, despite the apparent contemporary dominance of positivism and scientism, allow de Hirsch-Davies to claim that a 'nation must have great ideas and fruitful fantasies' and that to be true to itself it had 'to dream dreams and see visions', without damaging his reputation as a serious historian. Aestheticism and unreason were the hallmarks of both his nationalism and his historical writings. This tendency in his work took its most extravagant form when he wrote in *Yr Haul* in February 1907 that:

> while the unromantic and dry light of science and 'modern progress', as it is called, throws light over the practical inhabitants of the cities and midland plains of England, the fairies are yet alive on the slopes of Snowdonia and Cader Idris.

This revolt against 'scientific' historiography pointed the way to Saunders Lewis' classic article on Dafydd Nanmor in *Y Llenor* in 1927 and to Ambrose Bebb's historical *tour de force Machlud yr Oesoedd Canol* (1950). It was also what enabled J.E. Daniel to declare, without a twinge of embarrassment, in *Welsh Nationalism: What it stands for*, that 'it is not things that happened yesterday that explains the state of things today', but 'old, unhappy, far off things, and battles long ago'. The Wales of the depression era was suffering the effects of too much scientific government so that 'it is in the poetry of Taliesin and Dafydd Nanmore far more than in Special Areas Acts or Five Year Programmes that the salvation of Wales is to be found'.

Attempts to pinpoint the precise origins and nature of French right-wing influence on Lewis and Bebb, in this wider context, might seem a rather scholastic exercise. Yet for political rather than historical reasons, one suspects, it has become a major preoccupation particularly among nationalist intellectuals to dissociate Lewis, particularly, from a Jew-baiting movement which collaborated with the Vichy regime. Lewis himself has done little to clarify the matter, for scarcely any enlightenment can be gained from the direct statements that he has made. When he denied Maurras' influence on him, he offered for public consumption his debt to Paul Claudel, François Mauriac, Jacques Riviere and Étienne Gilson. However, his oft repeated acknowledgment of debt to Maurice Barrès is itself a strong indication that he was not averse to the basic principles of *Action Française*. More confusing is the fact that although Lewis denied Maurras and accepted Barrès, he followed the Maurrasien line of rejecting Barrès' romanticism and saw, with Maurras, a cultural and political salvation in a period of classical greatness in Catholic Europe. However, by 1927 such a position had become commonplace even among the Catholic intellectuals of France itself.

In this context, Lewis' own account of his conversion to Roman Catholicism as a recognition that the Mass was the only valid form of worship must be suspect. That is not to say that it had no part in the process, for Lewis' admiration of Tom Nefyn suggests that he felt that Nonconformity had wrongly banished the communion service to the edges of religious observance. Yet even Caerwyn Williams, whose approach to Saunders Lewis tends to be eulogistic, cannot accept such a simplistic explanation. He places, correctly, the conversion in the context of Lewis' total intellectual experience as part of his discovery of Europeanism and Medievalism. There can be no doubt that his conversion was political in the sense that it was part of a search for authority. Lewis saw, like Charles Maurras, de Hirsch-Davies and Wade-Evans that classicism and catholicism were identified with regulation and order. As Maurras had found these things in the Catholic France of Louis XIV, Lewis discovered them in the Catholic Wales of Dafydd Nanmor.

Although the breadth of inspiration which Saunders Lewis and his followers received from France may seem considerable, it is sometimes more apparent than real. In many cases close examination reveals that it finds its way back to *Action Francaise* or at least to the tradition that the movement drew its sustenance from . For example, Lewis' debt to Jules Lemaître as the father of impressionist literary criticism may seem far removed from politics. Yet there is no doubt that Lemaître was likely to appeal to Lewis as a lapsed republican who had by the time of the Dreyfus affair become, with Emile Faguet and the young Maurras, the bearer of a banner of literary criticism and political philosophy that had been raised by the right-wing and revanchist Ferdinand Brunetière. It was not that Lemaître simply shared the nationalism of Maurras and Barrès, but he was also very much rooted in his region—the Loiret. Politically this regionalism was welded firmly into an anti-statist royalism. In his only novel, *Les Rois*, Lemaître attributed Europe's ills to the collapse of monarchy and the onslaught of democracy. Like Brunetière and Maurras, Lemaître blamed the rationalism of the eighteenth century and the French Revolution for all the ills of the nineteenth and twentieth centuries.

Lemaître's close association with *Action Francaise* after its founding once more suggests that Lewis' hot denial of his admiration of the movement in 1927 was not as frank as it might have been. This is reinforced by his claim, in defence of Bebb, that the latter was influenced far more by Jacques Bainville than by Charles Maurras. The essential dishonesty of the claim lay in the fact that Maurras and Bainville were a two-headed political animal. Bainville was part of *Action Francaise* from its beginning, and his historical studies of the political institutions of France provided the pragmatic basis in history for *Action Francaise's* opposition to democracy and its proposed restoration of anachronistic corporativist forms.

The issue is made no clearer by the contributions of later commentators. J. E. Caerwyn Williams gives credence to Lewis' claim on behalf of Bebb by suggesting there were severe limits to Bebb's admiration of Maurras on the grounds that 'if Maurras' three hatreds, as it is said, were the Protestant Reformation, the French Revolution and Romanticism, one cannot imagine Mr Bebb seriously choosing those three as his own three hatreds'. Mr Williams fails to reconcile this with Saunders Lewis' claim, for Jacques Bainville's historical studies formed the base of Maurras' polemics and the three *bêtes noires* which he cannot imagine Bebb accepting were in fact Bainville's. Bainville's historiographical influence on Bebb was crystal clear to the extent that his stilted and polemical account of the historical relationship between Wales, the Crown and Parliament was closely modelled on Bainville's scheme of French history into which the history of Wales was forcibly thrust for anti-democratic and corporativist ends.

One cannot avoid the feeling that perhaps Saunders Lewis was taken aback by the vehemence of W.J. Gruffydd's attack on him and his colleague, Bebb, and hoped to divert attention from the infamous Maurras to lesser known members of the French right. While criticising Maurras for being anti-European, *Y Ddraig Goch* could refer to Jacques Bainville in June 1927 as 'one of Frances's most able political writers'. A month earlier it had hailed Robert Fabre-Luce as:

> the leader of the latest nationalist movement in France, a movement that embodies in itself the sure and valuable elements of the political leadership of Maurras, but which is also European in its spirit and places nationalism in a wide, liberal, international and civilised system . . . We are surprised to see how alike the aims of Fabre-Luce are to the teachings of *Y Ddraig Goch*.

The truth, had it been known, about Fabre-Luce would have been rather less palatable to political and intellectual circles in Wales. He was an extreme nationalist who became the disciple of the founder of the *Cagoule* (the *Comité Secret d'Action Revolutionnaire*), the renegade communist-turned-facist, Jacques Doriot.

The influence of France on the Welsh right wing from the 1880s onwards was certainly not 'wide', 'liberal', 'international' or 'civilised' in the normally accepted senses of those words. It represented rather an anti-democratic and authoritarian tradition which found its full expression in a group of intellectuals who gathered around Lewis and Bebb and which seemed to realise the Anglican reaction's hope of a cadre of cultured men who would operate exclusively within Wales, shunning the parliamentary system as 'alien' and stressing the need of a Welsh alternative based on an organic authoritative leadership.

Attempts like that of D. Tecwyn Lloyd to escape the orbit of the French right have proved futile, for although Mr Lloyd (in his essay on Saunders Lewis in Derec Llwyd Morgan's *Adnabod Deg*) has rendered valuable service in drawing our attention to the similarities between this group and Hilaire Belloc and the English Distributists, his attempts to attribute their ideas entirely to Leo XIII's encyclical *Rerum Novarum* are unconvincing. He ignores the mass of evidence which points to the fact that the anti-democratic and corporativist attitudes of the right in Wales were predominantly inherited from Europe by way of France. Even if one were to accept that *Rerum Novarum* could have played a part in their thinking in that it had become, by the early twentieth century, a part of the general reservoir of European rightist ideology, it would hardly be consistent with Mr. Lloyd's intentions. He appears to be labouring under the misapprehension that Leo's encyclical was a liberal attempt to steer a path between the right and the left, an alternative to the statism of capitalism and socialism. This confusion could arise from an association between the right and capitalism which was almost certainly absent from Leo's thinking. In the 1880s and 1890s such attempts to find alternative social orders were a rebellion as much against liberalism, the product of bourgeois capitalism and individualism, as it was against socialism. Rightism in the nineteenth century, even in Wales, was a conservative rejection of urbanism and capitalism and it is in this anti-liberal and anti-bourgeois context that Leo's encyclical must be seen. Thus, far from being an expression of liberalism it was its very negation. Like social catholicism in France it was an attempt to keep conservative peasants rooted in a conservative social order. Indeed, *Rerum Novarum* was largely inspired by La Tour du Pin's *Syndicats Agricoles*, and significantly, Charles Maurras described La Tour du Pin as 'the master'.

Thus insofar as European reactionism from the early nineteenth century onwards viewed the French Revolution of 1789 as the fount of all evil, Welsh conservatism was in the mainstream of European political thinking at least from 1880 onwards. That the French right should have played such a prominent part in developing the counter-revolutionary tradition is hardly surprising, nor is it any wonder that Welsh anti-liberal and anti-democratic elements should have tapped such a rich vein so widely and so consistently. Thus even though much enlightenment resulted from it, it could be argued that in focusing attention so precisely on the influence of *Action Française* on the nationalist right in 1927, W. J. Gruffydd's attack also obscured a much larger tradition in Welsh politics, and invested the Saunders Lewis-Ambrose Bebb group with an originality which they hardly merited.

Bibliographical note

Perhaps the main difficulty of the historian of ideas lies in the fact that the majority of the people whose ideas he examines are not systematic thinkers. Much of what they say is derivative and often based on a misunderstood or half-digested original. Such a problem arises with the Anglican accusation that their Nonconformist opponents were 'positivists'. It is difficult to decide whether the Anglican accusers misunderstood Auguste Comte or whether the application of the term was a deliberate calumny. Insofar as this is what the Anglicans thought the Nonconformists were, or at least affected to believe it, the term has been retained in the essay, although strictly speaking 'progressive' would be a more accurate description of the prevailing political ideas of the Liberal Nonconformists.

Much of the material which has gone to make up my over-all picture of Welsh political ideology between 1870 and 1930 has had of necessity to remain in the background. The sources of such information as I possess have been a range of newspapers, journals, pamphlets, monographs, both secular and denominational so wide that reference cannot be made to all of them here. In relation to Wales I will confine myself therefore to sources from which material actually used in the text has been taken.

Primary sources relating to Wales

1. *Nonconformist and liberal publications*
Seren Gomer: This Baptist journal was an early champion of democracy and Welsh national consciousness. It dealt with a wide

range of issues, religious and secular, domestic and foreign. Far
from being a denominational news sheet it was, for much of the
nineteenth century, virtually the sole source of information about
current affairs for many monoglot Welsh Baptists. It maintained a
staunchly liberal and democratic line and in the late nineteenth
century threw in its lot with *Cymru Fydd* and, as one might expect,
the cause of Church Disestablishment.

Y Tyst: A congregational newspaper which, like *Seren Gomer*,
dealt not merely with denominational matters but with political
issues at home and abroad.

Yr Ymofynnydd: The official organ of Welsh Unitarianism,
this journal maintained a particular interest in the affairs of France
which it reported in detail to its readers. Of the nonconformist
journals this was the most consistently radical and democratic and
until the 1900s it remained the most loyal to the traditional values
of individualism, rationalism and the Enlightenment. Its
commitment to Liberty Equality and Fraternity was unflinching as
was its belief in the idea of human material and spiritual progress
towards perfection. It maintained a purist *laissez-faire* Liberalism
at a time when others were yielding to the temptations of
interventionism. An abrupt change occurred in the 1900s
(coinciding with a change of editor) as the journal began to
support the trade-union movement and the Labour Party as the
main hopes of human progress.

The North Wales Observer and Express: A weekly, secular
newspaper, now defunct; this was radically liberal and maintained
a sustained attack on the *ancien régime* of Church and squirearchy
in the late nineteenth century.

2.   *Anglican publications*

Yr Haul: This was the monthly intellectual organ of the Anglican
Church in Wales. It opened its pages to all shades of Anglican
opinion, but generally favoured an anti-Anglicist approach. Since
its foundation in 1850, it had concerned itself with Church
defence, but its contents were varied. Like its Nonconformist
counterparts its scope of interests was wide and its pages throw
particular light on the state of mind of the leading laymen and
lower clergy of the Church who, both in an editorial role and as
contributors, kept the journal going. *Yr Haul* attempted to
'popularise' current historiographical and socio-political thinking
among Welsh Anglican scholars.

Y Cyfaill Eglwysig: This sister publication of *Yr Haul* was a monthly journal aimed at Anglican Sunday School teachers and the parochial Church Defence and Literary Societies. Its contents were therefore more 'popular' than those of *Yr Haul* and the journal forms an invaluable insight into Welsh Anglican thinking at a lower level in the late nineteenth and early twentieth centuries.

John Jenkins, Y Parch, *Moesoldeb Gwleidyddol* (1896). A valuable work on political morality and philosophy which received the blessing of the Bishop of St. David's who wrote the introduction.

The Rev. David Jones, *The Welsh Church and Welsh Nationality* (1893). One of many historical works which attempted to establish the national *bona fides* of the Anglican Church in Wales, and which led to an Anglican discovery of its own past. This historiographical Odyssey was to form the basis of a reactionary Welsh nationalism which blossomed around the turn of the century and which, through its three greatest exponents, J. Arthur Price, an Anglican barrister and two parish priests, the reverends A.W. Wade-Evans and J.E. de Hirsch-Davies, was to exert a powerful and profound influence on the early Welsh Nationalist Party.

3.   *Nondenominational intellectual journals*

Y Geninen: Founded in 1883, *Y Geninen* rapidly became a forum of debate on all aspects of Welsh life. Non-sectarian and national, it gave space to all comers and became an institution in the literary, political and religious life of Wales.

Wales: A short lived publication which took a rather anglicised 'drawing-room' look at the affairs of Wales. It did carry some significant articles during its short existence.

Welsh Review: Another rather short lived journal which appeared to aim at being an Anglo-Welsh version of *Y Geninen*.

Y Llenor: Founded in 1922 as the literary organ of *Cymdeithasau Cymraeg Y Colegau Cenedlaethol* (the Welsh Societies of the National Colleges), under the editorship of the academician, poet, essayist and liberal W.J. Gryffydd, it became a major and influential journal in Welsh intellectual circles. Although political controversy was never its objective, as literary output, criticism and historical writings became at times almost explicitly concerned with basic political and social attitudes in the twenties and thirties, W.J. Gruffydd found it difficult on occasion to exclude controversy of a political nature and had to fight hard to maintain his equanimity and neutrality as an editor.

His *bêtes noires* were the French traditionalists and the Welsh Nationalist right. Saunders Lewis, a cult figure in some nationalist circles, came in for sustained criticism by Gruffydd. Lewis was a founding member of the Welsh Nationalist Party who converted from Calvinistic Methodism to Roman Catholicism in 1932. He was president of the Party during the twenties and thirties and editor of the Party's official journal *Y Ddraig Goch*. He and a group of rightist intellectuals, notable among whom was W. Ambrose Bebb, dominated the philosophy of the party between the wars. Bebb, a fervent admirer of Mussolini and Franco (his admiration of Hitler was short-lived), and who stood as a nationalist candidate in 1945, had come under the influence of both Charles Maurras and *Action Française* and Charles Le Goffic, the Breton separatist, while teaching at the Sorbonne in the early twenties. He later became a teacher of history at the Normal College, Bangor.

Primary Sources relating to France

The history of the extreme right in France is well documented. Elitist and traditionalist writers left a huge number of essays, histories and novels which can prove by its very volume an embarrassment of sources to the historian of ideas. In a bibliography on a subject relating to Wales a representative selection must suffice.

J.-K. Huysman's novel *A Rebours* (1884) became the veritable handbook of the French Decadent movement which exemplified the aesthetic revolt of the right against urban and industrial society, while Maurice Barres' *Les Déracinés* (1897) is also a classic of its kind. Jules Lemaître's novel, *Les Rois* (n.d.) considered the twin evils of democracy and individualism and their effect on European stability.

More directly political was Barrès' *Scènes et doctrines du nationalisme* (n.d.), which was a classic exposition of extreme nationalism in France. A less extreme statement of Catholic right-wing ideas can be found in Emile Faguet's *Problèmes politiques du temps présent* (1900), while of the massive output of Paul Bourget, the most useful are *Pages de critique et de doctrine* (1910), *Nouvelles pages de critique et de doctrine* (1922) and a collection of articles which were written between 1880 and 1883 and published together in *Essaie de psychologie contemporaine*, (1924-28). A typical example of Jacques Bainville's historiography is his *Histoire de France* (1924).

Secondary sources relating to Wales

Most works on the subject of J. Saunders Lewis and his colleagues have appeared in Welsh. Only two works of any substance have appeared in English on Saunders Lewis, namely: B. Griffiths, *Saunders Lewis*, (1979) and A. R. Jones and Gwyn Thomas (eds.), *Presenting Saunders Lewis* (1973).

In the Welsh language of great interest are: Derec Ll. Morgan (ed.), *Adnabod Deg* (1977) which is a series of articles on leading nationalists of the interwar period. Outstanding in the collection is Gareth Miles' admirable essay on W. Ambrose Bebb.

J. E. Jones, *Tros Gymru*, 1970. This is a history of the nationalist party written by the late J. E. Jones who was a life time member of the party and a full time officer of the movement.

Two works of exceptional interest which throw light not merely on Saunders Lewis' life and ideas, but also on the state of mind of the authors themselves, are Pennar Davies, *Saunders Lewis: ei feddwl a'i waith* (1950). D. Tegwyn Lloyd and G.R. Hughes, *Saunders Lewis* (1975).

Secondary sources relating to the French right

Only a short selection of the vast amount of material available on the subject is included here. I have attempted to select works which give as wide a view as possible while at the same time covering those aspects of the subject referred to in the essay.

M. Anderson, *Conservative Politics in France* (1974).
M. Augé-Laribé *La Politique Agricole de la France de 1880 à 1940* (1950).
P. Bourdrel, *La Cagoule: 30 Ans de Complots* (1970)
P. Drieu de Rochelle, *Doriot ou la Vie d'un Ouvrier Francais* (1936).
H. Fontanille, *L'Oeuvre Social d'Albert de Mun* (1926).
R. Girardet, *Le Nationalisme Francais 1871-1914* (1966)
J. MacManners, *Church and State in France 1870-1914* (1972).
R. Remond, *La Droite en France* (1963).

The Language of Edwardian Politics
Peter Stead

In modern industrial societies, as G.M. Young succinctly observed, things tend to a culture. It may be added that within cultures there tends to be a language—a vocabulary, a rhetoric and a way of using words and phrases that is part of the very distinctiveness of that culture. Historians know that as they approach a culture they have to learn a new language and that sources are not only communicating direct information but also patterns in which key words and phrases and forms of emphasis begin to reveal the frame of mind or psychology of the age. What most historians first encounter is a public language which binds together the elements within a culture. To trace the spontaneous emergence and maturing of this public language is perhaps the first task of any social historian, and this study must of necessity become political for the language of a culture is usually a vital clue to its group and class politics.

Britain in the twentieth century has been characterised by a powerful and quite distinctive labour movement. It was the late Victorian and Edwardian periods which saw the birth of an independent working-class party and of a much larger and more powerful trade-union movement. Victorian politics had been dominated by social elites who had yet moulded a politics and culture that were truly national, that encouraged, prepared for and accepted 'the rise of labour' and, as recent studies have shown, held together into the war years. The Edwardian years did, however, witness a battle in which a number of small groups indicated that they fully understood the politics of the 'Victorian culture' and knew that there was now the potential within sub-cultures to create a new society. The language of Edwardian politics reveals the magnitude and passion of this struggle between elites and rebels, both of whom realised what Gramsci spelt out, that culture could be organised like any other practical activity and the understanding of reality manipulated. Both political

groups knew it was culture and reality that were at stake and not just parliamentary seats or a few extra shillings a week. The issues were immense and, as the battle was waged, both sides found that new efforts were required to bring life and meaning to the everyday language of politics. To be effective their language needed a new edge. The historian of Edwardian Britain finds himself moving from the everyday language of parliamentary politics and industrial relations into a battle over language in which culture and therefore, as Gramsci taught, truth and freedom were the real issues.

In March 1910 'Argus', the Welsh correspondent of the Social Democratic Federation's organ *Justice*, examined the election address of William Brace who had just been returned as the MP for South Glamorgan and concluded that it was 'a glib concoction of the worn platitudes of Radicalism which come gurgling from the mouths of superficial political reformers like buttermilk from a jug'. William Brace would hardly have accepted this harsh judgement on his election address which he had obviously had difficulty in composing. Like many other so-called 'Lib-Lab' MPs Brace did not have to worry very much about winning his constituency in a straight fight against the Tories but he did have to worry rather more about the language he would use in outlining his ideas and, indeed, in describing his candidature. He must surely have blushed at the accuracy of the opening phrase of Argus's attack, for what else could a Liberal do but concoct a credo out 'of the worn platitudes of Radicalism'? The actual politics of everyday life had shifted to become concerned with wages, with working conditions, with unemployment and with housing, but electoral politics were not about everyday reality but about the manipulation of a social consensus. The Liberals were inevitably talking a language of the past and theirs was a rhetoric designed to arouse and comfort, much as a stirring and familiar piece of music does. Brace, like other Lib-Labs and many Liberals in Wales and elsewhere had deliberately aimed at a concoction of platitudes because that had become the language of their politics. This was a language forged in earlier battles and what mattered now was not the small print but the overall sound of the phrases and, of course, of the particular voice in which they were being delivered. Familiarity was all.

Edwardian working men were much talked-at people for they spent a great deal of their leisure time listening to sermons, talks and public addresses, many of which could also be read at length in the many national and local papers. The fact that the medium had become the message and that listening had become a form of popular entertainment is revealed in the repetitive and wordy nature of these speeches. The historian can only concur with Argus's use of the term 'gurgling' and with Nun Nicholas' use of the word 'prattling' to describe the political mode of men who immediately became precise and technical when operating as professionals in the courts or in industrial bargaining. In 1908 Sir S. T. Evans told his constituents at Aberkenfig that the principles of Liberalism were 'to render justice to everybody, to remove all privileges, to redress all inequalities and to make the people so far as possible, or at any rate to give them the opportunity of being, a contented people and a successful nation'. In 1910 the appearance of Mabon's election address led the *Rhondda Leader* to conclude that their MP was

> the embodiment in which we have clothed our political views for a House of Commons representative. He is the very inclusion of every quality of personality, experience and capacity which has made for an ideal Welsh representative. This Welsh mining area is Labour in every aspiration but, since man cannot live on bread alone, the Rhondda mining electors are Nationalists, they are Nonconformists to an overwhelming degree, and the whole gamut of social reforms come within their ambition for a better Wales and a better living condition for the masses.

On and on went the hurdy-gurdy of Liberalism and Lib-Labism, always moving from the *esprit de corps* forged by the Welsh Non-conformist experience into the aspiration of an unspecified fulfillment. Occasionally however there would be a clue as to why the tune was again being played as, indeed, there was in this extract from the *Rhondda Leader*, for what was meant by that curious phrase that 'this Welsh mining area is Labour in every aspiration'?

The *Rhondda Leader* was illustrating the extent to which the word 'Labour' had become significant and powerful in the language of late Victorian and Edwardian politics. The growth of a national and recognisable pattern of working-class life, and the institutionalisation of collective bargaining, had helped to make the concept of 'Labour' one that was increasingly invoked. Here was a clear interest which was deserving of respect and which had to be represented in some form or other in public life. Few people doubted that 'Labour' was a reality but just to mention it, let alone describe it, was to give it more meaning and to make it into a more dynamic force. For Liberals the political dilemma was one in which Labour had to be recognised and yet contained. Their linguistic problem became one in which the word 'Labour' had to be uttered in a way that did not give it too much emotive power. The process of neutralising what was becoming a reality demanded a safe language—demanded, in fact, a rhetoric. For almost twenty years men who were essentially Liberals had to use a language and, in particular, the word 'Labour' to bind their supporters into the established pattern of politics, and in this process they were to be greatly helped by the national and local press. For years Mabon, the quintessential Lib-Lab, had stressed that 'as it was in the beginning so it shall ever be—Labour first', and his local paper was only too willing to admit that the Rhondda, just about to experience its most serious outbreak of class warfare, was 'Labour in every aspiration'.

Things were, of course, not that simple. In a situation in which several different political groups, all trade unions, and many newspapers were anxious to describe the scores of new working-class leaders as 'good labour men', or as 'popular labour leaders' it was, as the *Labour Annual* of 1896 admitted, 'somewhat difficult to say who and what are Labour representatives'. Such was the reality of Labour that it was bound to become an issue in late Victorian politics but it was Keir Hardie who saw that the rise of Labour made independent Labour politics an imperative, and his life's work became that of persuading those who recognised Labour, or thought of themselves as part of it, to vote for independent Labour candidates. Hardie faced a mammoth task but it was one to which he brought a full and varied armoury. After the Mid-Lanark by-election of 1888, his message was always that 'the attitude of the official Liberals made it unmistakably clear that they care nothing for the interests of Labour'. In propagating this simple argument however he relied on a very sophisticated political image in which he blended the language and morality of Victorian Radicalism and Nonconformity and his own physical appearance with a cultivated air of what the Lib-Labs always saw as 'insubordination'. With Keir Hardie the simple logic of independence originated in what was at first an innate but then a cultivated cheekiness. He was, as William Brace once bitterly complained, 'a law unto himself' and this was a far more important fact about Hardie than his Socialism.

Language though became his most powerful weapon. What he did in effect was to express his message of independence in a language which entertained in the accustomed way. Using his pretty well irresistible accent, he would tell his listeners anything they wanted to hear as long as it did not interfere with the idea of independence. To him the logic was simple, but he faced audiences and electors more susceptible to effect than to logic. The young Jack Jones heard him at Merthyr and recalled how 'his talk put us in different places to where the boss was living' for 'every word he spoke came from a bleeding heart'. Accent and emotion were, however, only a part of the story, for Keir Hardie, in arguing the need for 'independent' and 'direct' representatives of labour, was able to capture the very word 'labour'. The title of every political group formed by Hardie between 1888 and 1906 contained the word 'Labour' and his stress on the fact that labour was the very basis of independence gave the word a new meaning and legitimacy. He had no exclusive claim to the word but his use of it gradually weakened the original meaning and, more particularly, made the use of it by other groups seem deliberate, contrived and somewhat cynical. The beauty of Hardie's independent position was that he increasingly made the Lib-Labs look somewhat half-hearted and anomalous however much their support was numerically greater than his. He fully appreciated that in politics singularity was all and in establishing his quiddity the word 'Labour' was vital.

The leader-writer of the *South Wales Daily News* who wrote in 1906 that 'Independent Labour for one thing does not represent the Labour Party as a whole' must have known that he was working a fast one in using the term 'Labour Party' to mean labour, as must William Brace when he claimed that 'he stood for the establishment of a Parliamentary Labour Party, but . . . also for the policy of co-operation rather than isolation'. It is impossible to read the newspapers between 1906 and 1910 without being struck by the linguistic disingenuousness and floundering of men who, whilst being sure that the majority of electors were with them, could not quite find the words to define their position. Their anxiety was caused as much by the paradox as the threat. Keir Hardie's victory came psychologically rather than electorally.

Nobody expressed this anxiety more fully than William Brace who, though as distinguished and tested a miners' leader as any, had won a constituency where the miners' vote was less prominent than in those represented by his colleagues. He pointed out that he had been 'adopted by the Labour, Liberal, Free Church, Free Trade and Progressive forces in the constituency' whilst the *Rhondda Leader* which circulated in part of the division decided that it would 'call Mr Brace, a Radical of the most vigorous type' adding that 'a Radical is more than Labour and a little bit more tense than Liberal. Radical embraces both'. All this was an attempt to define accurately the candidate's position but the language of politics demands a shorthand, for no elector responds to identities established by a list or formula. The voter looks for an immediate tag as Keir Hardie appreciated. The Liberals searched around and, for a while, in the heady atmosphere of 1906 and its aftermath, they came up with 'Progressive'. The word was a God-send for Brace who now used the term 'Progressive forces' to define his support. *The South Wales Daily News*, aiming for that last word which would invest the struggle with the sanctity of a Holy War, thundered that 'the Labour leader who attacks Liberalism is false to Labour. He is not a Progressive'. The word was given a good airing and was as common in South Wales as Peter Clarke has shown it to have been in Lancashire, but it brought few tears to the eyes. Language, or rather the language of identification, was failing the Lib-Labs. Just to talk of Progressivism was to miss the directness of the Labour supporter who reminded his readers that it was 'useless offering the Welsh miner Labour wrapped in the swaddling clothes of Liberalism' for 'he knows it for make-believe'.

What was needed now was an opportunity for Liberals to indulge in language and if this could not be done in defence of a position then it would have to be done in criticism of the opponent's position. If a precise and emotive definition of Progression had proved to be elusive then a precise and emotive isolation of the enemy was a more than useful substitute.

Language was to play a part in the isolation of those who in any way challenged traditional political allegiances. What the business and political leadership did in conjunction with their press was to stress those characteristics which underlay the culture and also firmly relate the economic well-being of the community to the existing social and political norms. In South Wales there was an emphasis on Welshness and Nonconformity accompanied by a continuous stress on the varying fortunes of that coal trade which determined the prosperity of so many. In a situation in which a whole community was trained to depend on business forecasts much as cricketers depend on weather forecasts it became an obvious tactic to point to any group who were threatening to 'rock the boat'. In these crucial years after 1906 it was important to identify and isolate those who in later times would have been called 'extremists' but who, at that time, were termed 'advanced'. 'Advanced' men were at first those who formed 'a political element' within the trade union world and who were led by 'strangers to the Coal Trade', and then later they were more likely to be 'irresponsible' militants for whom collective bargaining took the form of 'shouting or blustering' and who were in the marvellous words of the *Colliery Guardian* 'playing ducks and drakes with their industry'. Whoever they were the 'advanced men', the new 'schools', had to be identified, denied wisdom and made to appear as dangerous outsiders.

There were several ways of using language to suggest the iniquity of the new men. As they were upsetting a delicate balance, a consensus of forces, they became identified as a 'section'. The almost sacrosanct nature of community feeling is perhaps most clearly detected in the way in which the word 'section' became such a powerful term of abuse. To belong to a 'section' was the ultimate offence against the community. Of all sections that of the 'direct' labour men was the most pernicious. In 1908 the *Colliery Guardian* pointed to the 'increased strength of the Socialist section' amongst the leadership of the South Wales Miners' Federation and warned that 'New men by new methods are carrying out a new policy. Whether that policy will bind the Federation together as the old policy has done, bringing up the South Wales membership to over 150,000 remains to be seen—but it is very questionable'. In 1909 the *Glamorgan Gazette* examined the activities of the Maesteg Urban District Council and regretted that 'only in recent years has the council been divided upon the election of labour members. As a rule sections on public bodies do not make for good-will and efficiency'. Perhaps the strongest condemnation of sectionalism came in the editorials of the *South Wales Daily News* (that paper for whom 'Labour' belonged 'inside the Liberal Party') for, knowing its readership's frame of reference, it warned that 'to encourage Ishmaelism is always a danger'.

The true nature of the 'section' was to be seen in its mode of activity, and when active it tended to be identified as an 'element'. An 'element', of course, was bound to operate in a very different

way from a more established political organisation, In 1909 one
ILP journalist reported that there was 'a disposition throughout
the whole area and in West Wales in particular to regard ILP
organisers as Machiavellian conspirators' and this was a theme
often taken up by the press in general. Socialism was always
'insidiously promulgated' and genuine Labour candidatures were
always 'engineered'. It has always to be suggested that there was
something underhand and sinister about all Labour activities. In
January 1910, when it was announced that Ben Tillett was going to
make it a three-cornered fight at Swansea, the *South Wales Daily
News* found it 'deplorable' that 'at almost the last moment there
interposes an element whose avowed object is to discredit the
champion of progress (Mr Alfred Mond) and to split the progressive vote'. Particularly deplorable was sectional activity in local
government where, as we have seen, there was a traditional myth
of non-political activity. In 1908 the *South Wales Daily News* was
delighted at being able to publicise complaints against a Labour
'caucus' on the Pontardawe Board of Guardians. One Guardian
had complained about the ILP's 'hole-and-corner' meetings and
another commented that 'they might as well carry *en bloc* the
resolution of the preliminary meeting held that morning by one
section of the Guardians at the Dynevor Arms'. Throughout the
Edwardian period the surest way to discredit opponents was to
suggest that they were behaving secretly and taking covert decisions.

This sustained attempt to depict the 'insiduous' nature of
sectional activity was at moments of urgency accompanied by
straightforward abuse. The epithet of judgement was all important
in Edwardian politics and the 'good Labour' man or occasionally
the 'mild Labour' man could always be contrasted with the
'advanced' and 'dangerous' types. When the danger had to be
spelled out the epithet could be spiced up. In 1913 an agent of the
Bute Estate brought to the attention of the Lord Lieutenant the
information that of the five men nominated for the bench by the
Aberdare Trades and Labour Council 'the first three are Socialists
of the most extreme republican type. The fourth is an innocent
person of no ability at all while the fifth is a decent enough labour
representative on our Local Council'. This accusation of
republicanism made in a private letter provides a good indication
of the language of innuendo that was resorted to at times of
crucial elections or threatened industrial unrest. The object of the

exercise was to suggest that the adherents of what was called 'the modern type of Socialism' were somewhat deficient in respect of Welsh patriotism, Christianity, sexual morality and enthusiasm for the Crown. What is perhaps surprising was the frequency with which these wilder criticisms of the Socialists were made by Nonconformist ministers. The politics of the Nonconformist clergy in Edwardian Wales were very complex. It may be surmised that the vast majority of preachers silently supported Liberalism but the minority which came out in support of the ILP were very frequently opposed in public by a number of outspoken anti-Socialist ministers whose language injected a particular bitterness into the news columns.

In 1907 the Reverend Cyngor Williams, noting that Socialists wanted to abolish private property, argued that 'the best workmen in the district were capitalists in a small scale' and he therefore doubted whether 'they were going to divide with loafers and spongers'. In the following year the Reverend J. T. Davies decided to take on the ILP leaders of the Ogmore Valley describing them as 'infidels and immoral men'. The most sustained intervention of ministers in politics came in the Mid-Glamorgan constituency where there was a prolonged campaign to depict the local miners' leader, Vernon Hartshorn, as a lapsed chapel-goer and, therefore, a man unsuited to represent the constituency. Following the by-election of 1910 in which he was defeated by the Liberal, Hartshorn complained of the way ministers had declared 'that every vote given to me was a vote for Atheism' and the *Labour Leader* described a Liberal pamphlet used in the election as being a 'farrago of abominable misrepresentation—a farrago purporting to show that Socialism means neither more or less than a campaign against Christianity, against marriage and the family'. But things were to get worse in Mid-Glamorgan for in the General Election some nine months later Hartshorn was opposed and beaten by the Reverend John Hugh Edwards whose supporters issued an eve-of-the-poll pamphlet asking 'What is Socialism?' to which the answer was given, 'It is crying for the moon. What are its first fruits in Mid Glam? Look around our churches. What is depleting them of our young men? Socialism.' This was a new kind of Liberal campaign and it led one Socialist to complain that 'never was the candidature of a political adventurer supported by more questionable means'. The tone of this new Nonconformity was taken up by the Socialists themselves and the Reverend J. H.

Edwards was told that 'clothed in the garb of religious rectitude, and wearing the Nationalist colours, you hide the grinning skeleton of a political hack'. Similar language was used in the Gower Constituency where the Reverend W. F. Phillips of the Young Liberal League fully revealed the new eagerness of that organisation to combat Socialism. To Phillips, Socialism was 'the party of revolution, the Party of new bogies and half-digested ideas' and Keir Hardie was 'a liar of the first water and a traitor to the country'. Such language indicated the liberal desire to strike back at the ILP but it also reflected the arrogance and narcissism of ministers to whom words came easily and who desired the same kind of publicity and fame which was being won by the charisma of the new men. In 1910 the Young Liberal League certainly mounted the most outspoken attack on all forms of Socialism. *Justice* referred to 'those antiquated ministerial bigots who are a living outrage upon the spirit and traditions of Evangelical Christianity' and said of W.F. Phillips that he had 'the mind of a gnat and the soul of a viper'.

If it was this intervention of what Hartshorn called the Welsh 'priesthood' which occasioned the bitterest verbal exchanges of the Edwardian period, there were other occasions when the conventions were put aside to allow a fresher language. One difficulty facing the historian of this period is that of getting past the formal language of the chapel, politics and social life into that vernacular spoken by a working class still only half-educated and preponderantly descended from Victorian labourers. It is impossible not to feel that the press and social leaders were attempting to impose a degree of sophistication on communities that still possessed a frontier and peasant rawness. There was a more basic language spoken at the workplace and at the pub—a language outlawed by the chapel and rarely recorded outside the crime columns of newspapers. It was in the various forms of industrial action that we can catch snatches of the vernacular and hints of an altogether more picturesque underworld vocabulary. In 1911 the six hundred miners on strike from the Tareni and Gleision pits at the top of the Swansea Valley, angered by the refusal of their union to give them aid, issued a manifesto in which they pointed out that they had not only 'grappled with our common enemy the capitalist but also with creatures whose interests are akin to the cobra and python, the most treacherous and poisonous reptiles of their species, who stalk in our midst in the guise of Labour friends'. This was the language normally used against that most hated section of the workforce, the non-unionists who, especially between 1906 and 1910, occasioned not only the traditional responses of group action such as the beating of tin kettles and pans, the blackening of faces and assault by women armed with brooms but also extreme verbal abuse. They were referred to as 'the non-unionist "pests", "rats", or "Dagoes".' The actions taken and the language used remind us of how near in time these Edwardians were to the days of the Scotch Cattle.

The language of the people may then have been very different from that of politicians and journalists but it is interesting to examine the way in which various personalities were able to bring a freshness and individuality to their language which enabled them to cut through the cliches. We have already seen that what others saw as his 'insubordination' and 'impertinence' were an important element in Keir Hardie's political persona. It was the accusation of insubordination from Liberals and from older labour leaders like Mabon and Brace which clinched the role he had created for himself. Mabon once called him the 'critic-general of everyone outside the pale of his own party' which was precisely of course, what he had set out to be. Hardie's successful manipulation of his insubordination usefully illustrates the way in which public figures could create an image and also a mode of speaking which gave them a distinctive position. It had to be carefully done for if 'insubordination' could be overdone by those who lacked Hardie's sense of how far to go, so too it was possible to over-reach in other directions. The age was quick to spot an authoritarian style and the epithet 'Czar-like' was the most common and the most emotive term of abuse that was currently available. It was probably in the interests of variety that in 1906 'one of the rank and file' in the South Wales Miners' Federation said of 'our fatuous leaders' that they were 'as imperious as the Bourbons'. The age was as quick to spot 'glibness' (and many of the Young Liberal League ministers were rumbled precisely because of this) and, perhaps even more, any form of pomposity. The assumption of any form of 'ex-cathedra' position without the full authority to back it up brought immediate ridicule. The Lib-Labs all too frequently put themselves in that position. Ben Tillett, that constant thorn in the side of the Welsh Lib-Labs, said at the 1912 TUC that 'Brace is always a roaring lion here but when he is outside and there is a fight on he is like a cooing dove'. Hartshorn was a leader who established his reputation by exposing the Lib-Labs, but his time was to come for the *Rhondda Bomb* spotted how in 1912 he had been 'flattered, praised and boomed' by the coal-owners and 'puffed into rapid and undeserved prominence'. They were later to wonder 'how far is Hartshorn's pose mere swanking swashbucklerism?'

It was a culture which loved to expose rhetoric and puncture pomposity but directness of approach and of language could be appreciated if backed up by intellect and achievement. Nobody loved to expose the cant of the period so much as the maverick coalowner D.A. Thomas who spoke from a position of power and in a language that reflected his scepticism. At a time when his Liberal colleagues were doing all they could to bolster the Lib-Labs his judgement was that 'the average Lib-Lab is little more than a perambulating gramophone wound up by the Liberal Whips and despatched on their peregrinations from the officers of the party caucus'. During the great Cambrian dispute at his collieries, Thomas went out of his way to praise the younger leaders at the expense of Mabon and this caused much resent-ment. One miner warned that 'we all know that all through his career Mr D.A. Thomas's chief delight has been to put cats among pigeons'. Hartshorn was to reply to a later ploy by asking Thomas to 'give us proof that he is something more than the impulsive spirit of mischief—the Puck of the coalfield'. His mischievousness was to cause untold suffering to the miners of his Combine and his economic values were best revealed in his judgement that the Minimum Wages Act represented 'a triumph for Syndicalism and a considerable leap in the direction of Socialistic darkness', but at the same time his detachment and irony placed him nicely outside the stuffiness and clichés of Edwardian politics. Nobody did more to expose the pretentiousness of Labour leaders for whilst he always spoke amicably of Hardie and Hartshorn, he once said of George Barker that 'like all great men [he] has his weaknesses and his weakness is that he is obsessed with the idea that the mantle of Napoleon has fallen upon him, that he is destined by Providence to lead a revolution in South Wales'. Like many others he thought that William Brace took himself 'too seriously' but admitted to 'a great liking' for him but not without adding that he doubted 'whether anyone has a higher opinion of him than I have, unless it be perhaps William himself'.

For all Keir Hardie's insubordination and D. A. Thomas's

mischievousness the language of Edwardian politics was fairly conventional and tended to proceed along well-established paths. Most public figures including Hardie and Thomas made safe noises, set out in part ot entertain and in part to confirm existing prejudices, and usually they ended up telling people what they wanted to hear. The truly advanced and militant leaders, were faced with the task of cutting through these cosy conventions of public life and the surest way of doing that was to present their message of revolt in an extreme language guaranteed to shock their Lib-Labish audiences. For almost twenty years Ben Tillett felt somewhat suffocated by the Mabonism that passed for labour leadership in Wales and he constantly attempted to rip through it. Speaking usually from his union base on the Swansea waterfront Tillett set out to make headlines. In 1907 he told his audience that 'I think most of the parsons if they were in Heaven would leave us better off'. Later that year he announced: 'Friends this is not a Christian country—Christianity died with Jesus Christ' and he went on to attack the 'Cecil class' who 'spent more money on wine for one dinner than the average working man could afford to spend in a month'. He could not be allowed to get away with this language and *The Cambrian* described it as 'a rabidly violent onslaught' and as being 'couched in a mood of such acerbity and vehemence of expression as we seldom hear nowadays'. Tillett's assault on Welsh complacency culminated in his candidature at Swansea in the first election of 1910—a candidature in which he felt 'justified in fighting for the forlorn, the robbed and the out-casts of capitalistic society'. As we have seen this candidature was bitterly denounced by the press and Tillett's failure provides a good illustration of how effectively extremists could be isolated.

Perhaps it took outsiders to talk the language of extremism for in those years of unrest which began in South Wales in 1910 few of the homegrown leaders could rival the speeches of Tillett at Swansea or of Captain Tupper in Cardiff. There was no doubt that the language of the almost unknown and mysterious Tupper not only took him into the law courts in an action against *The Daily Express* but helped to forge an unprecedented and impressive labour solidarity in Cardiff's dockland. *The Express* had quoted him as saying of the rich that 'we will take devlish good care we starve them out' and of a general strike that 'the bloodshed of French Revolution will be as a mere flea-bite'; but during the Cardiff strike in July he told his men that 'they were now one great compact mass of humanity united to fight the combine of capitalism' and it was not long before one of the miners' leaders was reflecting that 'if they had leaders in the coal trade like Captain Tupper' they would soon make progress with their demands. But in a sense the coal trade did have a local Captain Tupper for not only in 1910 and 1911 but throughout the Edwardian period C. B. Stanton of Aberdare had spoken a language quite unlike that of any politician or trade unionist. Stanton was the leader of the Aberdare miners and his whole industrial policy amounted to a declaration of war on the Powell Dyffryn Company and on the Conciliation procedures, whilst his candidature in the East Glamorgan Constituency in December 1910 rivalled Tillett's in its denunciation of Lib-Labism. When *Llais Llafur* once commented on a miners ballot that 'not more than about five per cent of the men who registered their votes cared a bilberry about materialism or Socialism, whether William Brace was a local preacher or Charlie Stanton was known to be guilty of the heinous crime of drinking a glass of beer', they were possibly suggesting that there were two very different types of miners' leader. If throughout the Edwardian years Brace spoke the platitudes of Lib-Labism then it was Stanton who had educated his audiences into the language of revolt.

Stanton was a big man who, as we have been slyly informed, liked his beer and who possessed what General Macready described as 'a powerful pleasantly-toned voice of which he rather enjoyed the sound'. At the time of the Powell Dyffryn strike in 1910 sections of the press became fascinated with this miners' agent who was so obviously dominating proceedings in the Aberdare Valley. The *Daily Mirror* found him to be 'a big handsome man—strikingly recalling Wilson Barrett as the Silver King' and as they watched him being cinematographed at Aberaman concluded that 'his romantic appearance and vigorous personality are chiefly responsible for having brought the mines in the district to a standstill'. *The Daily Express* found it easy to understand his 'hold over the minds of the men of Aberdare'. This was the man who had been the bogey of the South Wales press for so many years. He was, of course, as the *Colliery Guardian* made clear, 'a fair example of the irresponsible demagogue' who had done much to undermine conciliation and to create strikes first in Aberdare and then throughout the coalfield. Year after year this journal along with the rest of the Welsh press ran a campaign against this 'turbulent' man who 'evidently has the idea that he should manage the Powell Dyffryn Collieries'. They were condemning an uncompromising opponent who saw the much vaunted process of industrial conciliation as a 'peace at any price policy', but they were also condemning a political language that had no place in a culture bent on conciliation at all levels.

We too can appreciate the hold that Stanton had over his men for his powerful language leaps out of the pages of those Edwardian newspapers. He gave that army of shorthand writers who swarmed through the valleys more quotable quotes than D.A. Thomas, Ben Tillett, Keir Hardie and all the other personalities of the South Wales political scene put together. From about 1906 on, the rising tension in South Wales can be traced through Stanton's speeches. Nobody was more bitter and vocal in the war against non-unionists and he asked for them to be 'cleared out of their lodgings' and for the employers to be 'hammered to their knees' on this issue. He was amongst the first to suggest that the Welsh miners had bred a new kind of union establishment and he spoke of principles that 'were in danger of going to the devil' of a Federation that had become 'a money-making machine' and he warned his fellow Executive members that 'they were not paid to be Press representatives' and that it was time for them to 'stand side by side with him to do some dirty navvy work'. Stanton's tactics and his language came to fruition in 1910 and the Powell Dyffryn strike of that year was his finest hour. Far more than anybody thrown up by the more famous Cambrian strike of that same year Stanton was the spokesman of the Welsh unrest of 1910. A year earlier he had warned that 'the tyranny of the employers in some districts and the way in which they try in every way to crush the men is rapidly converting the men of South Wales to Socialism'. Nobody did more to emphasise how out of touch the older leaders had become; to Stanton they were 'fossilised' and their Federation 'had drifted into a condition of dry rot', and unlike them 'he did not go to either church or chapel to tout for votes'.

Stanton was a demagogue—someone who deliberately used the power of his voice, and personality and a well-chosen vocabulary to incite feeling. One can easily appreciate how, what was widely diagnosed as his 'irresponsibility' contributed to the unrest of those years, an unrest, by the way, summed up by Mabon as 'a passing emotion'. Successful demagogues however invite closer inspection and it would be foolish for the historian to dismiss Stanton. More than anyone else he explains why there was a rank-and-file revolt in Edwardian South Wales and he does that in a fuller way than the so-called 'Syndicalist' academics of the Rhondda. Ablett was not a public man and whilst his writings indicate what was discussed and learnt in classrooms, it is Stanton's speeches which help us to understand why many thousands of miners were by 1910 thinking that enough was enough. He preached head-on collision to an increasingly receptive audience but he did so in a language that displayed a keen intelligence and a tremendous ability to say the right thing at the right time. His language was a cutting-edge because it expressed well what was widely thought and at the same time took the argument and the listeners one step further. A platitude entertains and consolidates but a turn of phrase educates and creates. There was little hope for Mabon and his group after Stanton had described them as a 'fainthearted, over-cautious, creeping, crawling, cowardly set who pose as leaders but who do not lead'. At a time when there was much feeling in South Wales about the role of the police there was nobody else who could have said that a crowd had been 'brutalised' by a 'promotion-seeking, overfed, wanton and drunken police'. It was Stanton who saw that D. A. Thomas was 'posing as an up-to-date Liberal'. He was an important and effective leader who became a powerful figure because, as he himself pointed out, he had 'not sacrificed his individuality', because he was a professional who, as George Barker commented was 'always watchful and alert' and who, more than any miners' leader, had, in the words of *Justice*, 'a withering scorn for the mean, contemptible tricks with which the mine-owners endeavour to cheat the men'. And we may add that he did not have to 'prattle'. For this adventurer everything was an anti-climax after 1910 and in order to regain his power he became a war-mongering populist, but he had done his stuff. At a meeting of the Aberdare Urban District Council in 1906 he had referred to the 'shoddy' nature of colliery houses and in appealing for 'better class houses' he commented that 'the present workmen's dwellings street after street were much like boxes of dominoes. A man required to be very sober and it must be broad daylight before he could find his own house'. What I am saying is that Mabon and Brace could not have made that remark. Stanton helped to take South Wales out of the era of Cymru Fydd and into the era of Nye Bevan and Gwyn Thomas.

In 1910, however, the resources of civilisation were not exhausted. In four brief years the Progressive myth had been shattered and South Wales found itself centuries away from an era in which the complaint had been that 'the Labour leader who attacks Liberalism is false to Labour'. The political establishment who had worried over that 'modern brand of Socialism represented by the ILP' now had to contend with the power of Stanton's rhetoric, with the supreme logic of those who argued, with Ablett and Hodges, that 'the man who was right industrially was right politically' and with the fact of massive strikes and riots. This danger had to be nailed. It was not enough to talk of 'irresponsibility', 'insubordination' and of 'advanced men'—something strange and more emotive was needed. The answer was provided, of course, in the very word 'Syndicalism' and no word was more perfectly fitted for the task as it attributed genuine and widespread unrest to influences that were made to sound intellectual, subversive, foreign, insidious and clandestine. That great wave of unrest could all be explained in terms of the undue influence of 'Marxian' cliques preaching this 'extreme and dangerous' doctrine. Vernon Hartshorn who was as prominent as any miners' leader in the struggle for the Minimum Wage said that 'Syndicalism' was a 'bogey being used by the enemies of trades unionism' and Keir Hardie, recalling that it was only a few years since 'Socialism' itself had been a bogey, wryly commented that 'the Press had done more in two months to popularise Syndicalism and make it known than all its advocates could have accomplished in twenty years'.

Language then remained a vital part of that struggle we refer to as the 'rise of labour' right down to the end of the Edwardian period. The post-war years were to see the working-class culture of South Wales as the dominant force in the area's politics. Men nurtured in Hardie's ILP and in the union lodges had constructed a political language and vocabulary that was to hold sway for fifty years. It was a powerful and vital language but the questions as to when that language became a rhetoric, as to when those leaders fell into the danger of what Aneurin Bevan described as 'imprisoning reality in your description of it', as to when, in short, they began to 'prattle', are best examined on another occasion.

Bibliographical note

This essay developed in part out of an experience of Labour politics in the 1970s in which I was very conscious of having to learn a very specific language and one that did not always lend itself to my idiom. My sense of the Edwardian language comes from a wide reading of the contemporary press. For South Wales the *South Wales Daily News* was the great quarry of information; in its columns the Liberal viewpoint was expressed and defined and every attempt was made to accomodate labour; here the tensions of the age were best revealed and the manipulation of language most clearly illustrated. Of the fifty or so other newspapers which circulated in South Wales I always found the *Glamorgan Gazette* (Bridgend), *Llais Llafur* (Ystalyfera), and the *Aberdare Leader* the most informative, the most wide-ranging and the most entertaining. Labour's voice was heard in the pages of Hardie's *Labour Leader* and the SDF's *Justice*, whilst the *Western Mail* and even more the *Colliery Guardian* revealed what all the best coalowners were thinking.

I first tried to capture the cross-current of Edwardian politics in 'Working-Class Leadership in South Wales 1900-1920', *The Welsh History Review*, vol. 6, no. 3 (1973). Labour History has its own version of the Dangerfield controversy and the respective arguments are best outlined in P.F. Clarke, *Lancashire and the New Liberalism* (1971), and Ross McKibbin, *The Evolution of the Labour Party 1910-1924* (1974). In deciding as to whether Labour had made a crucial breakthrough in the Edwardian period it is important to remember that tactical and psychological victories like those won by Hardie were more vital than voting figures and that individuals did not always act politically as they acted industrially.

The Secret World of
the South Wales Miner:
The Relevance of Oral History
Hywel Francis

> Before 1640, the traditions I have been describing (Lollardy,
> Anabaptism, etc.) circulated verbally. Historians, themselves the
> products of a literary culture, relying so much on written or printed
> evidence, are always in danger of underestimating verbal
> transmission of ideas.
>
> Christopher Hill (1978)

> Oh we ran [pit papers in Aberdare in the 1920s] for about a year or
> more. And I don't know where they went to—you never kept them
> you see. In the Movement I never kept anything you see. We
> worked from day to day . . . We never thought of keeping a diary
> or mind if I had kept a diary it would have been very good
> now . . . And of course my political understanding was not high at
> the time really. You build it up over a period and there's much
> implication of things I didn't fully understand, I understood them
> a little perhaps.
>
> Max Goldberg (6 September 1972)

The importance of oral testimony to the contemporary social
historian is now undisputed. The use that is made of it, however,
can be highly controversial. In the absence of traditional
manuscript material, it can simply be a substitute and often an
invaluable one. More often it supplements other sources wherever
they are inadequate. The aim of this essay is to suggest that there is
a qualitative difference in oral evidence as a source and that
material already available on the South Wales coalfield amply
indicates this. Furthermore the methodology adopted to collect
such material and its analysis afford some important clues in the
tracing of an evolving class—if not *proletarian*—consciousness
among the working people of the South Wales mining valleys. It is
this last question which provides the core of my enquiry: what
kind of understanding do we have of the creation of what can be

described as a unique proletarian coalfield society in the twentieth century and how was this particular *collectivist* consciousness forged?

For the historian of the twentieth century to ignore oral evidence is tantamount to taking a decision to write off whole areas of human experience. Indeed there are human activities which can only satisfactorily be uncovered by collecting oral testimony. Most societies have their secret worlds whether out of necessity because of their clandestine, semi-legal or illegal qualities or because there is no written tradition as Jan Vansina has shown is the case amongst West African tribes. (Secret in the sense that Western observers are orientated away from the importance of collective, received memory.) But even in such an advanced, reasonably literate, industrial society as the mining valleys of South Wales between the wars, with its range of social and political institutions each spawning a multiplicity of primary and secondary historical sources, there is a world beyond this which is not, and cannot be, analysed or even chronicled without the intervention of oral testimony. It is only concealed because the historian may choose to ignore the value of human memory.

Where do we, for example, find evidence of child labour in the South Wales coalfield in the early part of the twentieth century? What kind of perceptive insight do we get of Aberdare in the 1900s from Max Goldberg:

> I had to work from when I was eight years of age. I worked in a barber's shop every night except a Tuesday night, and from eight o'clock Saturday morning until twelve o'clock Saturday night, I was so small I used to stand on the box to lather the men's faces you know, and I used to get one and six a week for that and the man I worked for he was so bad he used to make me, you know when I went in to have my tea, I had to have it standing up . . . I used to go up to the toilet to have a little rest you know and I used to cry you know. I remember crying, I would be tired out you know. So I left there, and then I worked in a grocer's and I had to work the same every evening and then Saturday all day and I got half a crown a week then. So it was a big help in the house you see.

How many historians would consider the last sentence to be the most important of the testimony? Does the detail of exploitation transcend the final judgement of the narrator?

Similarly Jim Evans' boyhood experience in the Rhymney

Valley during the first world war is again something of a revelation
and gives an added dimension to war-time food shortages:

> [I] started work in the Post Office as a telegram boy. I had been
> working for three years prior to that carrying out for the grocer:
> went down in the morning before school, sweeping out the shop,
> putting the sawdust down, delivering little orders on the way to
> school. Go down in the lunch hour again to see if there were any
> orders, then after going home, having tea and go to the grocer's
> and work until eight o'clock, nine o'clock in the night . . . Half a
> crown and an egg was my weekly wage but they were very, very
> meticulous about the egg. They used to shake it and make sure it
> was a good one because I was a good errand boy.

Such an accumulation of evidence gives a better understanding
not only of social conditions but of the history of the class itself.
The extent to which this very early work experience contributed to
a personal appreciation of exploitation as a class phenomenon is
much more of a central question than whether the working class *in
general* was ever *psychologically* conditioned by 'go thou and do
likewise'.

The discovery of such unchronicled experiences applies even
more forcibly, and in a universal sense, to women. Where, other
than through oral testimony, can the historian trace the industrial
and domestic work experience of women in this century in the
mining valleys of South Wales? A remarkable diversity, progress-
ing from a variety of mining jobs (surface and underground) to
employment in tinworks, brickworks, ammunition and clock
factories, were all encompassed in the first five decades of this
century in but one mining locality—Ystradgynlais. This was apart
from working on farms, in local shops, pubs, hotels and
'gwasanaethu' (domestic service) outside their own homes, in the
immediate area and beyond.

The whole distorted experience of South Wales in the inter-
war period is one which can easily be misinterpreted by the social
historian. Oral testimony can very often be the only corrective.
The demise of young women, trapped in a male-oriented,
economically depressed society, evades the grasp of the historian,
usually because there are no obvious sources. How, for example,
do we adequately trace that seemingly subterranean network
which tapped the limitless cheap female labour market within the
coalfield and resulted in that army of Welsh domestic servants in

the Home Counties? It is only by talking to such people that we begin to put flesh on the statistical bones which indicate the mammoth population changes between 1871 and 1951, particularly in the Rhondda. To understand coalfield society we must not only scrutinise Hunger Marching Tonypandy miners but also Mardy girls in service in Croydon in the 1920s:

> And they just received me from this girl and in I went; I felt awfully nervous and then she took me to my bedroom which was right up in the attic and told me to change into my afternoon uniform and to come down to make tea. Well if I hadn't been to this training centre, I wouldn't know the difference between afternoon tea and high tea, because we didn't have that kind of thing at home . . . They were both widows, the daughter had two sons, the older son which I called Mr Eric and the younger was Master Kenneth. They were supposed to be very religious people and I suppose they were. Anyway evening times we used to have a cooked meal and I would take my plate and have whatever was going. I never really had enough you know but I would never ask for more. I was too frightened to ask for more . . . I didn't feel I was part of the family at all. I felt I was the servant then you know and I was there to do my work and that was that . . . they didn't converse much with me at all, and when they did it was just to run the Welsh down . . . You wouldn't say that they were gentry because I met gentry after that and I found that they were far better, nicer people than they were.

But what of the complexities of class and nationality in faraway London society as seen through the eyes of the same Rhondda girl in service in a Clapham Common Welsh dairy:

> We used to go quite a lot on a Sunday evening after Chapel up to Hyde Park to the Welsh Corner there and we used to meet people from home and we used to have a wonderful time chatting and having news from home . . . There was a London Welsh Society because my master and mistress belonged to it, because they used to have luncheons and things, periodically you know, and they used to dress up. And I used to love to watch them dressing and I used to help the daughter, and I never went to anything like this. Mind you, they were very kind if there was any dramas or anything . . . I used to go with them by car.

Indeed, central to an understanding of this hidden world is the question of class (a theme which appears in all the above testimonies). The emergence of a proletariat should not be measured only (if at all) by the collation of statistical evidence on Parliamentary elections. Even within a seemingly homogeneous workforce moulded by a fairly straightforward economy there are complexities of race, language, religion, urbanisation, parochial loyalties, internal and external labour mobility, population movements and depths of class hostility in which oral testimony is either the only historical source or is the major indicator. (This is to say nothing of the effect upon valleys and communities of uneven economic development, private ownership patterns and differences in the quality of coal.) Furthermore, oral evidence very often gives a completely different insight into defining a working class. The quality of its consciousness is the interaction of so many variable strands: loyalty to such organisations as the Labour Party, the South Wales Miners' Federation or the Communist Party can often only be expressions of finely developed class instincts which manifest themselves in many other ways and whose roots are not always simple.

The semi-rural anthracite mining village of Abercrave in the Upper Swansea Valley is a classic example. It was one of the last pit villages in which the owners were not one or other of the massive coal combines, but families who lived locally. Their social and economic control was diffused and apparently all-embracing. The class tensions and relationships were liable, consequently, to be intense and perverse. One miner recalled:

The Morgans' and the Davies' . . . they were coalowners and they had such big families, big followings you know. And I mean, you couldn't open your mouth in that colliery without it was carried back you know . . . If they [the union] had a meeting, they [the owners] had their cronies coming to the meeting, and you'd know it would be out straight and back to the colliery owner . . .

Now those [miners] as a family . . . and good workmen all of them . . . exceptionally good men with an 'atchet . . . [one of the brothers] could kill a pig . . . He'd learnt that amount of trade although he was a miner trained . . . and of course he had these tools of a butcher, sharp knives, saw. And this under-manager . . . was playing around with other women you see, and this [miner] was living next door to one woman that he was carrying on with. And he made a statement to that effect. And now this under-manager was coming down this road, and he pulled him up and he said 'Listen now, you keep your mouth shut about me' . . . And one thing went from another, he waves his stick and he was going to hit [the miner] see. [The miner] stuck him with a knife . . . They took the case to the Assizes . . . and [he] was let off pretty lenient . . . But the renegades in Waunclawdd [colliery] when he was jailed for six months, these men . . . said 'Listen, we've got a butty now in jail and he done the right thing, a thing that a good many of us would have done . . . What about his wife and kiddies?' So we rose a levy in the lodge, as long as [he] was in jail . . . we decided to pay [his wife] the minimum wage . . . He came out and he thanked us . . . well they're both dead now . . .

. . . and then when his [the under-manager's] retirement came, he was ignored by the people in the village, and he felt it. He was a sorry sight, he was a capable man . . . he was a well spoken man, but he loaned himself to them, he was there only to make profits for the company.

Received oral tradition in the late 1970s relates that the same under-manager would insist that his chapel's programme for the Annual Gymanfa Ganu (Religious Singing Festival) would have a hymn which included the following verse:

> Er imi dwyllo'r byd
>   A llwyddo i guddio mai
> Rwy'n chwerw mron;
>   Er hyn i gyd
> Nid yw'm euogrwydd lai.

> (Although I have deceived the world
>   And succeeded in covering my faults
> I have a bitter breast;
>   Despite all this
> My guilt is none the less.)

It is significant in itself that the memory of this small episode should have survived for over half a century.

In such a relatively self-contained community, whose class structure was fairly simple, two important and inter-related phenomena had a profound effect on a sharpening class, trade-union and political consciousness amongst the workforce between the wars. Without the use of oral testimony, the full extent of these influences would be difficult to assess.

Firstly, the teaching of marxism under the banner of the National Council of Labour Colleges (NCLC), as elsewhere, undoubtedly helped to challenge the consensus, 'community', notions perpetrated by village elders, whether they be coalowners, their officials, chapel deacons or ageing lodge officers, The classes, conducted particularly by such an irreverent tutor as Nun Nicholas, bred a new generation of miners' leaders in the locality which partly resulted in members of the village playing a disproportionately large role in the wider affairs of the South Wales Miners' Federation (SWMF) and later the South Wales Area of the National Union of Mineworkers (NUM). That one of the lodges in the village was expelled from the SWMF for a period during the second world war in no way diminishes this long-term contribution although the enduring bitterness caused by the expulsion is measurable in a negative sense by the lack of oral evidence. Like family skeletons, past union disgrace can be erased from the collective memory.

Secondly, the small Spanish community which arrived, via Dowlais in 1911, had a leavening effect on industrial militancy in the area and particularly within the two local lodges of Abercrave and International. Oral tradition has it that they were the best trade unionists. One lodge secretary, who along with most of his generation in the village was considerably influenced by the uncomplicated philosophy of the hard-working Spaniards, was Dai Dan Evans:

> I've never found any Spaniard in arrears with his union contribution.... A shilling a fortnight, you could bank upon the Spaniards coming there to pay their contributions. And whenever there was a ballot held, they used to go on to the secretary and ask him—'Which of these is the Communist?' 'Communista', they said. Their vote was invariably for the Communist candidate.

Other dimensions of this unequivocal philosophy constantly burst through in this small ethnic community which took such great pride in its received historical tradition. A second generation Abercrave Spaniard recalled his father's outlook:

> 'The Sermon on the Mount, can you beat it?' he used to tell me . . . it was pure socialism. But organised religion was quite a different thing altogether. So what he said was this, 'If you don't learn anything bad by going to Sunday School or going to a church, or to a chapel, all right, fair enough, you can go.' And the priests used to come round and try to get us to go to the Catholic church which was then down in Pontardawe. And he used to

say . . . 'No, why should my children go all the way down to Pontardawe, when there's a church round the corner . . . if God is in your church, surely he must be in this church as well.' And for people who were being brought up, steeped in Catholicism, I think this was a very progressive way of thinking. And this was the philosophy we had at home. It was a philosophy of what I considered to be . . . true socialism . . . It was practised in the house you lived in . . . And of course in those days . . . you sat round the fire at night and you had your old story telling. My grandfather, my grandmother, my father and my mother, they used to tell us stories they had learned as children themselves round their fires in Spain as little children. So we learned through these stories, we learned the history of Spain, we learned about all the folk-lore of the parts of the country they lived in.

They took such philosophical values into the colliery. On seeing the under-manager spit in the face of a submissive collier one Spaniard was heard to say, 'If he did that in Spain, cemetry for him'. Their attitudes towards the colliery owners was nothing short of contemptuous and must have eroded the lingering effects of paternalism in the village: that their utterances are recalled over sixty years later is surely evidence of that. One group of young Spanish miners, on being criticised by the manager for not working regularly, are said to have replied; 'We've earned enough for our week's keep: food, for our lodge, and for our beer—they're not exploiting us any more'.

The complexity of working class politicisation and its relationship with particular immigrant groups is a question of crucial importance to an understanding of the dynamics of South Wales society in the early part of the twentieth century. What qualitative change occurred with the influx of Caernarvonshire quarrymen, Cardiganshire and Somerset farm-hands into the coalfield? What were the manifold inter-relationships between the groups and between them and the receiving community? Did they merge immediately or did they try to emulate the success of Irish catholics (as in Maesteg, Merthyr and Mountain Ash) and the Spaniards of Abercrave and Dowlais, by creating something of a community within a community?

Ben 'Sunshine' Davies recalls the impact of Rhondda life upon him in 1919. It was as if he was moving from one time-scale to another: leaping out of a remote, closed, almost feudal rural society, still dominated by the religiosity of a Nonconformist chapel which shut the only village pub soon after the Revival, into a twentieth century world:

> Well I think it was around the end of August or September we decided to leave Cardigan for Ferndale. I was at present serving on a farm on the cliffs of New Quay, a farm called Pendryn farm. I can well recall it was the beginning of the corn harvest and I had difficulty in extracting myself from my service with the farm but by a lot of arguments I did manage to get myself free to travel with my mother and my brothers to Ferndale with a view of starting underground as there was a demand for miners immediately after the war . . . I started . . . at the age of sixteen . . . I went as a butty to a Bristol chap by the name of George Cheetham, and he was very, very deep Bristol brogue with him and I was very Welshy, didn't speak much English in Cardigan although I could understand, but to express myself after was a bit difficult and especially with this person from Bristol. But as time wore on we became more acquainted with our discourse and we were able to communicate very well . . . My mother found that I was a bit homesick . . . I was given a holiday back to the country, Whitsun the following year. And after that visit back home I had a week's holiday and then the longing seemed to wear off because there was a lot of attraction in Ferndale . . . There was picture houses, then there was plenty of dramas and theatres again in the Workmen's Hall . . . and a nice billiard place there, bars to go into, a nice reading room . . . I found it very strange the first day that I went down [underground]. After reaching the pit bottom we walked down into the darkness with a little oil lamp and we were all having a 'spell' . . . And there they were chatting and explaining their differences and touching on different topics, some economics, others politics, others about their domestic troubles . . . I was astonished to hear such a lot of mixed arguments and people trying to explain things—some in Welsh, others in English, and we were boys then sitting altogether and listening attentively.

It was the same kind of tempestuous environment which Maximilian Stanislav Goldberg saw in Aberdare during the great war. Undoubtedly, the receiving community shaped his rebellious outlook but it was his Irish Catholic roots which sparked his interest in revolutionary politics:

> Well I was for Ireland. My mother was Irish and in the church. I got linked up with Irish chaps so I thought Irish. I didn't have any real political understanding but I thought Ireland was being badly

done by and therefore I lent my support to this. [I joined] the Irish Self-Determination League. It was the sort of counterpart to the Movement that was very active in Ireland . . . Well we held meetings and discussions and there used to be, if we could get any gunpowder or stuff like that we used to get it if we could, to send across . . . Yes, this was the beginning.

Out of Aberdare and Merthyr came the largest groups of Welsh volunteers for the International Brigades: arguably the highest form of proletarian consciousness. Within these groups, perhaps surprisingly, were many lapsed catholics of Irish origin. Certainly when the historian also examines the major Irish contribution towards the development of working-class organisations in many urban centres in South Wales, the roots of the Labour Movement are by no means only Radical Nonconformity (if at all).

In stark contrast to the dynamic cosmopolitan qualities of the central and eastern valleys, the rural anthracite coalfield to the west experienced a much slower rate of proletarianisation, largely reflecting the leisurely pace of economic development. The divide within the coalfield is highlighted by the perceptive observation of an anthracite miner:

> [Caerlan] was a small community of about twenty-eight houses including a farmhouse, a grocer, a barber's shop and a public house. It was at the top end of the Swansea Valley and . . . its ideas were polarised between two institutions, the Chapel and the public house. It was on the periphery of the coalfield . . . and that made it a very unique place so far as a large number of men who were working in the pits had their roots in the agricultural areas and therefore had not been proletarianised in the same way as the heart of the South Wales coalfield . . . You had some men with dual loyalties, loyalties to their old ideas . . . as farmers . . . Life to us in the Rhondda was exceedingly artificial . . . There was no trees on the mountains; all the animals that you had were domestic animals . . . There is not a farm to be seen anywhere . . . The tink of the damn pit, the tink of the tramcars on the road, that's all you would hear. Rhondda people are acclimatised to what I would say now is a very uncouth proletarian life . . . in the sense that there is nothing natural about it . . . people were clustered one on top of the other, you see, one road, the road and the river took the whole of the bottom of the valley.

At the very time Max Goldberg and Ben 'Sunshine' were entering the Aberdare and Rhondda valleys, the tightly-knit anthracite villages gave a different meaning to the 'all-Welsh rule', the closed-shop and to 'community politics':

> Cymraeg oedd pawb yn siarad yn y pentre, oedd dim Saeson wedi dod. Os fydde Sais yn dod 'ma, fydde chi'n gofyn i ambell i hen ddyn, "Pwy yw'r dyn na, chi'n nabod e?" "O nagw i, man from off somewhere." Dyn diarth. A cofiwch oedd gofyn bod e'n cered yn weddol o gwmmws, 'se dynon diarth yr amser hynny, a gwyr Cwmtwrch a gwyr Cwmllynfell, oe'n nhw'n parochial iawn, oedd dim lot o groeso i ddyn diarth . . . Gwedwch, hyd yn oed rhywun, na nhad i chi. Dod o Gwm Nedd, i Gwmtwrth. Dyn dwad oedd e chi'n gweld, oedd e'm yn native, oedd e ddim wedi ei eni a'i fagu yng Nghwmtwrch. Oedd gofyn bod chi wedi cael eich geni a'ch magu yma cyn bod chi'n o wyr Cwmtwrch neu Cwmllynfell. Os fydde chi'n dod o Gwynfe, neu fel oe'n i'n gweud wrthoch chi, Aberdar neu rywle, oedd un dyn yn gweud wrth nhad, "Cadw lygad ar hwnna, dim lot o olwg ar hwnna." A'n enwedig os oedd e'n siarad Saesneg. Oedd e fod i chael hi, fights mawr yn Cwmtwrch yn amser 'ny chi'n gweld. Oedd hi'n amser garw iawn yn Cwmtwrch. O, a cicio, oe'n nhw'n leicio cicio, fel ma nhw yn Yorkshire a Lancashire, os nag oe nhw'n gallu wado nhw ar ei dwylo, cwpwl o bunts oe nhw'n gael chi'n gweld, bechgyn diarth. Wedyn oedd gofyn bod nhw'n iwso'u pennau neu oe nhw ddim yn para'n hir 'ma.

> (Welsh was spoken by everybody in the village, there were no Englishmen. If an Englishman came here, you'd ask an old man, 'Who is that man, do you know him?' 'Oh no I don't, man from off somewhere.' A stranger. And remember it was necessary that he toed the line fairly well, if they were strangers, in those days, men from Cwmtwrch and men from Cwmllynfell, they were very parochial, there wasn't very much welcome for a stranger . . . Say—even someone—there's my father for you. Came from the Neath Valley to Cwmtwrch. [About fifteen miles.] He was a man who came in you see, he wasn't a native, he wasn't born and bred in Cwmtwrch. You had to be born and bred here before you were one of the people of Cwmtwrch or Cwmllynfell. If you came from Gwynfe, or as I was saying to you, Aberdare or somewhere, one man would say to my father, 'Keep an eye on him, I don't think much of him'. And especially if he spoke English. He was in for it, big fights in Cwmtwrch in those days you see. It was a very rough time in Cwmtwrch. Oh, and kicking, they liked to kick, as they do in Yorkshire and Lancashire, if they couldn't beat them with their hands, they'd have a couple of kicks you see, the strangers. Then it was important that they used their heads or they didn't last long here.)

Even into the 1930s non-Welsh speaking Welshmen from Abergavenny or Merthyr were considered English, and would have great difficulty in obtaining work in Cwmtwrch or Cwmllynfell collieries. Such apparent insularity (or was it working-class self-defence?) survived down to the late 1950s:

> But when the pit actually closed [in 1959] we had an Englishman on the Committee, and then we'd revert to English. But when the colliery was at its best they were even conducting the Annual Meeting and General Meetings in Cwmtwrch and Cwmllynfell Hall, every other in turns, and they would conduct all their affairs in Welsh even if the English were there.

The complexity of getting a 'start' at such collieries seemed to have the parochial support of owners and men:

> When there was s shortage of labour in Cwmllynfell Colliery, they employed a few extra from Cwmtwrch, not enough men say in Cwmllynfell village to man the pit, so they were having extra labour from Cwmtwrch, When there was more shortage after that, they were having men from Ystalyfera providing they could play in the Cwmllynfell band. And the Cwmtwrch people were having jobs in Brynhenllys and Cwmtwrch at one time providing they were prepared to pay Dr Owen, [the Cwmtwrch doctor who had shareholdings at a local colliery].

The extent to which such local customs and agreements were significant in holding back a more worldly perspective is difficult to assess. But in examining the industrial relations of the anthracite coalfield in the first decade of nationalisation, they cannot be ignored. Hidden, unwritten agreements between managers and men to deceive the coalowner had to come out now that the National Coal Board came into being. One manager recalled such attitudes as:

> 'Well I'm looking after my men, I'll treat them in the way I want to treat them, not what the coalowners . . . want to do, see . . . ' And that is the difficulty we found in the anthracite after nationalisation was to sort things out.

But even such apparently enduring localised attitudes had been eroded by internal mobility between the anthracite and the steam coalfields. The extent of 'tramping', and its contribution towards the breakdown of anthracite isolation is difficult to measure. But as with George Ewart Evans' discovery of those farm labourers who followed their barley to Burton-on-Trent, it needs an oral historian to ask the first questions and often to get the first answers.

'There are no Christians in Banwen' was an utterance, redolent with local nuance, used by a pit-manager to describe a workforce which aspired to shake off its deference to its 'betters'. Nothing could have been more appropriate. It was a statement which begs particular questions about the nature of all those communities across the coalfield in which the working class was now emerging in the early part of the twentieth century. To deny its different rates of retardation and development, its ethnic, regional and local roots is to deny it has a history at all.

Bibliographical note

All the interviews quoted in this essay are transcribed tape-recordings deposited at the South Wales Miners' Library, 50 Sketty Road, Swansea. They were collected (with one exception) by the Social Science Research Council financed South Wales Coalfield History Project during the period 1972-74. Leandro Macho's testimony was a recorded lecture at the Library entitled 'Growing up in Spanish Abercrave in the 1930s'. The interviews were of Ben 'Sunshine' Davies (Banwen), Dai Dan Evans (Cae'r lan, Abercrave), Jim Evans (Abercrave), David Francis (Onllwyn), Max Goldberg (Aberdare), Josiah Jones (Joe 'Brickman') (Cwmllynfell), Will 'Post' Rees (Cwmtwrch), Jim Vale (Abercrave), John Williams (Banwen) and Maria Williams (Mardy). The collection is almost entirely transcribed and indexed and has a very wide range of recollections on the South Wales coalfield in the twentieth century with special exphasis on male and female work experience, trade-union, political and workers' educational activities, anti-fascism, the Spanish Civil War. the 1926 lock-out and migration into the Valleys at the turn of this century. The project's *Final Report* (1974) gives a full account of its oral history programme. A further project, also financed by the SSRC, began in 1979 with the aim of collecting sound and video tapes on the period since 1945 within the coalfield.

Apart from historians of the late nineteenth and twentieth centuries, Christopher Hill is one of the very few who has given any attention to the significance of received oral tradition. His essay 'From Lollards to Levellers' in Maurice Cornforth (ed.), *Rebels and their Causes: Essays in Honour of A. L. Morton* (1978) has important insights.

The pioneer in the field of British oral history is George Ewart Evans, some of whose work on the South Wales miners is published in *From Mouths of Men* (1976). The first concerted exercise in the collecting of oral evidence in Wales was made by the Welsh Folk Museum under the guidance of Vincent Phillips. Although it has concentrated on folk lore, rural society and the Welsh language, it has accumulated some important material on coal mining. In particular, Lynn Davies' pamphlet *Aspects of Mining Folklore in Wales* (reprinted from *Folk Life* 9) and his *Geirfa Glowr* (1976)—the *Miner's Vocabulary*—are both valuable studies.

The most prominent British academic in the field is Dr Paul Thompson of the University of Essex, whose *The Voice of the Past: Oral History* (1978) is a comprehensive survey of oral history work throughout the world. It is also the best account of the importance of oral testimony to the social historian. He has a much simpler explanation of methodology than the nonetheless erudite *Oral Tradition* (1965) by Jan Vansina which focuses more exclusively on African tribal societies. Dr Thompson is also the editor of *Oral History*, the journal of the British Oral History Society which publishes articles, conference reports and work in progress. Amongst the most productive British groups have been the Centerprise Publishing Project which has concentrated on the community history of the East End.

A considerable amount of oral evidence is now being used in the social and labour history of the South Wales coalfield some of which is being published in *Llafur*, the journal of the Society for the Study of Welsh Labour History. Two theses which rely heavily on such testimony are Kim Howells, 'A View From Below: Tradition, Experience and Nationalisation in the South Wales Coalfield 1937-1957' (University of Warwick, 1979) and my own, 'The South Wales Miners and the Spanish Civil War: A Study in Internationalism' (University of Wales, 1977). *The Fed: A History of the South Wales Miners in the Twentieth Century* (1980) by David Smith and myself also makes considerable use of miners' recollections.

Undoubtedly oral history seems most widespread in the USA. A new American publication, *International Journal of Oral History* will probably bring the work of the American Oral History Association more to the attention of European labour historians and folklorists alike. American coalfield historians have long used oral testimony. Among more recent projects is *Patch/Work Voices: The Culture and Lore of a Mining People* (1977) by Dennis F. Brestensky, Evelyn A. Hovanec and Albert N. Skomra all of the Fayette Campus of Pennsylvania State University. Video and sound recording has also figured prominently in the work of the Highlander Research and Educational Center (Tennessee) which now has growing links with the South Wales Miners' Library. The Center published Matt Witt's *In Our Blood* (1979) which is an account of four American coalmining families who are the sons and daughters of European immigrants, of black field hands from the South, and Navajo Indians.

Victimisation, Accidents and Disease
Kim Howells

Some of the tales told of the injustices perpetrated by coalowners are lies, some are not. Often the details of injustice or outrage have become mangled by time. In the pits, as in all other work-places, men sought short cuts and the means of earning more money in less time and for less effort. Pit safety rules were by-passed and broken at least as often by the men as by management.

In their private conversations, miners will admit that pit accidents often are caused by their own errors of judgement. In public, however, they display a lot more reticence. Invariably they will shift the blame for accidents back onto the shoulders of those who employ miners to do their dangerous and dirty work. In these situations, a special order of 'moral justice' manifests itself. Demands are made that compensation for accidents be paid even when there is tacit agreement that the accidents in question were caused (in the immediate situation) by the mineworkers' negligence or wrongdoing. It is pointed out that the miners involved in particular accidents had almost certainly risked death many times previously—and often through no choice of their own. The risks, it is argued, are part and parcel of mining and the coalowners did themselves little good in the eyes of mining com-munities by attempting, when it suited their pockets, to forget this basic fact. No other single act was guaranteed to bring as much opprobrium upon the heads of the owners as did their opposition to the compensation claims filed against them by their injured or diseased employees and by the widows of pit accidents.

Sometimes, false claims were lodged against the owners. I have been informed, by several ex-claimants, of cases in which the fabrication of evidence against the owners was both elaborate and successful. What was conspicuously missing in all of these accounts was a sense of guilt on the part of the ex-claimants. Their past lies are rationalised away as constituting merely the means by which they 'got their own back' on the owners. Morality here has little to do with the accepted concepts of legal justice. It has everything to do with the fact that, in popular consciousness at least, the miner was seen as having been 'cheated all along the line'.

Memories of discontent over alleged under-payment of compensation for accident or disease have provided in the South Wales coalfield a residue of bitterness which is rivalled in intensity, though not in scope, only by the lingering indignation of men who believed themselves to have been unjustly victimised because of their political or trade-union beliefs. The owners, it is clear, were regarded as being 'fair game' for anyone with enough cheek or guile to overcome them in a court of law.

Recollections of grievances concerning compensation and victimisation have dominated most of the free-ranging discussions which I have recorded with ex-mineworkers. That this should be so is hardly surprising. Both types of grievance afforded the 'victim' a clearer insight into the class nature of society than he was likely to encounter anywhere else outside of the more radical of the contemporary political parties. Such experiences formed part of an overall mythology in which the coalowners were typecast as grasping individuals ready, at the drop of a writ, to snatch the last crust from the mouth of an orphan or widow of one of their victim-employees. It must be remembered, also, that, as Royden Harrison has commented: 'pre-existing class consciousness [may have disposed men] to expect and perceive victimisation and injustice even when they [were] not there'.

Such mythologising was not limited to the ranks of the miners and their families. The public pronouncements of the coalowners and their officials were shot through with what Professor Harrison has termed '. . . their lore of fact and fiction respecting malingerers, stupidity and carelessness' amongst their employees. It was amongst the employees, however, that such tales of alleged injustice flourished most obviously. This is hardly surprising, for when a miner was denied adequate compensation for a lost limb or damaged lungs he was denied even the bitter justice of a 'fair' sale of part of his productive capacity. Similarly, when he was victimised, he was prevented from selling the only commodity which he owned, his labour power. Both acts served to test, in the most strenuous fashion, the victim's conception of social and industrial justice in a capitalist society.

There can sometimes develop amongst those who see themselves as victims a desire to seek comfort through a ritual listing of the iniquities allegedly perpetrated upon them by their persecutors. Few workforces display a reticence to indulge in this trait, and this kind of myth-making was as common in South Wales as in any other coalfield. Tales of individual dignity shown in the face of managerial provocation, for example, could become decorated and supplemented until they emerged, perhaps a decade later, as acts of class heroism.

Similarly, it is not unreasonable to surmise that there must have taken place what Professor Harrison has envisaged as 'competitions at the bar to tell the best tale . . . of the iniquitous conduct of Powell Duffryn.' It does not pay to become too cynical, however, for the reality which spawned the myths was a hard one. By the end of the 1930s concepts such as those which advocated 'a fair day's work for a fair day's pay' and which attempted to instil within pitmen a sense of loyalty for their employers received diminishing sympathy as the decade dragged to a close. The Chairman of the huge Amalgamated Anthracite Company, F.A. Szarvasy, for example, felt that because the situation had become, by 1938, so 'strained', it was necessary for him to remind his employees that their interests lay firmly with the interests of the Company. He feared that the Company's workmen were, as he put it,

> mistaken in their conception of the main problems and that in their eagerness to fight against what they believed to be capitalistic principles of management they forgot what in fact they should be fighting for—namely, the protection of their own homes and livelihood, If you starved the hen you would in due course be compelled to go without eggs.

Szarvasy's worries cannot be interpreted as indicating that the anthracite coalfield was thronged with socialist revolutionaries. In the midst of capitalism's most acute crisis, the great majority of the workforce showed, by their actions, that they were prepared to abide by the laws and economy of the bourgeois state. It was almost certainly the case, that in the eyes of a great many Welsh miners and their families, society stood in need of the radical improvements which might result from a number of fundamental changes in the organisation of production. Nevertheless, the bourgeois state remained for them what Lukacs termed the 'natural basis of society'. It provided the 'ideological foundation of legality', but where its 'legality' was most suspect, so its ideology was most vulnerable. After all, there was obviously very little justice inherent in an act of victimisation perpetrated by a strong employer upon a weak employee. Such an act smacked of despotism—especially when it appeared that the employer was being aided by the apparent indifference of the state. It would have been extraordinary, indeed, if at such moments at least some of the victimised miners and their comrades did not ask themselves and each other 'Well, for whose benefit is the state organised and run?'

The lessons learned at the compensation courts were scarcely less instructive. They taught that if a man was active and strong, then he was of use to his employer for he was a source of production and profit. If, during the course of producing that profit he became disabled or diseased, then he was of no use to his employer. He became, instead, an economic burden, an 'unfortunate victim of circumstance', a creature to be cast aside with as little embarrassment to the employer as possible, but to be cast aside nonetheless, like any other piece of useless machinery.

In 1937, 175 men and boys were killed in the pits of South Wales, and 25,947 were injured. Expressed differently, five miners died and 680 were injured for every million tons of coal raised on the coalfield.

These deaths occurred despite the fact that the year witnessed no spectacular colliery 'disasters' of the kind so beloved by newspaper editors.

In April, 1937, Sir Alfred Faulkner, Permanent Under-Secretary for Mines, emphasised his disappointment that life had been made, as he put it, 'no safer in the mining industry' than it had been 'twenty years previously'. This was his contribution to a public debate within mining circles which attempted to explain why it was that the number of fatal accidents in South Wales in the first three months of 1937 had turned out to be double the number of such accidents in the first three months of 1936.

During April, 1937, for example, a Tredegar Justice of the Peace and coal employer, Mr David Evans, informed his fellow guests at an annual dinner organised by the South Wales Coalowners Association that there had been, within the past year (and as a direct result of the increased demand for coal) an influx of extra labour. This, he inferred, had brought with it grave problems of safety, for, 'Men who had been idle for years came back to work', perhaps having suffered in the meantime consider-able physical debilitation, and he had read of 'many cases in which such men had been *killed in the first few days.*' That, he suggested, 'might account for the accident ratio.'

David Evans' statement was an ambiguous one. Possibly, this was intentional. 'Physical debilitation' could be taken to have been caused either by a lack of muscular exercise resulting from unemployment, or by a lack of nourishment due to severely curtailed income. There may, of course, have been a less con-tentious explanation for the high death rate: namely, that the newly-hired colliers were simply short of practice and that in their haste to secure their first wage packets in years they ignored or forgot some of the most basic safety procedures. It is not unreasonable to assume that the most satisfactory explanation contains elements of all three theories.

However, it is not always the 'most satisfactory explanation' (as an 'objective' historian might see it) which achieves the greatest popularity; people perceiving of themselves as the victims of a harsh and unjust industrial society will seek different kinds of 'satisfactory explanations' for the ills which they suffer than will those whom they cast in the role of persecutors. In the minds of the 'victims' there existed a powerful association of images and ideas concerning unemployment, deprivation and the high rate of fatalities and injuries recorded at the coal face. By its very nature, this association did not have to reflect the true accident statistics with any great accuracy or sophistication, Violent death and serious injury were, quite literally, everyday occurrences in the mining communities. The vast majority of deaths would have occurred, in all probability, whether the individuals involved were physically debilitated or not; it needed only the merest hint that the deaths were in some way associated with prolonged depriva-tion to spark off a glow of vindication for the 'victim'-interpreta-tion in the minds of those who subscribed to it.

For the relationship between ideas about reality itself is not, of course, mechanical but dialectical. The mining population's image of the 'reality' of death at the coal face in South Wales dur-ing the 1930s was inextricably linked with its image of itself as the victim of blatant social injustice outside of the pits.

This link or association expressed itself with blunt clarity. The title of the Powell Duffryn Company was always shortened, in

185

common usage, to 'PDs'—an abbreviation which was invariably lengthened and transmuted during strikes or serious disputes into 'Poverty and Death'. The jibe was one which stuck : 'PDs equals Poverty and Death'.

This popular image of the controllers of the coal combine companies as callous individuals was reinforced in at least three important ways. The first concerned the attempts by the combine companies to end a practice which was accepted as 'normal' on the coalfield whereby workmen were allowed to leave the pits early in order that they might be able to attend the funerals of comrades killed in pit accidents. The second concerned the leniency with which coalowners and mine managers were treated in court cases after legal action had been brought against them for wilful breaches of mining safety regulations. The third concerns the common allegation that owners were guilty of hedging and delaying over compensation payments for accidents.

In May, 1937, seven Cambrian Colliery workmen appeared before Pontypridd magistrates in what the *Colliery Guardian* referred to as a 'test case'. Their pit had been acquired just a year earlier by the Powell Duffryn Company and the new owners accused the men of taking unauthorised leave of absence to attend the funeral of a fellow workman, killed some days previously, All were found guilty and fined.

A fortnight later, Oliver Harris, the General Secretary of the Federation, received notice from Edmund Stonelake, a Bwllfa miners' official informing him that a man had been killed at Bwllfa and that his comrades intended standing by the established Bwllfa custom of stopping work at three-quarter shift in order that they might attend the funeral. He added that he did not want to advise them to stop working and then get them fined for doing so.

Bwllfa No. 1, like the Cambrian pits, had been acquired by the Powell Duffryn Company in 1936 as a result of their merger with Welsh Associated Collieries. The enthusiasm of Bwllfa's new owners for 'disciplining' their employees was already well known to Stonelake and the rest of the Bwllfa workforce. They had experienced during the previous summer two portentous disputes arising from the company's refusal to recognise existing 'custom and practice'. Stonelake's letter makes it obvious that he and his committee knew perfectly well that if they adhered to the old custom of working only a three-quarter shift on the day of the funeral, then the company would almost certainly retaliate with court proceedings as they had done successfully in the Rhondda two weeks earlier.

Despite this threat, however, 'custom and practice' was faithfully adhered to. The local newspaper reported the events as follows:

> 600 miners on the day-shift at Bwllfa No. 1 colliery defied the management by walking out before 1 p.m., after working three-quarters of a turn, to attend the funeral of jovial, popular 'Billo' Griffiths, workmate fatally injured by a fall of side last week. It was, before the 'amalgamation' the custom of the Welsh Associated Collieries Co., to allow them the privilege to attend, by leaving early, the burials of victims of fatalities at the colliery. The new PD Associated management refuse the men this concession and 600 of them took matters into their own hands. Few will be found to blame them.

Deep passions were aroused by this issue. It was not merely a question of needing to 'show respect for the dead', although that desire played an important part in determining the men's actions; it was much more an expression of the indignation and distaste which the miners felt when confronted with the raw and blatant quality, as they saw it, of Powell Duffryn's brand of industrial exploitation. The newspaper report reflected this prevailing sense of hostility:

> The men claim that the old privileges stand despite the change of management. But more important than any law or tradition is the spirit of humanity which seems to be disappearing from our pits. Miners, automatons as they have to be underground, are not lacking in human feelings and emotions. A workmate has been taken suddenly (and who may be next?). They want to walk to his grave with him, sacrificing a quarter of a shift's pay, which means much these days. The colliery companies want more and more output in this boom period, and men try to respond. But the spirit of humanity must not perish. Humanity in industry is what the world needs.

The Powell Duffryn Company contended that a breach of contract under the 1937 Wages Agreement had been committed, and they served summonses on 27 of the Bwllfa workmen who had taken part in the Funeral walkout. The Bwllfa men were joined on strike by upwards of 200 other miners from some of the smaller drifts in the immediate vicinity of the No. 1 pit. On the following Thursday evening, the strikers assembled in the Trecynon Hall where they were advised by their local Federation officials to return to work and to forward all grievances to the Federation Executive Council in Cardiff who, the strikers were assured, would then take up the issues with management whilst work at the pit continued.

The local newspaper described the scenes at this meeting as 'deplorable'. The union officials were 'assailed by shouts of "Traitors", and other uncomplimentary remarks. Their advice was ignored, and the proceedings were marked by considerable disorder.'

Like the rest of the colliery lodges of the Aberdare Valley, the Bwllfa Lodge had not distinguished itself as being particularly militant since 1926, Why, then, the flare-up over funeral arrangements in 1937?

Well, it is almost certainly the case that this attempt by the new owners, Powell Duffryn, to eradicate the practice of sacrificing a quarter of a shift as a symbol of respect to fallen comrades was seen by the Bwllfa workforce as constituting but the most extreme of a whole series of attempts by the company to impose upon the pit systems of work and discipline which it considered alien.

It was no coincidence that the issue which drew forth from the workforce the most vehement criticism of employers and union officials was the emotive one of 'Blood on the Coal', for the image which every mining community holds of itself is coloured by its collective experience of death and disaster within its pits.

Most ex-Powell Duffryn miners that I interviewed, for example, expressed the belief that their employers chose to obey many of the safety regulations only when they deemed it worthwhile in terms of Powell Duffryn's operations to do so. Indeed, there is little doubt that, even by the late 1930s, the existing laws on mine safety were often imperfectly enforced, largely because the owners were unafraid of the possible consequences of transgression:

> The penalties for Breaches of the Coal Mines Act are so light [wrote one observer] that they hold no terrors for the company, and the average fine (including costs) imposed for breaches of the Act is about £4—which is about as serious a deterrent as a pin-prick to a rhinoceros.

Two incidents, both of which occurred in Powell Duffryn pits during June 1938, illustrate anomalies in the enforcement of mining regulations of the type which tended to cause scepticism and dissatisfaction amongst the coalfield's workforce.

On 6 June 1938, four men died as a result of a gas explosion in Tirherbert Colliery at the 'top end' of the Aberdare Valley. The explosion occurred when an accumulation of gas was ignited by an unauthorised instrument for testing the current in electric cables.

During the subsequent Coroner's Inquest, the jury was informed that the four victims had died when working in a heading roughly 20 inches high, along the floor of which ran an electric cable carrying 500 volts which was used to power a coal-cutter.

In giving evidence, HM Inspector of Mines, Captain Carey, said that in his opinion there had been insufficient ventilation to carry away any gas which might have escaped into the heading as a result of the operation of the coal-cutter. Captain Carey's opinion was seconded by the Chief Inspector of Mines in the Cardiff Division, Captain G. S. Rees, who had visited and inspected the scene of the accident some hours after it had occurred.

The Company denied that their ventilation system had been inadequate, and called upon their own pit officials as witnesses in an attempt to prove their case.

The Coroner, to the mystification of the Miners' Federation representatives present, informed his jury that it was 'quite a clear case'. He told them that they had to ask themselves whether they could attach 'any serious blame to anybody who was living for what had happened'. The jury retired for 35 minutes and then returned to the court to announce that, although 'more strict supervision should be kept over those in charge of the electrical apparatus', nevertheless, they felt that there was 'not sufficient evidence to attach the blame to anyone'. No Powell Duffryn director or official was censured or fined in any way.

Not satisfied with this verdict, the widows and dependents of the dead men were encouraged by the legal advisers of the Miners' Federation to press charges against the company for negligence and malpractice. This they did, their case appearing before the Stipendiary Magistrate, Mr J. Bowen Davies, K.C., at the Aberdare Police Court some three and a half months later.

Once again, the Inspectors of Mines expressed the view that, in their opinion, the company were guilty of providing insufficient ventilation. They also inferred that un-named, or unknown, Tirherbert Colliery officials, had probably removed certain vital evidence from the scene of the accident before they, the Inspectors, arrived at the colliery. (The missing evidence was a piece of electric flex and a sheet, or sheets, of brattice cloth—the latter used for ventilation purposes.) Once again, however, the court found in favour of the company.

Still extremely dissatisfied, the widows and dependents took their case to the Glamorgan Assizes. There, Mr Justice Lewis heard the plaintiff's counsel, Griffiths Williams, express the opinion that 'it was a highly suspicious feature of the case that the essential things which caused the explosion should be missing'. He suggested that 'Someone must have removed these things before the manager arrived on the scene.' It was also very strange, he added, that the very item which would have created a spark—the electrician's apparatus for testing currents—was never spotted by management or officials at any time before the explosion.

Answering Mr Justice Lewis, Griffith Williams agreed that he was suggesting, in fact, that the management, knowing that an illegal practice was going on in the mine, either took away or got somebody to take away that vital piece of evidence.

Justice Lewis told the court that the Powell Duffryn officials were 'not the sort of people who entirely, regardless of rules and regulations, would endanger the lives of workmen in that pit.' He expressed himself as satisfied, despite the evidence of the case before him, that illegal methods, such as the fatal testing of electrical currents which had led to the explosion, were not common practice at Tirherbert colliery nor in any of the other PD collieries. Nevertheless, he gave judgement in favour of the widows and dependents on the grounds that, as he put it, 'If half the evidence which had been given by the plaintiff's witnesses were true the management of the mine were guilty and had been guilty for years of the most callous and criminal disregard of the lives of the men working in that pit.'

Three of the widows received compensation sums of between £495 and £959; and the widow of Jones, the erring electrician, received nothing—on the grounds that it was her husband's use of illegal equipment which first ignited the explosion.

The second incident involving court proceedings can be told more simply. It occurred a few days after the Tirherbert explosion and involved three miners from Elliots Colliery in the Rhymney Valley. They were discovered by a Mines Inspector to be working in their headings with 'insufficient timbering' to support the roof. They appeared later in June 1938 before magistrates at New Tredegar and were fined between ten shillings and one pound each.

Neither of the two cases cited above were spectacular examples of miscarriages of justice. To find such a case, we have only to look at the Gresford explosion of 1934 which killed 265 men. The inquest into that disaster proved that breaches of the Coal Mines Act had been rife at the pit. Yet not one Gresford company official amongst all those directly or indirectly involved, went to prison or was heavily fined.

A charitable interpretation of the role of the courts in the fields of inquiry and litigation following mining accidents during the 1930s would be one which claimed that the judiciary were attempting to place the onus for safety onto individual workmen.

This was not the interpretation favoured by most mining families. There were many living in South Wales during the 1930s to whom the courts represented little more than institutionalised extensions of the coalowners' economic power. Such people regarded the courts as being venues incomparably more congenial to the rich than to the poor. Indeed, there prevailed amongst the workforce during these years a feeling that justice could be bought as easily as any other commodity by those who could afford it. One ex-miner expressed this feeling in the following way: 'The Law Courts of Britain', he said, 'are open to all, like the doors of the Ritz Hotel.'

What seems most to have galled working men and women was the apparent readiness of the courts, and especially of the local magistrates' courts, to accept automatically the words of the coalowners as being the words of completely honourable men, when they, the employees of the coalowners, knew them to be men who were as capable as the next of base and dishonourable actions. The average miner, it was felt, was, in the eyes of most local magistrates, guilty until proven innocent. The three prosecuted colliers of Elliots pit, for instance, would not have been held up by the mining workforce as the innocent victims of a biased judiciary. The prevailing sentiment would have been that the men were fined 'for their own good'. But the workforce also knew that one of the overriding causes of such transgressions of the law as that committed by the Elliots men was the system of work and payment which the coalowners operated in their pits. Low price lists, piecework, conveyor speed-ups and the competitive 'stent' encouraged men to cut corners and to take risks.

In the Gresford Enquiry, for instance, it was quite obvious that, in the final analysis, the cause of the disaster was, quite simply, the desire of the colliery owners and directors to maintain profits by increasing output and productivity. To do this, they allowed themselves the luxury of not bothering, as a great many other coalowners bothered, to slide around the safety regulations or to 'interpret them loosely'. At Gresford they simply disregarded them whenever it was deemed more profitable to do so. A Gresford under-manager, for instance, explaining to the Court of Enquiry why he had broken the regulations concerning shot-firing, said frankly: 'If all these men on the level of the main coal seam had to be withdrawn for every shot on that road, which I had considered quite safe personally, then the colliery would have to close. The Act could never be complied with.'

Such an admission would have shocked few miners in South Wales; for they, like their employers and managers, accepted that the taking of risks and constant occurrence of serious accidents underground were part of the 'inevitable' price to be paid for coal. As Federation members, miners fought collectively, and sometimes fought hard, to lessen that price, but few questioned the fundamental supposition—that the business of coal-getting 'naturally' entailed risk, injury and death. Generally speaking, it was only when management, acting on behalf of the owners, proceeded to violate certain ill-defined safety limits (which both they and the men would have recognised—usually through custom and practice) that sizable disputes occurred. Even then, the disputes which *did* occur tended often to reflect this pervading acceptance of risk and death, for they often involved accusations of cowardice or malingering being levelled at individual workers, or groups of workers, by management.

Wherever a job or task involves risk-taking and the possibility of violent death, codes of behaviour emerge which will contain passages dealing with bravery, cowardice, manliness, skill, toughness and strength. Coalmining abounds with such codes, and they were understood, interpreted and reapplied by management, often in a perceptive and highly successful fashion, to maintain or increase the productivity of pitmen. The latter became intolerant of management's manipulation of these codes when it appeared to them that their employers were insulting their dignity, and the dignity of those maimed and widowed as a result of colliery accidents, by utilising wealth and social standing to renege in Courts of Law on the unwritten agreements between management and men concerning the 'convenient' infringements of safety regulations by both sides at individual collieries.

At times like these, open expression was given by miners to their belief that the owners wanted to have their cake and to eat it. For not only did the latter demand, under threat of dismissal, that men worked in conditions which very often contravened the legal safety requirements, but also that, in the event of a serious accident, their employees should shoulder the blame for any contraventions which became evident during subsequent court proceedings.

It was not a cut and dried situation. Far from it. The dangers at work created in the Valleys a vital sense of community and comradeship. But, though the miners accepted risk and danger, they demanded, in return, recognition of that acceptance by the owners and by the courts. They demanded, in effect, that both the owners and the courts should recognise that, in the effort to produce coal profitably, safety regulations were very often sidestepped or ignored by both men *and* management.

When a mineowner denied responsibility for the death or disablement of an employee, he generally attempted to prove his case in court by shifting the blame for the accident onto the victim. This practice was 'morally' acceptable to the workforce only when it became obvious, during the course of accident inquests, that the victims had suffered as a direct result of their own foolishness—perhaps by lighting cigarettes underground or wandering up closed and gas-filled roadways. In cases other than these exceptional ones, however, the legal efforts of the coalowners were viewed with great suspicion and scepticism. For, not only was it generally believed by the coalfield's workforce that the owners could buy their way out of trouble by hiring sharp lawyers, but it was also believed that the judiciary were, as often as not, in the pockets of the coalowners. The controversy over the Tirherbert explosion of 1938 is a case in point.

The first attempt to prosecute the Powell Duffryn Company by the four widows of the Tirherbert victims took place, it will be remembered, at the Aberdare Police Court in March 1939. The attempt failed when the bench ruled that there was insufficient evidence against the company's named defendants: D. R. Llewellyn and Son, Ltd., (a subsidiary of Powell Duffryn; Sir D. R. Llewellyn and Mr W. M. Llewellyn, JP, were on the Board of Directors of Powell Duffryn) J. A. Price, the company agent, and Isaac L. Davies, the manager of Tirherbert.

In the light of the subsequent award made to the widows, against the company, at the Cardiff Assizes, this judgement by the Aberdare magistrates was quite remarkable—more so when it is taken into account that they dismissed, out of hand, charges brought against the company alleging that no safety lamps had been provided, as they should have been by law, on the coal cutting machine at the face where the men died, (a charge which the company did not bother to deny at the Cardiff Assizes) and that the dead electrician had been allowed, by management, to use, for many years, an illegal apparatus for the testing of electrical currents.

The ex-mineworkers and their families whom I interviewed in Aberdare seem never to have been particularly puzzled by such a judicial inconsistency. They explained them by referring to the 'link-up' which they say existed between the local courts and the owners.

This 'link-up', it is argued, worked invariably in favour of the employers, whether the cases before the courts concerned accident compensation or charges of evasion of employment. In the Tirherbert explosion case, this explanation seems extremely sound.

The magistrates present at the Aberdare hearing of the case were Mr J. Bowen-Davies, KC, Stipendiary of the old Miskin Higher Hundred, Mr E. J. Lewis of Hirwaun, and Mr J. Prowle.

Jack Prowle was, at the time of the Hearing, a Labour County Councillor. He had been, until 1926, a political and trade-union 'militant'. By 1929, however, he appears to have shifted his allegiance from the left to the extreme right of the Labour Party. The reasons for this shift have a direct bearing on his handling of the Tirherbert case.

In the words of a long-time observer of the Aberdare political scene, Prowle had become, during the three years following the great lock-out, '. . . hopelessly enmeshed with the

Llewellyns of Bwllfa and with the Banks family of Aberdare.' (The Llewellyns were the prominent coalowners and principal defendants in the Tirherbert case. The Banks were a well-to-do family of doctors and surgeons, related by marriage to the powerful Hann family, controllers, with the Llewellyns, of Powell Duffryn. In addition, Banks sat on the Aberdare Hospital Committee alongside W.M. Llewellyn). Prowle was alleged to have been, throughout the 1930s, a regular guest of the Llewellyn family at their musical and gastronomic soirees.

He did not, however, appear to have shared the Llewellyns' great enthusiasm for fox hunting and equestrian sports in general as did his companion on the Bench, Mr E. J. Lewis.

Just four months before the case was heard, the *Aberdare Leader* carried a report of the proceedings of the opening meet of the Bwllfa Hunt. Welcoming the cream of Glamorgan Society, as well as guests from other parts of Great Britain, was the Master of the Hunt, Alderman W. M. Llewellyn, JP, Director of Powell Duffryn. Amongst his distinguished guests was listed the Lewis family of Hirwaun, and chief amongst that family was Mr E. J. Lewis, proprietor of the Aberdare Steam Laundry and member of the Aberdare Police Court Bench. The journalist covering the fox hunt reported a colourful turnout, and pinpointed the first kill of the season as having occurred at Gellifalows Farm, barely two mile due north of Tirherbert Colliery.

Two months later, in January 1939, the same paper carried a page three headline which ran, 'Storm Over Stipendiary's "Lay-a-beds" Comment'. It reported that a resolution of protest to the Home Secretary, a public petition, a mass meeting of the unemployed, a boycott of the Police Court Bench by Labour magistrates, had been amongst the measures suggested at an angry meeting of the Aberdare Trades and Labour Council on Thursday 6 January as a protest against what the paper referred to as '. . . the remark recently made by Stipendiary J. Bowen Davies, KC about "lazy lie-abeds" which has already provoked a motion of criticism in the House of Commons by Labour MPs.'

The council meeting was marked by 'very outspoken discussion', during which several delegates, including Labour councillors, expressed their 'disgust at the reflection cast on the unemployed', (who happened to be the targets for Bowen-Davies's verbal castigation) and in which Aberdare's MP, George Hall, described the remark as 'contemptible and unworthy'.

The Chairman of the Trades and Labour Council, Councillor Tom Meredith, himself an unemployed miner, commented that 'a man sprung from the legal profession [Bowen-Davies was a qualified barrister] should be the last person in the world to talk about lie-abeds . . . These people never go to work until ten o'clock in the morning . . . Many of the unemployed, when they were working, had to get up at five in the morning.' To cries of 'Hear, hear.' Councillor Meredith added, 'I am one of the thousands who wish they had the privilege of getting out of bed earlier to go to work.' He went on the express surprise that a man who enjoyed such a high standard of life at the people's expense should talk in such a manner and insult people who did not have sufficient food, clothing and warmth.

Aberdare Labour Councillor William Lawrence quoted a remark which, he alleged, Bowen-Davies had made during a court case: 'It is inconceivable that a police officer should tell an untruth.'

'Saying this', argued Lawrence, 'gave the implication that the civilian, whoever he might be, was saying an untruth . . . There is an inarticulate feeling in Aberdare today that is difficult to express. The best thing that could happen to Aberdare is the removal of the Stipendiary.'

Councillor Sam Wilcox, supporting Lawrence, commented that he thought that Bowen-Davies aimed to '. . . wipe the floor with the working class', and that he was 'going too far' and should therefore be removed from office.

The Aberdare Council unanimously carried a resolution highly critical of Bowen-Davies's comments. He was not, however, removed from office.

The Stipendiary's contempt for the long-term unemployed was, of course, only an echo of similar allegations which emanated especially from the ranks of the coalowners and which attempted to 'play down' the distress caused by continuing high levels of unemployment by inferring that there were plenty of jobs available . . . for those with enough 'spirit' to get out and find them. It is hardly stretching speculation too far to suggest that Bowen Davies, and others in similar positions like him, were probably instrumental in popularizing this myth amongst the petit bourgeois elements of the Valleys' communities. They saw themselves as the hard-headed representatives of those in the

National Government who had 'struggled' in the face of widespread 'socialist hostility' for the previous eight years in the interests of British industrialists and financiers to cut back on public expenditure, and especially on the payment of unemployment benefit. Like the editors of the coalowners' mouthpiece, the *Colliery Guardian*, they wanted to '. . . destroy the pernicious fallacy that has been built up in the years of industrial stress, that the resources of the state may be usefully employed in keeping workmen off the labour market . . .'

These, then, were the three magistrates whom the state had entrusted with the task of judging, in a disinterested fashion, the Tirherbert widows' claim against the Llewellyns of Powell Duffryn. Two were personal friends of the Llewellyn family, and the third was a Stipendiary who, because of his inflexible support for the *status quo*, was denied even the confidence of the 'most respectable citizens' of Aberdare.

In his Presidential Address to the South Wales Miners Annual Conference in 1944, Horner referred to the terms of payment as compensation for miners' widows:

> Recent legislation [he informed his audience] has provided an increase from £300 to £400 for widows, We are not content, we never will be, until compensation is equal to wages. Weekly compensation is the wage of a disabled man. Why should it be less than if he remained able to proceed to his work? Again, the dependants' compensation should be in lieu of wages, and there can be no justification for widows and orphans having to exist on incomes far below that which they previously received. .

He declared that he had always considered the struggle for compensation to be 'equally important with wages' and he was not exaggerating. The controversies aroused by the non-payment of compensation served not only to highlight moral and ethical considerations regarding the cost of life and limb; they also strengthened the miners' healthy sense of collective paranoia—their sense of being the victims of a conspiracy hatched by coalowners and sycophantic functionaries and blessed by the state's courts and government.

197

Bibliographical note

The following are the chief primary sources used in this study:-

Aberdare Leader
Colliery Guardian

Aberdare Labour Party: Ward Minute Books Correspondence and Papers 1935—1957.
Tape Transcripts listed in the *Final Report of the (First) South Wales Coalfield History Project* (Library, University College, Swansea.)
Tape Transcripts listed in the working index of the (Second) South Wales Coalfield Project, South Wales Miners' Library, Swansea. Both these Coalfield Projects have been financed by the Social Science Research Council.
Bwllfa Lodge/SWMF Headquarters Correspondence. (Library, University College, Swansea.)
Insights and information, in almost equal measure, were taken from the works and thoughts of those listed below:
V.L. Allen 'Ideology, Class Consciousness and Experience; the Case of the British Miners.' University of Leeds paper (March, 1975).
M. Heinemann *Britain's Coal* (London, 1944).
Georg Lukacs *History and Class Consciousness* (London, 1971).
Royden Harrison. Unpublished correspondence with the author, 1977.
         Fuller details on sources and the context from which this particular essay derives can be traced in my unpublished thesis: K.S. Howells 'A View From Below: Tradition, Experience and Nationalisation in the South Wales Coalfield, 1937—1957.' (University of Warwick PhD Thesis, 1979.)

Notes from the Margin:
Class and Society in
Nineteenth Century Gwynedd
Merfyn Jones

The three northernmost of the western counties of Wales—Anglesey, Caernarvonshire and Merioneth—since 1974 re-parcelled under the historic name of Gwynedd (a name with the ring of clashing swords about it) are today noteworthy for their high unemployment, low incomes, caravan parks and for the fact that they provide the Welsh language with its last besieged fortress. Gwynedd is a marginal county much dependent upon regional funds; marginal to England and marginal too to that other country of Glamorgan and Gwent. The future threatens with more tourism, trees and nuclear energy (there are already two nuclear plants). The coastline blossoms into bungalows for Lancashire's retired; what was once a great industry is reduced to a line of amusement parks; the mumbling caretaker's voice echoes in the 'advance', and empty, factory. From 1951 until 1974 the three westernmost constituencies returned Labour members. In 1966 all four constituencies (Anglesey, Caernarvon, Conway, Merioneth) were Labour, but by 1979 two Plaid Cymru and two Conservative members were returned and Labour's thirty-year domination crashed. Whole parts of the region are fast becoming English, not anglicised but English, and the defenders of the fortress are reaching for their pikes. Significantly Gwynedd is characterised not only by extremely low levels of incomes but also, at the other end of the scale, by a large proportion in receipt of huge sums of unearned income. It is an area of wealth as well as of poverty.Snowdon presides over a broken-backed and demoralised kingdom, a suitable case for regional aid.

Gwynedd appears to fit well into the theories of distance: a peripheral area containing an ethnic minority, mountainous, remote and culturally divided: the key to its predicament must surely lie somewhere within its relationship to the metropolitan core. The factories lie empty because they are too far from materials and markets; a regional solidarity, graced by the term 'nationalism', emerges to confound the marginalist future. In such an analysis the crucial relationships become those obtaining between core and periphery rather then those between social classes. Many of the theorists who have considered these notions have been at pains to combine class and spatial relationships in their analyses but the political articulation of their theories has tended to emphasise the regional aspects of the problem at the expense of class relationships. In this essay it will be argued that whereas spatial factors are important they have not been as crucial to the history of Gwynedd as has often been assumed. The development and decline of Gwynedd can be more satisfactorily analysed by emphasising the particularly distinctive class relationships which obtained in the area.

Related to the theories of marginality are the beguiling myths of 'backwardness', of pre-capitalist modes of production preserved in remote (and often mountainous) areas even in the era of advanced capitalism. It is, of course, right to emphasise the uneven development of capitalism; the world can hardly be understood at all without such an emphasis. However, in this particular context the notion of backward Gwynedd as opposed to advanced Glamorgan is not helpful. On the contrary it involves a serious and fundamental distortion of its history.

For Gwynedd also was present at the making of the modern world and capitalist social relations, based upon the capitalist mode of production, were established in the area from an early date; the area witnessed, albeit in minature, a classic example of the transformation wrought during the industrial revolution and the assumed backwardness of the social structure, certainly from the mid-nineteenth century onwards, is a myth. Further, the particularity of the class relationships which became so important in the area stem in large measure from factors internal to the region and not from any overriding relationship with the core. By the early nineteenth century Gwynedd was locked into the modern world. The vicissitudes in its fortunes since then have been the result of the history of the capitalist process as it operated in that area and of the struggle between social classes involved in that process. The problems are not those associated with an absence of modernisation but, on the contrary, with the consequences of a modernisation which is itself decayed and incapable.

The early history of industrialisation in Gwynedd embraces changes in many traditional occupations such as woollen production and shipbuilding but is dominated by two extractive industries—copper and slate (another extractive industry, dolerite quarrying, was also significant) and the slate industry was preponderant in the area's economy for over a century. Extractive industries are of course typical of many underdeveloped economies, but two points need to be made in the case of Gwynedd to qualify any simple equation between extractive industry and economic dependence. In the first place copper mining led to the downstream development of the smelting industry and to the manufacture of copper-based commodities, and if smelting was not carried on near the source of the ore that was because that process required to be close to another extractive industry—coal mining. Secondly, both copper and slate mining or quarrying involve more than removing the ore or stone from the ground. Copper was burnt at the mine in order to remove sulphurous gases whereas slates were actually in a sense manufactured after the slabs of the material had been removed from the ground. It is therefore misleading to think of slate as being merely an extractive industry comparable to coal. The skilled workforce in the industry was actually involved, in factory conditions, in making a marketable commodity, roofing slates. Their consciousness of themselves as craftsmen was to be a crucial factor in developments in the industry.

If slate came to exert the deepest and longest-lasting influence on the area copper surely exerted the more dramatic. Copper was mined in several locations throughout North Wales but the significant developments were those related to the Parys Mountain and Mona mines in Anglesey which, along with similar, more modest, developments in slate suceeded in modernising much of the area's economy and society during the last decades of the eighteenth century. By 1780 the Parys and Mona mines were giant enterprises employing over 1,200 men and women, the growth of the town of Amlwch was closely associated with the industry and Anglesey's ore dominated the British and indeed the world copper market. This empire was controlled by one of the leading entrepreneurs of the industrial revolution, a man acknowledged as such by his contemporaries, Thomas Williams of Llanidan (1737-1802). Thomas Williams was an Anglesey lawyer who, through involving himself in a long legal battle between parties contesting ownership of copper mines, became the controller of the mines himself. He was a ruthless and feared bourgeois who, by 1792, had came to control not only his Anglesey mines but also the rival copper mines of Cornwall. He also owned smelting works and mills in Swansea, Flintshire, south Lancashire and the Thames valley, chemical works outside Liverpool, offices and warehouses in London, Liverpool and Birmingham and a bank based in Chester; from 1790 until 1802 he was member of parliament for Great Marlow. In 1799, when his empire was already crumbling, it has been authoritatively estimated that he was worth some £800,000. Thomas Williams was as responsible as any man in Britain for the development and the triumph of the capitalist order; he was not part of a regional backwardness, on the contrary, he for a time engineered the virtual monopoly-control of a whole industry.

The adventures of Richard Pennant (1737?-1808) in the slate industry seem modest by comparison but their consequences were even more widespread. Pennant started to develop the Penrhyn Quarries in Caernarvonshire in the 1780s; within a decade he had revolutionised the production of slate, built roads from the quarries to the sea and developed his own port. By the 1820s the quarries employed 900 men, by the middle of the century almost 2,000 were employed there. The owners of the Penrhyn quarries came subsequently to adopt the style and manners of the landed aristocracy but Pennant himself had not been of this caste, and his wealth was founded not on his own landed inheritance (though this does not apply to his wife) but on the money he and his father had made as Liverpool merchants. He was one of the most eminent of Liverpool's merchant princes and was for many years a member of parliament for that rapidly developing urban centre; his fortune was based on plantations in the West Indies. There is an important social and political distinction to be drawn between the commercial and industrial sections of the bourgeoisie (Pennant's original capital was largely merchant capital); but this should not detract from the influence of his audacious entrepreneurial methods on the opening-up of Gwynedd.

Similar men, with similar sources of capital, later developed the slate industry in Blaenau Ffestiniog and Dyffryn Nantlle. Most of them were Lancashire businessmen. Samuel Holland (1803-92) came to Blaenau Ffestiniog from Liverpool in 1821 and stayed to see the barren mountainside transformed into one of the largest towns in North Wales; he also became Liberal MP for the county of Merioneth. In addition the slate industry attracted considerable speculatory finance capital (Nathan Rothschild himself became involved in the industry in the 1820s). Innumerable small quarries and mines benefited also from local capital accumulated in shipping and other business ventures; this was particularly true of the Dyffryn Nantlle district where one of the giants of Welsh non-conformity, John Jones Talysarn was deeply involved in quarrying ventures.

Of the major slate quarries only the Dinorwic Quarries near Llanberis were owned by an uncomplicated landowner (Assheton Smith of the Vaynol estate), and even they were originally opened up between 1787 and 1809 by a partnership of lawyers. Other local landowners, such as the Ormsby-Gores and Lord Newborough, were involved in the industry but they did not typify the early slate-masters. The slate-owners were a different class whose wealth and experience were based on trade and manufacture, in every sense a 'modern' class. During the course of the nineteenth century, however, because of the enormous profits gained from the slate industry, sections of this group were able to build their mock castles and create their estates and move closer to the styles of the country gentleman. This trend was most visible and important in the case of the Penrhyn family which, due as much to complicated inheritance as to social aspiration, became increasingly aristocratic in manner and style resulting, in 1866, in the ennobling of Edward Gordon Douglas Pennant (he was actually a Douglas, the Pennant was assumed) when he became Baron Penrhyn of Llandegai. The pretensions of the Castle could not however disguise the fact that the elegant landowners were also businessmen. Their social adaptation to aristocratic conventions was of course, entirely typical of the British bourgeoisie. In this respect the Liberal politics of Samuel Holland, the Greaves family and other slate owners is as significant as the high-Toryism of Penrhyn Castle.

Capitalism in Gwynedd then was not a late development, a consequence which followed upon the maturity of capitalism in England, but was a part of the capitalist transformation which was completed during the industrial revolution and, in the figure of Thomas Williams, made an enormous contribution to the entrepreneurial energies of that early industrial capitalism. The process was on a smaller scale, of course, compared with what happened elsewhere (though this should not be overemphasised) and was, as elsewhere, incomplete in many respects, a point to which we shall return later. But the area cannot, in this historical period at least, be unlocked from the 'core' of which it was a part. This simultaneous development of capitalist processes of production owes much to the fact that Gwynedd was not as remote an area as has often been assumed. Remote from Merthyr Tydfil perhaps (Merthyr of course was a pretty 'remote' place itself) but not from Liverpool, one of the nineteenth century world's leading seaports and commercial centres, nor from the new industrial society being built so dramatically in Lancashire. The development of Gwynedd, and indeed of the whole of North Wales, is and was intimately linked to the south Lancashire and north Cheshire economy. The slate and copper industries prospered in Gwynedd because the area was *not* remote. It enjoyed short and easy sea routes to what was the most advanced economy in the world. Once the few, but difficult, miles from slate quarry to the sea were overcome, and by 1836 that most remote of towns, Blaenau Ffestiniog, was connected by rail to the sea at Portmadoc, Gwynedd enjoyed not poor but, on the contrary, excellent communications. By the 1820s several shipping companies were offering a daily steamer service from Liverpool to the Menai Straits. Because of the importance to the British state of the Irish connection via Holyhead land transport was also good: the Menai Suspension Bridge, designed by Telford, was opened in 1827; the mainline railway from Holyhead to Chester was operational by 1848. Gwynedd was indisputably part of the world's first industrial society.

The economic developments had a profound effect on class relations and the making of a working class in the region, the creation of a force of 'free' labour, followed familiar lines. Slate had long been quarried and worked in parts of Snowdonia by groups of independent quarriers many of whom worked on a part-time basis. In order for production to be organised on a fully capitalist basis these quarriers had to be removed and transformed into wage labourers. Tenant farmers and others had also to be recruited to this labour force and also became free labour. In order to achieve this the slate owners used the law, Enclosure Acts and their economic power. The independent quarriers were bought out or otherwise removed, the mountain land was enclosed, the workers started to construct their villages around their independent and nonconformist chapels—Bethesda, Ebenezer, Cesarea, Carmel and other towns and villages were created. The process was resisted, at times violently (particularly in the Cilgwyn area of Nantlle and in Dinorwic) but the new order triumphed. Capitalism in Gwynedd created not only a modern industry but also a working class.

This working class has often been characterised as backward and weak and been unfavourably compared with the advanced organisation and ideas of the working class, and particularly of the miners, in South Wales. From the first decade of the twentieth century onwards the contrast between the political consciousness of north and south does indeed become qualitatively marked and significant, although the aggresiveness of the miners and the compromising of the quarrymen can both be overdone, and one slate-quarryman, George Fretwell of Penygroes in Caernarvonshire, did give his life for the Spanish Republic along with his coal-mining comrades. Further the labour movement in Gwynedd did achieve singular, if temporary, political victories such as the election of R.T. Jones, General Secretary of the North Wales Quarrymen's Union as Labour MP for Caernarvonshire in 1922. In the nineteenth century, particularly in the latter half of that century, the contrast between north and south is nowhere as marked for, despite the fact that almost all the historians who have written about the slate-quarrymen (including the present writer), blinded by the myths of backwardness, have sought to explain the weakness of working-class organisation and consciousness in the region, the relevant question which should be asked is not related to the anaemia which supposedly characterises Gwynedd's working-class consciousness. The real historical problem is the surprising resilience and survival of trade-union organisation, particularly amongst the slate-quarrymen.

Few sections of the British working class could in the 1970s celebrate a century of continuous organisation. North Wales quarrymen were amongst them for in 1974 the few quarrymen that were left commemorated the stirring and crucial developments of a century earlier. The North Wales Quarrymen's Union (NWQU) was born in 1874 on a storm which irresistibly shifted the balance of class forces in the region; as soon as the union was founded its members were locked out by the two major concerns in the industry—Dinorwic and Penrhyn—but were nevertheless able to win sweeping victories over both employers. In Penrhyn they achieved not only the establishment of a union-controlled quarry-committee but also the removal of an entire management which had run the quarry for almost half a century. Their opponents, and on this occasion the losers, Lord Penrhyn and Assheton Smith, were two of the wealthiest and most powerful men in Wales. During the next quarter of a century the quarrymen were engaged in a prolonged and desperate resistance to a ruthless employers' offensive. Throughout the winter of 1885 the Dinorwic men stayed out in a struggle which was repeated even more dramatically in the Penrhyn Quarries where 2,800 men were locked out for eleven months in 1896-97 and then for three years from November 1900. The Penrhyn disputes, fought above all else for the right to organise, deserve in themselves a chapter in the history of British labour; they witnessed a rare level of working-class organisation and courage and were significant episodes in the national development of labour occuring as they did shortly after the Conciliation Act of 1896, and during the years of the national anti-trade-union offensive. The cause of the Penrhyn quarrymen and their families was a national labour crusade: in Bethnal Green, a district in which £300 was raised in collections for the struggle in Gwynedd, £25 was subscribed in farthings. Twenty four thousand people would need to contribute a farthing each to reach the sum of £25.

Dozens of trade-union organisations were founded in Britain in the mid-1870s, the NWQU was one of the few to survive. Despite this startling fact, clearly in need of explanation, historians have been more concerned with the weaknesses of the NWQU , which admittedly did not succeed in organising all slate quarrymen in the region until the first world war. This has produced an interesting discussion, despite its misplaced questioning and several significant answers have been offered. Two of them would seem relevant here: that the union's weakness is related to the general backwardness of the area and, in particular, to the quarryman's relationship with the land; that Welsh culture and politics emphasised national/regional allegiance as opposed to class solidarity.

These issues raise fundamental issues of interpretation. The cottager-worker is a dilemma for the historians of many industries, not least of coal mining: to what degree was a man's status as a 'free' labourer affected by the fact that he was also a tenant farmer or smallholder? The empirical evidence in Gwynedd offers little justification for the assumption that quarrymen who also worked in some way on the land were in any way significantly less class-conscious than those who did not; some medium-sized quarries in cottager country were amongst the best organised and militant in the industry whereas a large concern like the Oakeley mine in Blaenau Ffestiniog, drawing much of its labour from the terraces of that town, had a relatively aquiescent and compliant work force. Neither is there any evidence to suggest that the rift which appeared in the Penrhyn men's ranks in 1901 was in any way related to relationship to the land. What appears to have been the case, in fact, is that the quarry revolutionised the consciousness of the countryside so that men who were also cottagers thought of themselves primarily as quarrymen. So at least in men's minds the advanced sector of the local economy was that which laid down the determinants of consciousness. They were not shackled to the backwardness of the farm but to the modernising dynamic of the quarry. The only section of the workforce to which this would not seem to apply were the unskilled weekly migrants into the quarries (where they stayed in barracks), especially those from Anglesey, but apart from this possible exception even apparently quite rural parishes were in fact dominated by the ethos of the quarry. In this context it is worth noting that the men who worked in the Dinorwic quarries in the late nineteenth century, although recruited overwhelmingly from the immediate district, were drawn from over sixty different hamlets and villages, many of them miles distant. The slate industry dominated much more than the distinctive streets of the industrial villages from which it drew most of its labour and whose inhabitants' relations with the land in any case rarely went even as far as digging an allotment.

A significant proportion of the population of Gwynedd was of course involved entirely in agriculture, an agriculture moreover which was characterised by the most brutal poverty as families endeavoured to make a living from ever-hostile heaths and hills. The writ of industry most certainly did not prevail everywhere and the existence of a class of poor tenant farmers is of crucial political importance in the history of the region. Their world was a different one from that of the quarrymen and other workers and at times the contrast between the two was dramatically visible: the village-dwelling quarrymen always exhibited a certain contempt for the purely rural population referring to them as sheep (y mê-mês) or pigs (Moch Sir Fon). They dressed, ate and thought differently; in the election of 1885 the Blaenau Ffestiniog quarrymen went so far as to stand their own independent Liberal candidate against the rural based official machine. It is not being suggested here that the rural population were unimportant and by-passed by history. The point is that different modes·of production, offering a complex, constant but changing relationship coexisted within the region. Gwynedd itself cannot be characterised as a regionally coherent backward bloc, the crucial relationship was not that between this region and the core but rather the relationship between classes within and outside the region.

The other objection which is twin related to the question of their relationship with the land raises the significance of the prevalence of the Welsh language and of its political culture. This too is a problematic area. Gwynedd has always been a largely Welsh-speaking area and the slate-quarrying communities in particular were almost entirely Welsh speaking, in the nineteenth century. More than this they were effectively monoglot communities in which relatively few people had any real grasp of the English language: industrial negotiations were carried on through interpreters. People lived in an entirely Welsh-language culture at work, in prayer, at home; they read their newspapers in Welsh and sang their hymns in the same language, the North Wales Quarrymen's Union conducted all its meetings in the Welsh language. Despite this situation, however, the inability of so many people to understand English offered few defences to the marauding encroachment of a British culture normally transmitted through the medium of English including, of course, much (although not all) of that culture's chauvinistic boastings. The Welsh language, unlike many other minority and 'backward' cultures, offered few barriers to the extension of British and imperialist values, a fact which might offer a clue to its astonishing survival; it was an inconvenience but not, until possibly the 1960s, a threat, This is not the place to discuss the complexities of how this situation arose but it is worth emphasising that many of the cultural heroes of the Welsh language helped to transmit English content into a Celtic form so that, despite the distinctive characteristics of Welsh calvinism, many of its leading figures, such as Lewis Edwards, must be seen as the brokers for British (often Scottish) values. Such men 'modernised' Welsh culture to such a degree that it offered few problems to the new system.

The mistaken discussion about the backwardness of

Gwynedd's nineteenth century workers has therefore succeeded in raising significant issues which take us to the roots of the class relationships prevailing in the region. Those class relationships operated within a modern capitalist economy and society rather than in some remote backwater sheltered from the currents of history; this does not mean that the region did not exhibit distinctive and indeed unique patterns of social cohesion and conflict. To quote Marx:

> It is always the direct relationship of the owners of the conditions of production to the direct producers . . . which reveal the innermost secret, the hidden basis of the entire social structure . . . This does not however prevent the same economic basis—the same from the standpoint of its main conditions—due to the innumerable different empirical circumstances, natural environment, racial relations, external historical influences etc. from showing infinite variations and gradations in appearance which can be ascertained only by an analysis of the empirically given circumstances.

No man was more aware of the peculiarities of Gwynedd than the second Baron Penrhyn, George Sholto Douglas Pennant (1836-1907); a militant aristocrat he could never quite understand nor forgive the sour change that was taking place within his domain during the late nineteenth century. When the electors of Caernarvonshire rejected him in the election of 1880 he suggested that the problem resided in the fact that he was surrounded by Welsh liars. 'Caernarvonshire', he said, then, 'stands on top of the list . . . as a lying county'. During the evidence which he gave to the Royal Commission on Land in Wales and Monmouthshire in 1893 he outlined another theory to explain the cussedness of the Welsh: the rocky and mountainous terrain made fox hunting something less than the socially cohesive ritual which in his estimation it was elsewhere. Without horses, fox hunting does indeed lose much of its charm and stone boundary walls and boulder-strewn slopes offered an unacceptably stern challenge for horse and rider, wistfully recalling the hedges and the soft rich earth of southern England. This was Lord Penrhyn's puzzled variant on the core-periphery argument. A note of paranoia crept into the Castle Keep. A paranoia which is understandable given the savage political battle which raged in Gwynedd during the closing decades of the nineteenth century as Welsh liberalism, clamorous and aggressive, sought to dismantle the Castle's political power. Penrhyn fought back at every stage by defending every committee, every Local Board, replying to every article, countering argument with argument, letter with letter. When he lost his parliamentary seat he kept fighting, he formed his Property Defence Association, he got himself elected onto the new County Council there to argue face to face with his radical adversaries and he resisted trade unionism with an enthusiasm bordering on hysteria. Libelled and calumnied in a language he did not understand he expounded improbable explanations in order to account for the sharp contrast between his isolated and threatened position when compared with the easy power of his aristocratic friends and relatives elsewhere in the kingdom. Even his paternalism failed: 'we are perfectly willing', said the Penrhyn quarrymen's representatives in 1874, in a brave and explicit redefinition of relationships, 'that his lordship should keep his charities to himself—if those in any way interfere with him in his giving us proper wages'. He would not recognise that his own Castle, and all it represented, was one of the central reasons for the 'peculiarities' of the Welsh.

Many factors must be taken into account when discussing the 'empirically given circumstances' of nineteenth century Gwynedd. Some have already been discussed briefly here: the Welsh language; the numbers of tenant farmers. Others can only be mentioned in passing: the labour process characteristic of the slate industry, particularly its wages-payment system; the homogeneity of the region's working class and the significance of a small but vitally important group of middle-class English immigrants; the motivating drive of nonconformity. But the central fact was the concentration of wealth. This was the open wound in Gwynedd society which resulted in the bitter resentment and viciousness of its politics. The ownership of land in Gwynedd in the late nineteenth century was more concentrated than anywhere else in England and Wales. In Caernarvonshire in 1887 only 4.2 per cent of farm holdings (4.6 per cent of acreage) were owner-occupied, thirty-five families owned three quarters of the land of the county, the five most powerful of them owned half the land area. Lord Penrhyn owned 48,000 acres in 1883 and had an annual rental of £63,000 from his Caernarvonshire property. The two families who owned the Penrhyn and Vaynol estates shared between them half the slate industry of Gwynedd and quarter of the land of Caernarvonshire. This was the Gwynedd distortion.

The progress of the aspirant middle class was blocked by the sheer economic power of the few men who had originally developed the resources of the region; they reacted with a strident and vigorous politics and with a vision of a populist and nonconformist Wales which was a formidable, if sectarian, ideological construct; the mighty and powerful were stripped of their Welsh citizenship, were excluded by words and by force of argument. That ideological construct, the Welsh radical tradition, drove back the Castle and in a relentless political struggle claimed the future of Wales. But the Castle had made their Wales; the idea could be banished but the reality could not.

The political definitions of radical liberalism, however inadequate its analysis, sculpted the human shape of Gwynedd. We have talked a good deal here of modes of production and economic relations, and they are the keys to an understanding of any history or place, but history is about classes, class relationships and class struggle. It is men and women who change the world not Dalek-like modes of production. The ideas in the minds of men and women cannot be discounted. The fact however remains that the distinctiveness of Gwynedd owed much to those whom radicalism, and subsequently nationalism, wished to exclude. It was this distinctiveness which so crucially affected the consciousness of the Gwynedd working class.

The workers of Gwynedd were drafted into the Liberal army and for a time willingly accepted middle-class and radical leadership. For a quarter of a century even the North Wales Quarrymen's Union was controlled by a middle-class radical clique the most prominent of whom was W.J. Parry, mistakenly sanctified by one marxist historian in a Popular Frontist daze as 'the Quarryman's Champion'. The importance of this middle-class leadership should not be overestimated, however, since it says more of the nature of Gwynedd's middle-class radicalism than it does about the quarrymen; Parry's beliefs and actions differed little from those of William Abraham, leader of the South Wales miners. More significantly the particular class configurations and the prevailing political notions obtaining in Gwynedd refused to allow ·the development of 'normal' trade union relationships and led finally to the dramatic and dreadful industrial battles in Penrhyn.

The slate quarrymen were typical of the 'better class' of Victorian working men, conscious of their skill, proud of their respectability. They crowded to work dressed in bowler hats, white trousers and carrying umbrellas. Their organisation, the NWQU, which they defended against overweening power with such ferocious tenacity, followed a pattern of development familiar to any student of British trade unionism. Founded in the boom of the 1870s, it survived the depression of the eighties, blossomed briefly in the boom of 1889-91, fought fiercely against the employers' offensive of the nineties, moved increasingly toward Labourism and finally amalgamated with the Transport and General Workers Union in 1922. A 'normal' working class with its friendly societies and its trade unionism was, however, not admissible in the Gwynedd of the late nineteenth century since its meaning was subsumed in the general political warfare. As a weapon of radicalism, poised to strike at the point of profit, it was intolerable to the employers; as the standard bearer of an alternative power structure and an alternative political culture it posed, even in its seemingly moderate demands, a fundamental challenge to the Castle. Industrial disputes, often caused by the details of wages and conditions, became, in the peculiar conditions of Gwynedd, challenges to the established order. British trade union leaders and government officials looked on in uncomprehending disbelief at the savagery of the battle; its intensity had its roots in the thin and acid soil of Gwynedd and can only be understood in terms of the local conditions which affected the struggle. But the struggle, though it also at every point involved the outside world, was within the region, between classes, not between the region and the metropolitan core.

There is a new orthodoxy abroad which reduces Wales to a footnote in the discourses of the sociology of underdevelopment. This orthodoxy has wafted almost inadvertently from across the Atlantic like a bedraggled and gale-blown petrel; the eagerness with which it has been received and absorbed into current political vocabulary suggests that the model-makers have served us well in making explicit a notion that has long been loitering amongst us. The recent posturings of this new orthodoxy, particularly the vulgar reformism which conceals itself behind much of the current discussion of regional problems and regional aid, have provoked this essay. Its aim has been two-fold, to emphasise the distinctiveness of a Welsh region but also to insist that the desperate problems of Gwynedd are not some irregularity in the relationship of a metropolitan system to its peripheries which is susceptible to correction or re-definition through notions of national independence or through appeals for regional aid. Gwynedd was, and is, not only a place (where isn't?) but also a part of a process; its past and present can hardly be understood without that perspective.

Bibliographical note

This contribution has been concerned with the lack of historical validity underlining some of the assumptions so current in political and economic discussions in Wales rather than with a body of theoretical literature. The literature on core-periphery relations is vast and hardly underdeveloped; of particular relevance to Wales is Michael Hechter, *Internal Colonialism—The Celtic Fringe in British National Development 1536-1966* (1975) which only partially derives from economic theories of dependency. His work attempts to present a theory of ethnicity and ethnic change in which the survival of a Welsh culture is viewed as a reaction to the economic domination of Wales by England which takes the form of a cultural division of labour. Other interpretations are offered by Tom Nairn in *The Break-Up of Britain*, (1977) and by Gwyn A. Williams in *When Was Wales?* (BBC Wales Annual Lecture, 1979), a lecture which was delivered whilst the present study was being written and which should be compulsory reading for all interested in Wales. Of the present crop of Welsh members of parliament only Dafydd Elis Thomas (Plaid Cymru, Merioneth) has shown any inclination to examine the crisis of Wales by using the analytical tools of marxism and, in particular, the concept of the uneven and combined development of capitalism (see, for example his 'Cymru-Be Nesa?' in *Cyffro*, Summer 1979).

This essay approaches the history of Wales via a discussion of one of its regions—Gwynedd. Perhaps because so many of us who come from that area can never leave it alone, the area's history is relatively well researched; there are excellent county historical societies and a Gwynedd Archive Service which is admirably conscientious and productive. A. H. Dodd, *The Industrial Revolution in North Wales*, first published in 1933, remains one of the finest accounts of the regional impact of industrialisation anywhere in Britain and, in the light of its scholarship, it is curious that so

much misapprehension remained. On the modern politics of
Gwynedd, Cyril Parry, *The Radical Tradition in Welsh Politics : a study
of Liberal and Labour politics in Gwynedd 1900-1920* (1970) and I. G.
Jones, 'Merioneth Politics in mid-nineteenth century' *Journal of the
Merioneth Historical and Record Society* No *IV* are both outstanding
studies. Despite some grave factual inaccuracies Tom Davies 'The
Arfon Quarries', *Planet* No. 30 (1976) is an important and
pioneering attempt at analysing regional policy. Other works of
particular relevance here are J. Roose Williams, *Quarryman's
Champion, the Life and activities of William John Parry of Coetmar* (1978)
and Jean Lindsay, *A History of the North Wales Slate Industry* (1974).
For an account of the business ventures of Thomas Williams see J.
R. Harris, *The Copper King* (1964). Finally many of the peremptorily
stated asides contained in this essay are discussed, with rather
more empirical detail, in R. Merfyn Jones, *The North Wales
Quarrymen 1874-1922* (University of Wales Press, Studies in Welsh
History, forthcoming). Gwynedd society in the twentieth century is
presently being studied by Dafydd Roberts of University College,
Aberystwyth and our knowledge and understanding of the area
should be greatly increased by his completed research.

Wales Through the Looking-Glass
David Smith

> One thing was certain : That the white kitten had had nothing to do
> with it : it was the black kitten's fault entirely ... So to punish it she
> held it up to the Looking-glass that it might see how sulky it
> was—'and if you're not good directly I'll put you through into
> Looking-glass House. How would you like that?'

The problem for the self-righteous Alices of this world is that the
black kitten will always like it fine; the central nub of modern
Welsh history is that once Wales went through the looking-glass
there was no return, for this was not fiction nor fantasy but the
most drastic alteration of Welsh sensibilities that ever occurred.
Even now, it is difficult to comprehend the dramatic growth of
industry and population in the South : from the 1870s, at a time of
general depression in the British economy, South Wales was as
prime an investment area as American railroads or African gold
mines. Between 1871 and 1911 the population of Wales increased
from under one and a half million to just under two and a half
million. In 1871 the combined population of Glamorgan and
Monmouthshire was a third of the total; in the decades that
followed, every other Welsh county, apart from Carmarthen which
had an expansion of 60,000 in its new coalfield, either had small
increases in population (Caernarfonshire, Denbigh and Flint) or
static population or, indeed, dramatic loss of numbers. By 1911
Glamorgan and Monmouth had a population in excess of the
whole total of 1871, over one and a half million, and if we add the
industrial portions of Carmarthenshire we can say that two-thirds
of the inhabitants of Wales lived in this southern belt. It was a
demographic shift that might even have deterred Moses in his
anxiety to leave Egypt. The Welsh indeed had often considered
themselves in the nineteenth century as a special addition to the
tribes of Israel and, like most small nations in that century, had

found emigration a means of entry into the modern world. The irony, and it is a particularly teasing one, of Welsh industrialisation is that the Welsh had no longer to seek modernity elsewhere. The Welsh tribe wandered into Egypt and there mixed with other rural immigrants. Behind them they left a secluded pastoral country of sparsely populated uplands and the occasional small town. To this day the traveller who comes off the Brecon Beacons and into Cefn-Coed-y-Cymmer enters a world as abruptly different as any Dr Who discovers. For a quarter of a century, at least, one generation of Welsh men and women were travelling in time as well as space. Dropping down into Merthyr, itself the first Welsh urban experience of any note, they were confronted by a higgledy-piggledy riot of buildings and architectural styles strung out along valleys in places that were, in any normal sense, topographically lunatic. But this was not a normal place. Here public houses were built of a gargantuan dimension that implied the thirst for alcohol was insatiable, and it was, whilst chapels were thrown up as if they were going out of fashion—and they did. Where there had been silence, there was cacophonous noise, where there had been relative immobility there was now an intricate network of railway lines mocking landscape problems with arching viaducts and looming grey-stone embankment walls around whose basic convenience roads and streets were constructed. In the high streets yawning emporia offered the flotsam and jetsam washed up by the industrial economy—ready-made clothes and boots, convenience foods, handy goods and ornaments, entertainment in music hall and boxing booth, milk deliveries and newspapers and magazines. The society had the stumbling vitality of a blind man on a spree. The economic and political detail attached to this unprecedented social explosion has received attention from a number of historians anxious to refute Matthew Arnold's libel of the Celt as 'always ready to react against the despotism of fact'. Less attention has been paid, however, to the idea or concept of Wales that was touted in the late nineteenth century. The conflict between the reality of what was, within a generation, the majority Welsh experience and the ideal cultural image of what it was to be Welsh, spun around the twin poles of the existence of the novel society in the south and how it could be managed. Wales had come fully into the reckoning of the wider British world once more; in the sixteenth century for reasons of state—politics, war and strategic diplomacy; in the nineteenth century because of an increasingly vital part within the imperial economy. The disposition of the people was a crucial question. The Welsh, even before they came to analyse themselves, were discovered by others.

In 1860 the anonymous author of *Murray's Handbook for Travellers in South Wales* commented:

> The character of the mining section of the Welsh population has wonderfully improved in the last 10 or 15 years, which must be a source of congratulation to those who remember the lawlessness and ignorance which characterised Chartism, and the fearful riots to which it gave birth. Of course, where the amount of labour is so enormous, misunderstandings will often arise, which if not adjusted cause strikes and bitter feelings between master and man; . . . their improvement must be ascribed principally to education and the force of public opinion, which amongst this class of people is a powerful motive. It must be confessed that Dissenters have been the principal agents in humanising and softening the mass.
>
> Serious crime is absent but there is often to be met with a sad want of truth and straightforwardness, and a love of prevarication . . . for the rest the Welsh are a kindly, generous and impulsive race, often gifted with a lively imagination . . . and . . . a strong love of music.
>
> In South Wales, the use of the English language is certainly very much increased to the detriment of the Welsh, and as the pushing forward of new railways breaks down the barriers of isolation, so we may expect the latter dialect to become less common.

There is, there, co-mingled with congratulation, a gentle exhortation to keep up the good, civilising work. But as late as 1881 the American consul at Cardiff (the post itself being a significant comment) was deeply concerned because 'North Wales is pretty well known; but South Wales is *terra incognita* to most Englishmen. To bury oneself in some remote village of South Wales appears to be a Londoner's strongest expression of complete isolation from the world; yet the most remote of these villages is nearer than Australia or the Society Islands'. He proceeded to extol the rural beauty of old South Wales, not forgetting the 'clean, handsome' sea-port town of Cardiff. It is only when he comes to Merthyr that he is a little uncertain, though even there, amidst the changes of the modern world his sentimental American eye finds some pristine Welsh beauty:

> The peasants of Wales, like those of most lands cling less strenuously to their distinctive costume in these latter days than they were wont to do. Formerly a farmer's wife or daughter who should make her appearance at market or church . . . without wearing a tall beaver hat would have been deemed careless of her personal appearance . . .; so that 20 years ago these were seen in every direction in Merthyr market, as well as the distinctive long cloaks of bright colours, and the occasional scuttle-shaped bonnets. Nowadays the fashion is so greatly relaxed that we see but few of these in Merthyr market. The headcoverings of the women are chiefly mushroom hats of dark straw, or close-fitting bonnets of black crape, always with a lace cap or muslin underneath.
>
> There are, however, some specimens still to be seen of the Welsh peasant costume as it has been for generations past; notably a comely young woman behind a vegetable stall, who wears the full costume in all its glory. She is a pink of neatness, and her beaver is superb. I at once christen her the Pride of the Market, and if ever I go to live in Merthyr Tydfil, I shall buy my vegetable marrows of none but her.

The plaintive note of disappointment sounds all the more clearly in the tantalising glimpse of genuine Welsh costume Wirt Sykes was given. The phenomenon of a garb no longer totally native is one that travellers into emergent peasant countries would bemoan again, in the Spain of the 1920s or the Rumania of the 1930s. The willingness, indeed the desire, of peasant populations to shed their picturesque uniform has been, however, even more disturbing for those of their fellow countrymen whose own novel social position was defined by their own distinctiveness from peasant life. A peasantry which was not necessarily isolated as rural but rather linked into urban, industrial development cannot be seen as a part (a lower yet whole, integral part) on the scale of progressive social development. Worse still when, as in Wales, the country changes predominantly peasant characteristics within a forced generation. Hence the encouragement of the wearing of Welsh costume as a self-consciously Welsh characteristic amongst schoolchildren from the late nineteenth century, in the new board schools of the sprawling townships, where a Welsh 'clerisy' traced out the elements of higher Welsh culture. The 'clerisy' was a wedge of preachers, teachers, printers, shopkeepers and lawyers rather than a broad-based bourgeoisie (the Welsh strain here, until recently anyway, has always been rather thin). It was the almost incidental by-product of the Welsh educational tradition and of nineteenth century growth, briefly refulgent with the hopeful confluence of the two. It was conscious of its own roots in a ruptured Welsh history, its ideal was one of service through the example of its own leadership and its self-conception was as the sociological apogee of Welsh radicalism and nonconformity. It was consumed with the guilt of an achievement that implicitly denied its own origins and, thus, fiercely protective of the images and myths of a Welsh past whose crowning glory and seed-bed was the 'gwerin', a cultured self-sufficient folk. The irony, the crucifying dilemma of that emergent Welsh middle class was that their own lives, modes of dress and habits of thought, were living denials of their own past. The pictorial representation of Wales at this time, a subject hardly touched except in the fine-art sense, is instructive—the Welsh past is feminine, matriarchal, the future heroic, masculine, virile. In cartoons the divide is between benevolent, be-costumed Dame Wales and, say, her champion Lloyd George as Arthur or, as his egg-whitened hair lengthened, a genial Merlin. Or, take Cernew Vosper's famous painting of 1908, *Salem*—the assembled, plainly but traditionally dressed, worshippers in their bare pews and the very old lady, reverently clutching the Bible, and also in costume in the centre—the frugal best of Welsh peasant worship in a genre painting. But, of course, she is wearing a magnificent, intricately coloured shawl and, whatever the painter's intentions in colour and design, this straightforward example of bourgeois art (I mean in intention and execution) led, within the divided society it was meant to depict as assured, to a glut of legends on the old woman's vanity in arriving so splendidly dressed, so late. The vanity was proved, in the popular mind, by the alleged intrusion of the shape of the Devil himself into the shawl's pattern. The storm that broke around the first genuine piece of Anglo-Welsh literature, Caradoc Evans' *My People* in 1915, stemmed, at a different layer of the strata, from a deep psychological need to pitchfork out his mean vignettes of a sly, crabbed Welsh peasantry, which smeared with ink the hagiographic portraits the clerisy had hung in their minds. So long as they were confident of those household deities, burnished at eisteddfodau, recalled in chapel and concert, they could, in fact, allow the drift away from the realities that had once lain behind the outward emblems.

This was, from mid-century onwards, the time for the full emergence of a native Welsh commercial class as the shopocracy of the early nineteenth century learned how to generate and invest its own capital—most of those late nineteenth century coalowners and shipping magnates were basing themselves on an already acquired fortune. The often crucial role that Wales comes to play in British politics from, say, 1880-1920, is not incidental to this shift in economic status. The Liberal Party needed Wales every bit as much as most Welshmen thought Wales was best served by the Liberal Party. There are connections to be made between the growth of a dynamic Welsh industrial economy with its bustling, commercial class and the promotion of what were labelled, with increasing self-consciousness, 'Welsh qualities', 'Welsh ideals', between the foundation of a National University to foster these ideals and the projection of a nationalist Wales within an imperial system.

From the 1890s there appeared a flood of popular accounts of Welsh history, for the new schools and for the general reader. They contain the expected run-through of Welsh princes, the revolt of Owain Glyndŵr, the emphasis on the Welshness of the Tudors, the Methodist Revival and so on. Then they came to their own day in a ringing coda at the end: the heroic response of the nineteenth century is seen as the provision of educational opportunities, the coming of a National University, a National Library, a National Museum, and Welsh sections of government. The heroes are philanthropic industrialists, religious dignitaries, patriotic politicians of a liberal persuasion, educational reformers and humane civil servants. Rural discontent, Chartism and any other blurring of the picture are moved to one side for it is not history that concerns them but rather the cultivation of a necessary social myth; for, after all, what kind of people would be needed to oil the machinery of a thriving, open, commercial society?—an elite, administrative and political, whose own committment, in the deepest and most genuine cultural sense, would be as wholeheartedly dedicated to their idea of Welsh society as their daily response would be pragmatic. They owed their place in the sun to their being from Wales. The independence of Wales would, then, be one of recognition, a place earned and accorded in the imperial family of nations; no longer merely a Welsh-speaking, brown-bread eating, impoverished rural backwater.

The foundation of the University of Wales was an integral

part of that social aspiration. One of its prime movers was Sir Hugh Owen, born a farmer's son in Anglesey and thereafter a prominent government official in mid-nineteenth century London. He, along with other expatriate Welshmen, became intent on doing something for their fellow countrymen left behind, mostly in the way of establishing schools. A university was seen as the pinnacle of that agitation, and he is acknowledged as one of the principal founders and fund-raisers for the first University College, in Aberystwyth in 1872. The detail matters less than the connections:—

Sir Hugh was a member, in London, of a Welsh Calvinistic Methodist Chapel, a body instrumental in the 1830s in establishing the London Welsh Provident Society for the encouragement of thrift. And, just to make sure, they added the Metropolitan Welsh Total Abstinence Society. If we jump to 1861 we find him founding the Social Science section of the National Eisteddfod. A year later, 1862, Dr Thomas Nicholas, of Carmarthen Presbyterian College, draws up, at Sir Hugh's invitation (after a meeting in the Freemason's Tavern in London) an address to the friends of education in Wales. The appeal focused attention on the recent rapid increase in the 'demand for educated talent, for scientific acquirements, for engineering skills' which resulted from the phenomenal growth of Welsh industry—'her mines, manufactories, railways and shipping interests.' Fears of Welsh separatism were played down and instead the argument for funds was couched in the assertion that the 'hope of Wales lay in nearer approximation to England in general culture and in commercial enterprise.'

Wales did find a political role within the British nation-state, an economic importance within the empire and the subsequent accretion of social prestige. It was a distinction that had fallen earlier on Scotland, and for related reasons, bringing into the forefront of British life an array of Scottish lawyers, politicians and engineers, not to mention philosophers and novelists. This is why Lloyd George's success at Westminster could be appropriated, back in Wales, as a part of national prestige, at least after 1900; in 1890 he had been denounced by O. M. Edwards as a 'screamer', a complainer against land laws, tithes and education instead of one who applied constant, steady effort. Edwards concluded that he would come to his senses and '. . . by sound judgement and perseverance in well-doing . . . be such a member that the borough will be as proud of him as Merioneth is of T. E. Ellis'. The awe in which Tom Ellis was held can only be fully appreciated if his career is seen as the glorious summation of a process of political and cultural control reaching down through the revolutions in franchise reform, local government acts and educational provision that had marked out Welsh life.

T. E. Ellis, in his own person, came to represent the aspirations and attainments of the Welsh elite, even in his apparent apostacy in accepting the role of Whip for the parliamentary Liberal Party, underlining the new Welsh virtues of administrative capacity and mature responsibility. The contradictory tendencies in his career are subsumed by the power of traits wider than his own personality. There is, in him, no denial of what he conceives as the heritage of the Welsh countryside nor of his own introduction to English *mores* and civilisation at Oxford—it is equality for the full development of Welsh virtues that he seeks. In 1890, recovering on a sick-bed in Egypt, he set out his thoughts on Wales' needs, her hopes, and the responsibility of her sons and daughters . . .

> . . . Even if we get a church free from the government, and the schools and the land in the hands of the people, that would only be freedom without unity. In order to attain unity we must have a parliament, a university and a Temple.
> Education—Freedom—Unity.

It is a slogan akin to the metaphorical language soon to be used by labour leaders urging recognition of Labour's rights in proportion to Labour's revelation of maturity and dignity. Tom Ellis wanted Wales to reveal her worth in the empire as he had done himself in Oxford. It was in South Africa in 1891 that he praised 'the business houses of Swansea, Cardiff and Newport' and waxed eloquent about 'the collective energies of Welsh miners and quarrymen' and their fight 'for great principles'. This was the motor of modern Wales as he stressed again in 1892 when, in replying to the toast of the British Empire Club in London, 'The Principality of Wales', he said 'The more Wales has the power of initiative and decision in her own affairs, the more closely will she be bound to the very texture of the imperial fabric'.

But this was the inescapable paradox—that very economic vitality which gave substance to Welsh political confidence was undercutting the social basis on which this notion of Welsh unity was dependent. In 1897 Ellis attacked, with some fervour, the suggestion that cosmopolitan Cardiff be a Welsh capital, taking comfort only in the fact that as Liverpool is 'the material capital of North Wales' so Cardiff was 'the material capital of South Wales'. And thus having expelled 'materialism', though not its fruits, outside the real boundaries he felt able to hope for unity through education in the parts that remained. It was a vision of Wales in which the material wealth of new developments should be used to enrich a traditional life, itself, in the myth-making, almost stripped of blemish. At Liverpool in 1894 he spoke of the social life of rural Wales, and what threatened it:

> The drain from the Welsh rural districts into industrial Wales and into England has been so great that during the last decade the decline in the population in the nine preponderatingly agricultural counties has been quite marked and in some counties even alarming. The greater the migration from rural Wales to industrial Wales and to England, the more necessary it is that our country districts should receive the benefits of wholesome thought and fruitful activity. For the city is always recruited from the country . . . [whence] come the leaders of Welsh thought and movements, the makers of our nation . . . rural Wales has different modes of thought, different ideals, different spheres of activity, in a word a different civilisation from that of England. In some respects, this great national revival which is called Nonconformity has changed the character of the people. The old turbulence is gone, though exciting moments in the tithe war and coal strike showed that the hot Celtic blood still needs restraint. There is finer ore for the making of Welsh national wealth in its peasant and cottage homes even than in its rocks and hills . . .

The social philosophy behind Welsh liberalism was its conviction that it represented a community of interest; that was not so far from the truth. However, community, no matter how imbued with Welsh radicalism, Welsh culture and Welsh nonconformity, could not survive intact the pressures of internal conflicting interests. The examples from South Wales from the 1893 Hauliers' Strike to the disturbances of 1910-11 abound—it can be made even more clearly if we take in the dispute in the Penrhyn Quarries that led to a three year lock out. The North Wales quarrymen were in 1900, like the mining communities of the south, a Welsh-speaking, liberal-voting, chapel-going working class. Unlike the miners they were a small enclave in a predominantly rural hinterland and had relied on a middle-class leadership for their Union. The lock-out was regarded by their traditional liberal leadership as yet another example of insensitivity to Welsh requirements but in fact it was a basic struggle for the right to organise their own labour both as trade unionists and as craftsmen. It was a bitter conflict about wages and hours taking place amongst men differentiated by diet, clothes and work from the surrounding villages and yet still caught up in the older cultural patterns. The failure of their fight also undercut the poised society which they had created since the older patterns of community could not, by their very nature, sustain a proletariat, and the quarrymen, uprooted if not rootless, were becoming that by 1903. Even religious revivalism could not reunite their sundered communities.

The religious revival of 1904-5 is fascinating as a unique Welsh phenomenon expressive of the bewilderment people felt in this period. The first generation Welsh proletariat, whether in Merthyr from the 1830s, or South Wales as a whole from the 1870s, was indivisibly, in its individual human components, both rural and urban in experience. There was a human connection between North and West and South Wales because the economic differentiation that was in the process of happening had not yet separated out, had not divorced known experience in the minds and bodies of most of those immigrants, had not yet traced a linguistic divide. The lightning salvation the revival promised was doubly welcome then in that it came through individual grace and without the benefit of rules of authority which were singularly absent in the new towns. The power of Welsh nonconformity in its established guise was in dispute by the first decade of the twentieth century. One of the central features of the revival was the rejection by both Evan Roberts the collier, blacksmith and lay preacher, and his many followers of the pretensions to authority expressed by a theocracy burdened like so many latter-day academics with more letters after their names than thoughts in their heads. Time and again the confessions called forth in the meetings refer to the personal dilemmas of emigration felt by a first generation removed from the land and guilty about their own implicit rejection of a former way of life.

The only other nation with the same range of evangelical protestant revivalism in the nineteenth century is the United States and, forgetting the scale of things, there is a remarkable resemblance between two rural nations in 1800 who spawn fierce denouncers of cities, convince themselves of the manifest destiny of their country safe in the hands of rural tradition and end up by 1900 well on the path to an overwhelmingly urban future. Revivalism is a frontier sport and the Welsh one spread from the geographical divide between rural and industrial Wales. The popular dislocation glimpsed in these startling events is repeated in the militancy of much of the labour troubles, spilling over the disciplining agencies of trade unionism.

The question of control was paramount. The Welsh working class also adopted an ethos of respectablility—being in local parlance, 'tidy'—that derived from the cultural image set out by the Welsh middle class. The latter was, along with Catalan and Balkan groups, one of the late additions to the European bourgeoisie in that century of spectacular bourgeois achievement. Cultural overlordship was almost complete, tricked out with the bulbous frontages of select housing and memorial statues to heroes of war and commerce, insistently there in the adaptation of the universal bourgeois uniform of black undertakers' frock-coat, top-hat or bowler, spats or laced boots and starched wing-collar. This was the dress of respectability and of achievement. When the Welsh working class after, say, the Senghennyd disaster in 1913 when 439 died, discarded their hob-nail boots, flannel shirts, moleskin trousers and yorks they marched in funeral processions garbed in the uniform, black and respectable, reserved for Sundays and funerals by them, but the everyday wear of their betters. The careful insistent payment of pennies for the insurance is the most touching revelation of the importance of death as a social symbol for working-class families (and something common to Lancashire weavers and Parisian artisans). Indeed the ritual worried the 1917 Commissioners into Industrial Unrest, who speculated on the role of underpaid insurance agents since 'the hundreds of discontented insurance agents visiting thousands of homes, at frequent and regular intervals may infect a large portion of the community...with their own spirit of discontent'. The 'proper' funeral was a mark of respect for human life that humanity could not achieve when alive. This was equality in the face of death. The Welsh working class accepted that they were only to wear their working clothes at work or in private; on the street, in public, at ceremonial moments they would wear the clothes of the bourgeois.

After the first world war, when so much broke down (the vestiges of religiosity, the power of liberalism, the stability of the Welsh language, the power of the economy, the very optimism of the society) that symbolism, on occasion and briefly, could be reversed—the dressing-up and jazz bands of the lock-outs of the 1920s were gaiety in the face of disaster, not serious, and so roundly condemned by those who expected a proper response. Their full significance eludes us as yet. And A. J. Cook from the Rhondda who became General Secretary of the Miners in 1924 and led them into the General Strike of 1926, a man who was the mouthpiece not so much of the miners' mind as of their heart and guts; Cook, as an official dressed in coat and suit with waistcoat, celluloid collar and tie, up on a platform before an assembled crowd, would strip, divest himself of the uniform of assumed equality. He would rip off his collar and tie, reverse his jacket, roll up his trousers, put his cap on back to front. The press called him a lunatic, a mob-orator frothing at the mouth but the men loved him for it. He was becoming a miner again in front of them—deliberately making himself look ridiculous in the eyes of outsiders, deliberately declaring himself a part of communities whose work and wages, whose rates of infant mortality, silicosis, maternal mortality and TB were truly lunatic. Normality usually won—when Caradog's Côr Mawr sang before Victoria, when the Williamstown Male Voice won their third National in 1918 they were, miners all, in dress-suits and white-starched shirts. Before mechanisation in the pits a stall-system of working the coal encouraged individual pride in craftsmanship just as it exposed men to a wage system nailed to their individual productivity in variable seams. The underlying energies of this society were geared to individual betterment. Its *raison d'être* was profit but it was held together, and successfully for the most part, by a social cement that encouranged collective endeavour in the technicalities of choral music, brass-band playing and, of course, rugby.

The combination of industrial society and spectator sport is fairly clear. Indeed, what was odd in the Welsh experience was not the absorption of association football from industrial Lancashire and Yorkshire into North Wales but the manner in which an amateur public-school game took root, in such a lasting fashion, in the South. Indeed rugby in its early days was not well-liked by those who saw it as another aspect of the intrusion of a non-Welsh secular world. Its administrators in the 1890s were insistent on its role as a South Walian sport even to the extent of agreeing to con- tribute to national charities and the National Eisteddfod only when those were situated in South Wales. Very many of the early international players had dual qualifications. The Welsh Rugby Union defined international rugby as being representative of the *game* in South Wales football not of geographical or racial characteristics. Most of the early clubs owed their existence to doctors or students, of one kind or another, returned from English universities, with subsequent facilities provided by industrialists and businessmen. Very few working men had much say in the development of the clubs. On the other hand this game did allow an aspiring middle class in South Wales to claim parity with the game of more established hierarchies in England, Scotland and Ireland. It followed that the dispute over 'broken- time' and professionalism that split northern rugby union (with its assertive working men and self-confident middle class) from southern in England would have no counterpart in Wales where the organisation was firmly in hands that wished to foster amateur, communal values. (After 1900 it is soccer that brings professional sport firmly into South Wales.) The Welsh Rugby Union, founded in 1881, adopted a scarlet jersey and, after much debate, replaced the white leek on a black jersey of the old South Wales Football Union, with the deferential three feathers of the Prince of Wales. Within two decades Welsh rugby, despite its imitative stance as progressively innovatory as its thrusting society, had revolutionised three-quarter play and, down to 1914, swept all the honours on the board. Nothing succeeds, as they say, like success. Rugby was integrated into the concept of Welshness; the team of 1905, the only ones to defeat the All Blacks, were immortalised as heroic Welshmen, not just rugby players. There were frequent attempts to instil a sense of responsibility and fair play into the wilder reaches of the game—many clubs were closed by the WRU for varying periods before 1914, because of violence and disorderly conduct, usually caused by the spectators. And there was a clear determination to play a social role by giving money to the new intermediate or grammar schools to foster the game, by encouraging public school players to join clubs on leav- ing. The WRU closed grounds for a fortnight on the death of Queen Victoria; they sent funds to the Boer War. The new Wales was, in important respects, profoundly pro-imperialist—the Empire of nations was, after all, its own highest justification for within the imperial framework could be made the *Welsh* contribution.

Rugby in Wales provided many with participation but many more with the consumption of leisure. Its progress was heralded by the press, avid for its own provincial role, as was that of the Religious Revival (which closed many clubs down), whilst its combination of virtues as essentially a community game were extolled (forwards and backs, skill and strength, rich man, poor man). By 1914 the game was securely established, its career synonymous with the growth of coalfield society, but also, by then, not solely its representative as soccer spread, causing anxiety in circles by no means confined to sporting men. The magazine *The Welsh Outlook*, edited by Thomas Jones (1870-1955) who may be considered the unofficial Prime Minister of Wales for much of his life, carried a weighty comment in its second number of February 1914:

> In the sense that nationality is a community of memories so is Rugby football the national game. The names of the giants are on the lips of the people: there are traditions in Rugby that will rouse a crusading fire: there is merit of past achievement that sustains as nations are upheld by victories. The Association Code in Wales is new and alien and comes in on the back of its popularity elsewhere: it is the game of the alien of the valleys whose immigration and de-nationalising tendency is one of the major problems of our country. It is best reported in alien newspapers . . . Wales possesses in Rugby football a game which is immeasurably more valuable than the popular code of the other countries...it has made a democracy (i.e. the common man) not only familiar with an amateur sport of distinguished rank but is in reality a discovery of democracy which acts as participant and patron...A game democratic and amateur is a rare thing—a unique thing to be cherished, and therefore the concern of thinking men who value the complex influences making for higher levels of citizenship.

It was a similar 'concern' by 'thinking men' which led them to deplore the anti-leadership actions of Welsh miners implicit in riotous assembly and unofficial strikes, explicit in the 'No Leadership' proposals of *The Miners' Next Step* of 1912. Nothing was so inimical to the social darwinism that colours the philosophy of the time as the repeated onslaughts on the moderation of miners' agents and Lib-Lab MPs.

In 1916, a year after the South Wales miners have defied their own leadership and a war-time government's anti-strike regulations in order to increase their wages, Tom Jones is proposing post-war reconstruction for Wales.

'Once the war is over' he wrote 'industrial warfare will be resumed ever more sharply. The University should stand for the public good against all class or sectional interests, it should be a "great reconciling force".' Within a year, and despite his desire to see Tom Jones installed as Principal at Aberystwyth, David Davies, heir to the Ocean Coal Company fortune, proved willing to endorse Jones' candidature for the same post at Cardiff on the grounds that Cardiff was 'a more important arena' than Aberystwyth and, if appointed, Jones could do a great deal to ease the difficult labour problems besetting South Wales.

There was good reason why both Tom Jones, and his patron, should be well-informed about those problems. They were both well-acquainted with Daniel Lleufer Thomas, the stipendiary magistrate for the Rhondda, whom Tom Jones described as 'one of the most useful Welshmen of his generation'—he was a man involved in university administration, the foundation of the National Museum, town planning, housing schemes and other social services. In addition, and it is to the link between the social idealism of such men and their necessarily understated political stance that I am pointing, he was the principal co-ordinator of the famous 1917 Government Enquiry into Industrial Unrest in South Wales. That report concluded by advocating better housing, more education, better cultural facilities and an end to the 1916 Entertainment Tax—with blood on the coal why curb the circuses? Lleufer Thomas was also stipendiary magistrate for Pontypridd and Rhondda for 25 years. 'In these courts' said Tom Jones in a funeral tribute, 'he was confronted every week with the most sordid and squalid phases of our fallen human nature, and it says much for the tolerance of his mind and the bigness of his heart that he retained a perpetual breath of hope for the common man and the common good.' The common man has to be linked with the common good because if the encouragement of the good qualities or, at least, the hopeful image of the former is abandoned then the latter, the common good, is also at risk.

Thomas Jones was, both in words and in actions, the chief articulator of the rationale of a Welsh social darwinism that mostly took itself for granted. He had gone, in a manner that would have pleased Samuel Smiles, from working as a clerk in the Rhymney

Valley to the new College in Aberystwyth in the 1890s. He had progressed, via theology and christian socialism, to research at Glasgow University and on to a chair in Economics in Belfast. In 1910, with Davies' money behind him, he had resigned to run the National Memorial Association to combat tuberculosis. Jones' career now blossomed in the sunshine of that Welsh presence centre stage: he became Secretary of the Welsh National Insurance Commission, and on into the Cabinet Secretariat to serve, in turn, Lloyd George, Bonar Law, Ramsay MacDonald and Baldwin. His was, par excellence, the intellectual and administrative moderation of the 'social engineer' whose influence in America he so much admired. His face was firmly set throughout against any fever, be it environmental or just mental. After 1926 he poured his energies into the foundation of Coleg Harlech as a non-sectarian counter-balance to the insidious effects of independent working-class education in South Wales. As early as 1904, in the midst of a tirade against unofficial strikes, he struck his key-note:

> In every town in this populous valley (Rhymney) there should be a
> well-equipped Social Institute. It should be in closest touch with
> the elementary and intermediate schools of the district, and with
> the University College and Public Free Library at Cardiff. It should
> be in charge, not of an invalid collier for whom a post has to be
> found, not of one chosen because he was a Baptist or a Methodist,
> but in charge of a scholar with a passion for books, and capable of
> communicating his enthusiasm to others. For preference he should
> be a university graduate who has risen from the ranks . . . the
> leaders of the future. Don't spend all your money on books and
> buildings, and a pound a week on a lame caretaker. Sprinkle half a
> dozen cultured enthusiasts between Rhymney and
> Caerphilly . . . Pay them a living wage, and you'll get a big
> dividend on your investment. They'll plant a love of noble
> literature in your boys, and teach them the true uses of prosperity.
> If they are men of moral courage and telescopic vision, they will do
> something to prevent this expanding valley becoming a second
> Rhondda.

1904 was the year of revivalism not of the social engineer. It was the year when Dr R. S. Stewart, the Deputy Medical Superintendent of the Glamorgan County Asylum published his findings in the prestigious *Journal of Mental Science* on the relationship between wages, lunacy and crime in South Wales from the 1870s. He found that the steady rate of increase of lunacy was much higher for Glamorgan than any county in England and that the rate fluctuated according to economic indices. Dr Stewart was convinced that 'good times' led to an excess of eating and drinking as well as to a decline in productivity so that prosperity had not brought about the pursuit of moral excellence. Worse, it was dragging the working class down: 'There are two sliding scales, that of wages and of lunacy, going hand in hand. Whenever wages rise there is a concomitant increase in insanity, and vice versa, but the fall is never commensurate with the fall in wages and thence the steady upward movement in insanity which is observable.' Dr Stewart did hold out the hope that 'acute temporary stress', such as that which accompanied the six months lock-out of 1898, had 'a bracing tonic effect' that was accompanied 'by evidence of increased self-control.' It was to this possibility that Thomas Jones addressed himself in 1914 when from Barry, the coal-exporting town built in a decade to ship out Davies' coal, he founded and edited the monthly *Welsh Outlook*. The magazine defended moderate trade unionism against belligerent employers and insisted on the value of the Workers' Educational Association and of the university settlement movement in the fight against the spread of rank and file agitation and marxist pedagogues. A close supporter was Principal Burrows of the University College of South Wales and Monmouthshire who told university settlement volunteers in 1914 that

> Settlements and their like are the translations into terms of modern life of the friendly personal relations between individuals that did at least something in our villages to sweeten life and blunt the edge of political differences . . . There is a small section of the working class which . . . preaches the class war . . . They, too, do not love settlements or the WEA and have been known to call them the last . . . and most subtle defence by which capital seeks to deflect the straight path of revolution. But, after all, the working classes are English or Welsh like you. Blood is thicker than class.

If, despite all these well-intentioned efforts, expectations still fell away there remained the explanation of abnormality and of the unnatural influence of those same aliens who were undercutting the national game. For Rhys Davies, the novelist, writing in 1937 of the riots he had witnessed as a boy in Tonypandy in 1910, they were the work of 'a section of the industrialised race

... composed of ... rootless ruffians and barbarous *aliens,* particularly Irishmen who were ... bored with the monotony of work'; whereas, the chapels alone preserved 'the Welsh spirit' and 'offered the ancient Welsh foods [of "spiritual and artistic tendencies"] in abundance to thousands of souls who might have been utterly ruined and corrupted in the brutal new towns.' Those who had lost this spirit, in what he calls 'the sack of Tonypandy' were an 'enraged mob', 'slavering and barbaric-eyed.'

He could have been writing about mad dogs. What is important is not the lack of any real knowledge of events but the unstated reversal of the image—a 'good' working class is a docile one, certainly a respectable one possessed of the higher values of bourgeois frugality and thoughtfulness. The 1917 Enquiry detected such qualities in *Welsh* workers and thought that the propensity to strike lay with the alien immigrants; Welshmen, they declared, were more respectful too, when other Welshmen gave the orders (the overseers in ante-bellum plantations in America were invariably black). The definition of 'Welsh' here in use is one of social behaviour, desired or required, masquerading as a racial characteristic. South Wales, put in the position of losing primary Welsh characteristics of liberal radicalism, active nonconformity, small-scale existence and even the language itself, was increasingly liable, therefore, to go out of control. Even Tom Jones could lose his cool:

> These miners' leaders [he wrote in 1951] dealt with an inflammable population easily ignited by what they felt to be injustice, and although tamed and civilised by religion and tradition, and upheld and guarded in decent behaviour by social props and fences, primitive barbaric instincts were never far from below the surface and these could most easily be released by an excess of alcohol. Wild orgies of violence sometimes disfigured the hymn-singing valleys as in the Llanelli area in August 1911 when the police proved unable to control the mob, the Riot Act was read, the troops fired and killed several in the crowd and wounded others. Strikers and sympathisers for miles around gathered to avenge their comrades and maddened with drink proceeded to create pandemonium ... In North Wales the social structure was better balanced between agriculture, industry and well-to-do visitors from Liverpool, Manchester and the Midlands. Everyone enjoyed more elbow-room. It had rarely been necessary to order troops into that area to quell or shoot a turbulent mob.

If we listen to the assumptions of necessity behind the prose rather than to its inaccuracy on details, both for Llanelli and North Wales, a world of meaning comes through that takes us back to the self-congratulatory hopes of our traveller in 1860 and on to Tom Ellis' conviction that the values of rural Wales can be spread, only to abut in Tom Jones' despair at the denial of 'wise leaders' as he casts a wistful glance to North Wales. An imbalanced South Wales becomes, in this view, literally unbalanced.

And what happens, then, after the apparent stability of the British export economy buckles and the coal industry contracts as rapidly as it had expanded? Certainly after 1918 that old liberal-nationalist Wales was no longer able to disseminate its own image soon to be dismissed anyway by the rise of a more fiercely intellectual and political nationalism; at the same time the nature of class antagonism became more insistently overt. South Wales in the 1920s was no longer a boisterous youngster in need of discipline but an embarrassing nuisance now played out. In 1935 Tom Jones wrote a famous pamphlet with the ringing title 'What's wrong with South Wales?' He may have been a degree or two ironical when he suggested moving the entire population east to the Midlands and turning the coalfield into a vast industrial museum but he was quite consistent in his conviction that the only solution lay in mitigation by 'relief and recreation.' His diagnosis was not just of material decay. He worked hard to establish Coleg Harlech as a place where carefully selected unemployed men could be given a change of surroundings and wholesome food for six months at a time. Craft activites could be encouraged—carpentry, book-binding, athletic activities to fit them, in Jones' words, 'for leadership of the occupational centres, of which there are now over two hundred in Wales.' The miners, he concluded in 1933,

> had lost their standards and authorities. They achieved power with very little preparation and at a moment when they were deserting the culture . . . of the chapel. Standing over against the miners' home life in the old days were two authorities—the minister of religion and the employer of labour, and for both there was usually a real respect. The miner was contented because his responsibilities were limited and clearly defined. What was asked of him he did.

Tom Jones' activities were at least more humane than the desire of the Rev. J. Vyrnwy Morgan of Cwmavon who advocated, in 1925, the enforcement of birth control along with a sterilisation of those unfit to produce children in South Wales—

> because of the bearing of this indiscriminate propagation of children, merely for the gratification of the animal passions, which unlike the spiritual faculties, seem to gain a superfluity of power, the more they are exercised and transmitted, upon the economic life of the miners, as well as upon health and morals, . . . coincident with the rapid spread of Communistic-Socialism in South Wales there has been a progressive mental and moral deterioration, more especially among the younger section of the community who are extreme socialists.

There was little compassion for those who had, it seemed, ignored such good advice. And yet the people of South Wales continued to resist. In early 1935 for weekend after weekend in pouring rain hundreds of thousands marched to protest the government's new Means Test Bill and, in the only successful direct action of the 1930s, they succeeded in having it stopped. This was not a matter of praise for some. Saunders Lewis, the first President of Plaid Cymru, told an audience in Aberdare, one of those valley communities where unemployment was over 30 per cent of the insured population, that English money should be rejected and 'Welsh self-help' embraced instead. He declared that South Wales' Utopian ideals would lead to 'evil consequences and moral rotteness' whereas 'The Welsh Nationalist Party offered...the simple life instead of the Pentecostal Utopianism that was the curse of the country.' Plaid Cymru also advocated the de-industrialisation of Wales along with the introduction of a corporate, distributist economy on a small scale. The language used now is derived from a contemporary European sensibility out to denounce the machine, the state, urbanism and the rootless. South Wales becomes an exemplar of the disease. Lewis wrote venomously in 1939:

> The tramway climbs from Merthyr to Dowlais,
> Slime of a snail on a heap of slag;
> Here once was Wales, and now
> Derelict cinemas and rain on the barren tips
> ....
> We cannot bleed like the men that have been,
> And our hands, they would be like hands if they had thumbs;

Let our feet be shattered by a fall, and all we'll do is grovel to a
clinic,
And raise our caps to a wooden leg and insurance and a Mond
pension;
We have neither language nor dialect, we feel no insult,
And the masterpiece that we gave to history is our country's MP's.
....
. . . on Olympus, in Wall Street, nineteen-twenty-nine,
At their infinitely scientific task of guiding the profits of fate,
The gods decreed, with their feet in the Aubusson carpets,
And their Hebrew snouts in the quarter's statistics,
That the day had come to restrict credit in the universe of gold.

Lewis' elevation to the Pantheon of Heroes has led his admirers to
explain away his meaning in this poem through glosses as
intellectually contorted as they are embarrassingly naive. The
febrile visionary, unlike his more liberal acolytes, has not withdrawn his slander on 'the proletarian flood' who creep 'greasily
civil to the chip shops', nor his disdain for 'Man's faith in man.' In
the case of the frustrated poet it was a contemporary world that *did*
struggle and did survive in all its concrete, multifarious humanity
that was the crushing, insupportable rejection that he must spurn
with false accusations of passivity; in the case of the defenders of
the indefensible, it is charitable to assume that they have closed
their minds to the history of Wales. The abstract definition of
Wales adumbrated by Saunders Lewis had no room for the actual
human experience that had raged in South Wales: its economic
collapse in 1939 was, it seemed, absolute, and not for him the
dialectic forced on an earlier generation of bourgeois idealists by
the combination of relative prosperity and urban Welshmen. The
myth, however, only carries weight when it is in some sort of
relationship with reality: Lewis bore no relationship to the reality
of South Wales though he had a germinating one in the minds of a
section of the Welsh intelligentsia, deprived of their inheritance in
every sense. Paradoxically, Plaid Cymru, now become firmly
another social-democratic party, was in the 1970s in connection
with a contemporary reality that remains antithetical to the golden
social order Lewis dreamed about.

It is hard to resist the conclusion that it is the twentieth
century itself, having visited these momentous changes on Wales,
which has to be expelled or, at least, de-natured if that organic,

ordered Wales, cultivated and quiescent, were to be conjured down from the clouds.

By a quirk of fate that industrial process which accomplished the survival of Welsh-speaking communities by draining off excess population, and further stimulated Welsh cultural endeavour in the towns and the press, has led us to a point where any easy definition of people and country, leave alone nation, is impossible in Wales no matter how ardently some may desire to ignore the fact. The very existence of looking-glass Wales is an affront to the new theocracy as they swing linguistic incense to disperse the bad smell. It is not just a badge, an emblem that is offered, but salvation into a new life. If the Welsh language is to be used as a mark of organic wholeness, of spiritual differentiation from those who left the Edenic Garden then South Wales will continue to be the Samaria of the never-never land of Canaan.

And yet that unique South Walian culture is also dissolving. We should be wary of the coalfield myth, too, as it filters down into the masochistic nostalgia of fingering coffee-table photograph books or glorifies times easier to remember, and write about, than to live through.

The predominant image of South Wales in the interwar years is of grey misery, waste and hopeless pleas for help. It is the image contemporaries constructed after 1926. But it is quite false, as distorted a picture as that portrayed in 1939 in the most successful book ever written about Wales—*How Green Was My Valley*,—which is a lament for a world that never existed, that blames the wretched conditions of the 1930s on that very spirit of collective endeavour which salvaged so much that was at risk in the 1930s. Its power comes from its ability to simplify reality and so, because of the desire for a meaning or an answer, it comforts.

Historians are not comforters and must not be simplifiers. There must be explanation of the confusion of image and reality so that analysis of the living contradictions with which people had to contend may emerge. The process can be seen in close-up in the growth of the village of Maerdy at the top end of the Rhondda fach. From a collection of huts around a couple of pits in the 1870s, it becomes a thriving, Welsh, chapel-going society of about 6,000 people by the early 1900s. It was very much a respectable, moderate place beloved of Tom Jones and his ilk. In 1897 Jim Connell, the composer of 'The Red Flag', spoke at a hall in Maerdy and so upset the audience with his wild socialist ideas that most of them left the meeting. In 1899 when the colliery directors gave a party for the village, the men presented them with gold and silver mounted walking sticks whilst, in 1905, the Institute was opened with management's blessing. This was a place and a time intent on achievement—in the home, in their work, in their politics, within the established framework of the image of progress set by a wider society. The schools, elementary at first, later the superb grammar schools, set a tone, provided ladders of success, of escape, for a whole people.

But, and side by side with all this, came the pressures of other realities that led Maerdy men and women into riots and looting, to support of Communist leaders and the designation of their village, now after 1926 devastated by almost complete unemployment, by the nickname of *Little Moscow*. A red village, then, in which nonetheless there were religious groups from Baptists to spiritualists, film shows and dances, so-called 'Communist' soccer teams and 'red' boy scouts. The society that was being born within the old one was, so long as it lived, in the image of the parent body, connected to its reality despite striving to give it a new shape.

Since 1945, as the economy and society of Wales altered yet again, there has been fostered a new, false image, cosy and heart-warming, sentimental and nostalgic about the past. Television adaptations of the golden past, all the more golden for being hardships from which we have apparently moved, are soaked up; Max Boyce is loved as he takes a basically decent, rugby-loving, beer-drinking picture of the Welsh proletariat across the border, bearing the vestiges of that distinctiveness like sporrans and haggis, the present identification marks. That is the image now. And the reality is uniform housing estates, lego-block cities, sodium lighting that changes the colour of the moon, and steel and glass shop fronts as in Burnley and Leicester and Tooting High Street and the planet X. The railways have gone for motorway tubes of fluorescent brightness that convey a coalfield of commuters to the new centres of work on the coast. And for the convenience, now, of the motor car white-tiled subways burrow through the towns, passageways as sterile as the dead pedestrian precincts they serve; and Wrexham is Llanelli, and Pontypridd shall be Cwmbran, and only the daubers, the writers on walls came to proclaim their self-given identities—Pie, Tweet and Pan from Trehafod; Chopper and Screw from Aberbeeg, the

Aberaman Boot Boys who rule, OK?, and the quiet, but insistent, Pigeon who once filled a whole wall himself. Their assertion is a feeble one, but it is a human response in what has become an obliterating townscape.

It is still a question of control, of direction of energies, of which human values are to be opposed to those which dictate the shape of our societies. It is time to disentangle myth and image from reality so that the latter can be seen whole. Present delusions have past roots. The history of Wales is far more complex than we have hitherto realised; there are historical reasons for this blindness. They, too, will need to be disinterred. In the meantime, before the dissection of the historiography of Wales, the historical understanding of the social process by which Wales has entered into her present ambiguous state is a vital necessity. The mists of Hegelian rhetoric, of a willed idealism about Wales, even the celebratory invocation of an internationalist working class that was certainly more quick with life than its opponents ever were, must all give way to an emphasis on the ambivalent, contradictory, lived history of the people of Wales whose experience, albeit patterned, cannot be summed up by the preciosity of words like 'community' or 'nation' nor by the flag waving of phrases like 'inferiority complex' or 'class consciousness.' The craft of the historian is an arduous one. The humility of the historian in the light of the human past must seem insufferably arrogant to those who only wish to raid it for use. But then the responsibility of the historian is not to them, nor is their present likely to flourish so long as they ignore the past that only speaks when its integrity is recognised and articulated.

Bibliographical note

The preceding essay is an attempt to interpret some of the interpreters of that urban, industrial experience which has, over the last century, altered the culture of most Welsh people and affected all of them to a considerable degree. My viewpoint and argument are based on a reading of newspapers, official papers and sundry other contemporary sources from novels to topographical guides to journals and memoirs. It would have been impossible to adopt this essay's radical perspective if it were not for the works on Welsh history produced in the last twenty five years. It is no exaggeration to say that the founding of the *Welsh History Review* in 1960 opened a path through the sea; since 1972 *Llafur* has, in a different yet complementary way, added its voice. This book itself is a co-operative fruit of the seeds sown by the Society for the Study of Welsh Labour history—'llafur' indeed means not only 'labour' but 'the fruits of labour.'

The main contemporary sources used or quoted in the text are Wirt Sykes *Rambles and Studies in Old South Wales* (London, 1881); J. Vyrnwy Morgan *Welsh Political and Educational Leaders in the Victorian Era* (Cardiff, 1908) and *The Welsh Mind in Evolution* (London, 1925); T. E. Ellis *Speeches and Addresses* (Wrexham, 1912); R. S. Stewart 'The Relationship of Wages, Lunacy and Crime in South Wales' in *Journal of Mental Science* Vol. 50. (1904); Thomas Jones *A Theme with Variations* (1933), *Rhymney Memories* (1938), *Leeks and Daffodils* (1942), and *Welsh Broth* (1950); the translation of Saunders Lewis's poem is taken from Alun R. Jones and Gwyn Thomas (eds.), *Presenting Saunders Lewis* (Cardiff, 1973).

Secondary sources are now plentiful. Foremost among political historians of Wales both for his pioneering scholarship and his limpid, yet weighty, articles and books on all aspects of Welsh history is Kenneth O. Morgan. His *Wales in British Politics, 1868-1922* (Cardiff, 1963; Revised edition, 1970) is as indispensable as his new history of Wales from the late 19th century (to appear in 1980) will doubtless prove to be. Earlier sketches of Welsh history and culture by K. O. Morgan and others can be found in the useful R. Brinley Jones (ed.), *Anatomy of Wales* (1972). Tom Ellis's life and times are recounted in Neville Masterman, *The Forerunner* (Llandybie, 1972) whilst some of Thomas Jones's multi-faceted career is explained by E. L. Ellis, *The University College of Wales, Aberystwyth 1872-1972* (Cardiff, 1972) and by Peter Stead in *Coleg Harlech* (Cardiff, 1978). The essential, real counter-balance to the manufactured, idealist notion of Wales can be traced in Hywel Francis and David Smith, *The Fed: A History of the South Wales Miners in the Twentieth Century* (London, 1980).